SICK TO DEBT

SICK TO

DEBT

How Smarter
Markets Lead
to Better Care

Peter A. Ubel, MD

Yale UNIVERSITY PRESS
New Haven & London

Published with assistance from the foundation established in memory of James Wesley Cooper of the Class of 1865, Yale College.

Yale University Press books may be purchased in quantity for educational, business, or promotional use. For information, please e-mail sales.press@yale.edu (U.S. office) or sales@yaleup.co.uk (U.K. office).

Set in Galliard type by IDS Infotech Ltd., Chandigarh, India.
Printed in the United States of America.

Library of Congress Control Number: 2019934886
ISBN 978-0-300-23846-4 (hardcover : alk. paper)

A catalogue record for this book is available from the British Library.

This paper meets the requirements of ANSI/NISO Z39.48-1992 (Permanence of Paper).

10 9 8 7 6 5 4 3 2 1

CONTENTS

SICK TO DEBT

INTRODUCTION: ANOTHER BOOK ABOUT HEALTHCARE?

Nothing seemed to be wrong with Alfie Evans when he was born in May 2016. But several months later, he began experiencing progressively severe seizures, which eventually left him in a semi-vegetative state. Doctors couldn't agree on why Alfie was sick, but they were unanimous in concluding that his condition was terminal: that keeping him on life support would be "unkind and inhumane."[1] When Alfie's parents fought to continue treating him, a series of courts overruled their wishes, with one judge writing that the child's brain had "eroded, leaving only water and CSF [cerebrospinal fluid]."

Alfie Evans's tragic story captured international attention, in part because it galvanized growing discontent among the British population with the stinginess of the nation's healthcare system. Following the recession that began in 2008, the British government had frozen its healthcare budgets, despite the increasing medical needs of its population.[2] The budget tightening left some Brits so frustrated with the system that they began calling for a complete overhaul. Kailash Chand, a general practitioner in the United Kingdom, described the national health system as being in "the worst winter crisis of its 70-year history."[3]

The U.K. healthcare system is far from alone in creating discontent. Canadians are disturbed by parts of their system, too. Consider a letter Dr. Joy Hatley received from one of her patients that she shared on Twitter in 2017: "This letter is to inform you that we have received your referral for [redacted]. Our current wait time for a new patient referral is approximately 4.5 years."

Hatley is a pediatric neurologist in Canada, one of many providers who publicized their frustration with their nation's healthcare system through a Twitter campaign carrying the hashtag "#CanadaWAITS." As part of that campaign, Sue Robbins tweeted her frustration at having to wait "three excruciating months for a breast cancer diagnosis." Barbara Shantz complained about a two-and-a-half-year wait to get speech therapy for her "son with global growing developmental delays."[4]

Wait times have been growing in Canada for decades. According to a report out of Fraser University, Canadians already had to wait a median of more than nine weeks to see a specialist in 1993; that time grew to more than twenty-one weeks by 2017.[5] Some wait times are even longer than that, with Canadians waiting a median of almost thirty-eight weeks to see an orthopedic surgeon. It has gotten so bad that Brian Day, former president of the Canadian Medical Association, has sued the government over its ban on private insurance.[6]

But it hasn't gotten bad enough in either Britain or Canada to make people living in those countries wish their healthcare system was more like that of the United States. For all its flaws, the Canadian healthcare system is loved by most citizens. In fact, when the Canadian Broadcasting System conducted a poll in 2004 to name the greatest Canadian of all time, people didn't choose famous actors like Michael J. Fox, William Shatner, or Ryan Gosling; they didn't pick internationally acclaimed musicians like Celine Dion or Neil Young; they didn't even select Wayne Gretzky, "The Great One." Instead, they chose Tommy Douglas, the Scottish-born politician who established Canada's system of universal healthcare coverage. Danielle Martin, a physician in Toronto who has written about many of the flaws of the Canadian healthcare system, still finds solace by thinking of the country's southern neighbor: "When we compare ourselves to the U.S., we feel great."[7] Brits have access to similar solace. While only 61 percent of people in the United Kingdom are satisfied with their healthcare system, that proportion still dwarfs satisfaction rates in the United States, which don't even reach 30 percent.[8] This low rate of satisfaction results in large part from an astounding fact about the U.S. healthcare system—it somehow manages to simultaneously provide less healthcare coverage than any other developed country, while spending more on that healthcare.

Although Americans are united in their dissatisfaction, they remain divided about how to fix their healthcare system. They elect politicians to overhaul the system, only to complain when they try to do so. Since President Obama's healthcare plan went into effect, American attitudes toward healthcare reform have become even more polarized, with Republicans working to dismantle Obamacare, and with an increasing number of Democrats embracing "Medicare for All."

So why would I even consider writing a book about how to improve the American healthcare system? Well, it's not because I pretend to have all the solutions. I guarantee that even after this book sells millions of copies, the U.S. healthcare system will still be a mess. Healthcare is hard: it costs a lot of money and people still get sick and die.

Nor did I write this book because I thought I could convince you of a specific liberal or conservative approach to healthcare reform that you'd be crazy not to embrace. Plenty of experts on both sides of the political spectrum have offered their take on how to fix the system. For example, some experts on the political left seem to believe we can improve the system by ridding it of the profit motive. In *An American Sickness*, former *New York Times* reporter Elisabeth Rosenthal accuses the country's healthcare system of attending "more or less single mindedly to its own profits."[9] She points out that the United States has a rapidly growing for-profit hospital industry, often reimbursed by for-profit insurance companies, with providers enriching themselves at the expense of their patients. In *Deadly Spin*, Wendell Potter expresses outrage at American health insurance companies for pursuing profits at the expense of their customers, remarking with contempt that the average insurance company CEO brings in almost $12 million a year.[10] It is this anger over unhealthy profits that compels many experts on the left to call for the kind of single-payer system found in Canada and the United Kingdom, with hospitals and medical clinics motivated by the desire to provide high-quality care rather than the obligation to return healthy profits to their shareholders.[11]

Experts on the political right don't blame markets for undermining the way the American healthcare system functions; instead, they blame the *lack* of market forces. They point out that in normal markets, consumer scrutiny forces everyone from cell phone manufacturers to landscaping companies to hold down their prices while maintaining or improving the quality of their offerings. It is consumer markets that explain why people can purchase a $300 cell phone today that has more computing power than a $3,000 personal computer would have offered in 1989. American conservatives contend that the U.S. healthcare system should be reformed to more closely resemble these traditional consumer markets, with patients scrutinizing the cost and quality of healthcare goods and services before purchasing them. In such a system, patients would demand low-cost, high-quality healthcare, thereby forcing hospitals, insurance companies, and the pharmaceutical industry to become more efficient. In line with this idea of consumer healthcare markets, House Majority Leader Paul Ryan drafted the Patients' Choice Act prior to the 2016 election, and Congressman Tom Price drafted the Patient Empowerment Act.[12] Both bills called for patients to have more "skin in the game": to face the kind of out-of-pocket expenses that would incentivize them to scrutinize their medical care.

I wrote *Sick to Debt* because I don't think these ideas—from either the left or the right—are going to work. Under "Medicare for All," the United States would spend its way to fiscal doom, unless we dramatically change the way Medicare functions. While adopting a single-payer system would create administrative efficiencies, those would quickly be consumed by the added cost of covering tens of millions of Americans who lack insurance.[13] Moreover, Medicare spending has been growing at an unsustainable clip for decades, and out-of-pocket expenses for Medicare enrollees have been growing, too.[14] An analysis by Harvard health economist Kate Baicker estimates that over the course of a decade, one in six Medicare enrollees can expect annual out-of-pocket expenses to exceed $5,000.[15] To put that in perspective, Social Security pays out an average benefit of about $15,000 a year, putting that $5,000 beyond the means of many elderly Americans.

Under "Consumer Markets for All," individual patients would spend their way to financial misery unless we dramatically change the way we empower healthcare consumers. Healthcare consumerism is based on a naïve view of patients as rational decision makers in need of more financial "skin in the game," so they can savvily scrutinize the cost and quality of their healthcare alternatives. As a physician and behavioral scientist, I have spent almost three decades exploring the irrational forces influencing medical decisions. Building on insights from fields like behavioral economics, I have discovered a range of psychological phenomena that undermine the ability of patients to make such savvy healthcare choices.[16] It is critical to understand these phenomena if we are going to understand how medical markets will work if they become more like traditional consumer markets.

I also wrote this book because I'm worried about what will happen to our country if we don't rein in healthcare spending. In 2016, the United States spent almost 20 percent of its gross domestic product (GDP) on healthcare; Germany and the United Kingdom spent less than 10 percent.[17] The United States spends more than other developed countries, in part because of high prices.[18] Physician fees for hip replacement procedures are threefold higher in the United States than in France, and primary care office visits are two to three times more expensive than in Australia.[19] For a patient with rheumatoid arthritis in the United States, a month of treatment with a medication called Humira runs over $2,500; the same drug costs less than $900 in Switzerland. A magnetic resonance imaging (MRI) scan priced at $1,100 in the United States costs only $215 in Australia.[20] I wrote this book to identify ways to control this spending.

I am worried about healthcare spending not because it has exceeded some magical percentage of our GDP, but because I regularly witness the human cost of that spending. On August 1, 2007, thirteen people died when an eight-lane bridge collapsed in Minneapolis, a bridge I crossed dozens of times when I attended the University of Minnesota Medical School. Before the tragedy, the bridge had been rated as structurally deficient by the U.S. Department of Transportation, but tight government budgets delayed plans to replace it.[21] When I heard the news, I thought of friends still living in Minnesota who could have been crossing the bridge when it collapsed. I wondered if my profession was at fault for those thirteen deaths, and whether the rising cost of healthcare had forced the Minnesota Highway Department to postpone those repairs; with the state's Medicaid costs growing, and with a legislature hesitant to raise taxes, something had to give.[22] For similar reasons, I worry that the low teacher morale in my children's public schools can be blamed on healthcare spending. In North Carolina, the state government refused to give teachers cost of living increases because it, too, was overwhelmed by Medicaid expenses. I even blame the decline of American manufacturing, at least partially, on the crippling cost of providing healthcare benefits for American laborers.

American businesses pick up the tab for almost a quarter of the nation's healthcare expenses, putting them at a competitive disadvantage compared with companies operating in less expensive healthcare systems.[23]

I'm also concerned about the direct impact high healthcare costs have on patients' lives. Regardless of whether you agree that our country's bridges, schools, and manufacturers are being harmed by high healthcare spending, it is impossible to deny the crippling financial impact of health-care costs on people with acute or chronic illnesses.[24] Too often, when Americans get sick, they are forced to decide whether to pay their mortgage or their medical bills, with many even struggling to pay for groceries.

America is becoming "sick to debt," with no simple cure for our spend-ing ills.

Which brings me to the final, and perhaps most important, reason I wrote this book. In tackling high spending in the United States, and in determin-ing the proper role of markets in our healthcare system, we need to under-stand how policies play out at the bedside. Many people know more than I do about accountable care organizations, bundled payment plans, and other healthcare policies. Many have more expertise in health economics, medical management, and other topics relevant to figuring out how we can reduce American healthcare spending. But over the past two and a half decades, I've probably obsessed over the ways patients and clinicians make healthcare choices as much as any human on the planet. I practiced medicine for twenty years, providing me the great honor of helping thousands of patients make important medical decisions. I've also spent (too much) time on the other end of the stethoscope, figuring out which healthcare interventions will or will not cure my various ailments shared and, of late, obsessing over the costs of those interventions. I've also conducted hundreds of empirical research projects, exploring the factors that influence people's medical decisions. In the past half-dozen years, I led the largest study to date exploring how doc-tors and patients factor healthcare costs into medical decisions.[25]

In writing this book, I plan to advance debates about how, or whether, to bring market discipline to medical decisions. In doing so, I will provide insights relevant to healthcare policies favored by liberals, as well as those favored by conservatives.

In the first part of the book, I will lay out the promise of healthcare consumerism. I will explain why asking patients to cover some portion of their healthcare expenses holds the potential to better align the healthcare system with people's goals and values. But I will also lay out the pitfalls of such consumerism, with an emphasis on the psychologic and economic forces that undermine the way doctors and patients make medical decisions.

In the second part of the book, I will present a series of ways to improve the functioning of healthcare markets, so they better empower patients to make healthcare choices that promote their best interests. I will draw upon proposals being championed, too often, in isolation, and explain why we need a mixture of reforms that better align patients' out-of-pocket expenses with the value of their healthcare.

But I'm getting ahead of myself. It's time to see why so many pundits believe consumer markets hold the solution to America's healthcare woes, and why I—as a physician and behavioral scientist—think such solutions will require much smarter markets than those experts endorse.

WHEN MEDICAL MARKETS MEET
HUMAN NATURE

1

CAN AMERICANS SHOP THEIR WAY TO MORE
AFFORDABLE CARE?

Rachel Chong didn't feel right. Her stomach felt unsettled, and she had no appetite, her weight now five pounds lighter than normal. Then suddenly, the unsettling feeling was overtaken by dramatic pain, like a small grenade had exploded inside her abdomen. She rushed to the hospital. The look on her face and the way she avoided major bodily movements were probably what compelled the doctors to rush her to the operating room. An aggressive cancer had punctured a hole in her intestines.

Chong's colon cancer had been stealthily growing inside her body for years. Part of the cancer grew outward, into the lumen, the hollow portion of her colon. If the cancer had been any bigger, it might have blocked her intestine, an emergency in its own right. But instead, Chong experienced another kind of emergency: her cancer had grown inward, puncturing a hole in the lining of her colon, through which hundreds of millions of bacteria spilled forth, invading the normally sterile spaces inside her abdomen. She underwent emergency surgery to repair the puncture.

A few weeks later, Chong sat in an oncology clinic, joined by her husband and their two adult sons. They met with an oncologist, who explained that Chong's tumor was stage three; it hadn't spread outside her colon and was potentially curable with chemotherapy. "We know that if we do not give chemotherapy, your chance for relapse is more than 70 percent," Chong's oncologist explained. Then he described her chemotherapy choices. One approach would require her to come to the hospital, for three days in a row per treatment cycle, and they would "attach a bag on your body. You go home for twenty-four hours while the medicine is pumped into your body." She would need to come back a number of times for the three-day-by-twenty-four-hour infusions.

In the second approach, she would receive a combination of pills and injections, which would be administered over a couple of hours in the hospital clinic. "You would receive an injection every three weeks, followed by two weeks of oral medication at home. This method is more convenient, because there is no need for a line to be inserted, no need to bring home any pump." He explained they had only recently begun offering this more convenient treatment regimen, now that it was known to work as well as the more traditional approach.

Chong and her family liked the idea of the more convenient treatment, but the oncologist wanted to make sure they understood its burdens: "It has a risk of diarrhea."

"Mmhm."

"And of numbness, and nerve damage."

"Nerve damage?" her son replied.

"Yes. These are the two biggest [risks]."

The oncologist went on to describe other unpleasant side effects, such as fever, dry skin, and even the risk of her hands turning black. And then the conversation took a twist: Chong's oncologist told her the chemotherapy, which would consist of Xelox, a combination of the drugs capecitabine and oxaliplatin, would cost about $2,000. "Two thousand dollars per month?" her son replied, who began calculating how much would be covered by insurance, and how much they would be responsible for: "Six months is twelve to thirteen thousand dollars. About thirteen or fourteen thousand dollars." He turned to the oncologist, laughing, "Excuse me. How come the drug is so expensive?"

Realizing how much this would burden the family, the oncologist picked up the phone and spoke with the clinic's billing specialist: "Sorry to disturb you, I just want to check. For her Xelox . . . per month, how much is it again?" A pause while he listened. "She's subsidized . . . okay, yeah . . . how do we do that? One vial is how much? Fifty milligrams is nothing, right? . . . Oh no, fifty milligrams is half. Okay, sorry." The conversation continued until he figured out a way to get the chemotherapy without bankrupting Chong and her family.

Pretty amazing interaction. A woman had life-threatening cancer and her doctor spent almost as much time discussing the cost of her care as he spent discussing what that care would entail. I bet you didn't think patients in the United States, when faced with advanced cancer, sat in their doctors' offices discussing health economics.

You are largely correct. In the United States, such conversations are relatively rare.[1] But this conversation occurred in Singapore, where such discussions are ubiquitous, because Singaporeans routinely pay out of pocket for a significant portion of their medical care.[2] When my research team read twenty transcripts of oncology clinic appointments in Singapore, we discovered, without exception, that the patient, the patient's family, or the oncologist brought up the cost of care. Some experts believe that this patient/consumer scrutiny explains why Singaporeans spend only 4 percent of their GDP on healthcare, versus Americans, who spend almost 20 percent.[3]

Some experts believe if the United States wants to lower its healthcare costs, it should become more like Singapore, where patients have an incentive to scrutinize the cost of their medical care.[4] That's certainly the opinion of conservative healthcare expert Avik Roy, who says Singapore's "market-based healthcare system puts America's to shame."[5] That's also the conclusion David Goldhill came to in 2007, after spending several disturbing weeks watching his father succumb to what should have been a treatable illness.[6]

Goldhill's father had been admitted to the hospital with what looked like mild pneumonia, the kind that typically responds to a few days of intravenous (IV) antibiotics. But Goldhill's father contracted a second, more serious infection, one that might have been spread through contact with contaminated equipment or the unwashed hands of his doctors or nurses. Goldhill stayed by his father's side, increasingly concerned about the quality of medical care his father was receiving. In fact, twice Goldhill had to intervene to prevent hospital staff from taking his father to the operating room for surgical procedures that *other* patients were supposed to receive.

As CEO of the Game Show Network, Goldhill witnessed his father's poor hospital care through the eyes of a businessman. But he didn't go on a mission to bring continuous quality improvement methods to hospitals;

he didn't call on hospitals to reduce errors by investing in information technology. Instead, he concluded that American patients need to have more financial responsibility for the cost of their medical care. Goldhill became convinced the American healthcare industry wasn't focused on offering low-cost, high-quality services because patients weren't demanding them. Take Goldhill's father, for example. The hospital charged $650,000 for the five-week hospital stay. The Goldhill family's portion of the bill was only $992. They didn't have "skin in the game"—they didn't face enough out-of-pocket expenses to have reason to scrutinize the cost and quality of their father's medical care.[7]

Whether or not he knew it, Goldhill was concerned about an ancient problem.

The High Cost of Free Care

One of the reasons people go to doctors is to find out what illness or condition is causing their symptoms. Plato would not approve of these kinds of appointments. In *The Republic*, the ancient philosopher even accused physicians of inventing "fluxes and flatulences" to convince people of their need for medical care.[8] Plato was concerned about people who used illness as an excuse to miss work: "If anyone prescribes for him a long course of treatment with swathing about the head and their accompaniments, he hastily says that he has no leisure to be sick, and that such a life of preoccupation with his illness and neglect of the work that lies before him isn't worth living."

Plato's concern was echoed by another ancient source of wisdom— Homer. Not the famous poet, but the one of *Simpsons* fame. In one episode, Homer and his family arrive in Canada. Homer is about to cross a busy intersection when his daughter, Lisa, urgently warns him, "Dad. No. It says don't walk." Nonplussed, Homer replies: "It doesn't matter, they have free healthcare," after which he gets hit by a motor vehicle and gleefully proclaims, "I'm rich!" confident he will face no medical bills for his many injuries.[9]

Receiving free medical care doesn't cause people to hurl themselves in front of speeding vehicles. (It's funny because it's *not* true!) But it does cause people to claim they are sick when they might otherwise shrug off their ailments. In fact, the very first national healthcare system quickly found itself face to face with the problems Plato bemoaned.

It was the latter half of the nineteenth century, and German industry was expanding rapidly. The number of German factory workers skyrocketed from two hundred thousand in 1867 to twelve million by the turn of the century.[10] As a result of this industrialization, many Germans were forced to move from small farming communities to larger cities, where extended family could not as easily care for their needs. If a rural farmer broke his wrist, his family and neighbors could take over his chores until he recovered. But if a factory worker in the city broke his wrist, he couldn't count on friends and neighbors to do his work for him, leaving him without income until he healed. The industrialization of Germany's economy was increasingly leaving Germans one injury or illness away from financial ruin.

In recognition of this problem, Germany's chancellor, Otto von Bismarck, passed a law in 1883 requiring large factories and professional guilds to enroll workers in "sickness funds," to care for employees' financial needs when they were too sick to work.[11] Notably, money from the sickness funds was not used to pay hospital or physician fees. That's because in Bismarck's time, when people got sick, it wasn't hospital bills that bankrupted them. It was lost wages. Sickness funds weren't health insurance plans; they were more like temporary unemployment benefits. A man covered by a sickness fund could expect financial assistance for up to three months if he became too ill to work.

Plato could have warned Bismarck what would come next. Before Bismarck's law, most German men worked even when they were sick or injured; they were "it's just a flesh wound" tough. But after the law, they became less likely to shrug off ailments, calling in sick at double the previous rate.[12] And their illnesses lasted longer, rising from an average of two weeks in duration to three. Germany wasn't alone in experiencing a rash of worker ailments. Denmark established its own sickness funds shortly after Bismarck's legislation and over the next decade saw expenditures for sick workers increase eightfold, as workers became familiar with the benefits of the new law.[13] With funds available to subsidize their time away from work, the price of missing work was dramatically reduced, and workers responded accordingly. Some workers probably feigned illness. Other workers missed work for illnesses they would have previously shrugged off. Yet others who, before the law, might have missed three or four days of work due to illness might now miss six or seven.

Economists have a name for the phenomenon bothering Plato and bedeviling Germany and Denmark—they call it moral hazard.[14] It is moral hazard that concerns people like David Goldhill, who fret that lowering the price of medical care (through overly generous insurance) reduces people's motivation to think critically about their healthcare needs. Goldhill isn't worried about people jumping in front of moving cars or skipping work for minor illnesses. He is worried about people demanding more medical care than they need or care that is not worth the associated cost. Consider the barely used medical equipment littering my third-floor closet. There's the ice machine that ran cold water over my shoulder in the week following my rotator cuff surgery. I tried to return the machine, but the orthopedic clinic told me: "Your insurance has already paid. It's yours!" There are the crutches I used after hip surgery, and the walking boot I needed for a month after ankle surgery. (Yes, I am falling apart.) All this equipment is still in top condition. Dozens of other people could benefit from it, for the small price of cleaning it up. But I have no financial incentive to return the equipment, and indeed would have to spend valuable time trying to figure out who would even take it off my hands.

Or consider the ultrasounds my wife received during her two pregnancies. At the time she was pregnant, there was no evidence that ultrasounds during uncomplicated pregnancies improved the health of either mothers or their children. In fact, the best studies suggested it was of no benefit at all.[15] But our insurance company covered the full cost of those ultrasounds, which meant that other people who enrolled in our plans subsidized the cost of our first baby pictures.

Generous insurance coverage reduces people's out-of-pocket expenses, and they respond by demanding more medical care than they otherwise would have demanded, without carefully scrutinizing the cost of such care. It is reminiscent of the line from *Field of Dreams*—"If you build it, they will come"—with a twist: if you pay for it, they will consume it. When Singapore created its healthcare system in 1983, its prime minister, Lee Kuan Yew, was determined to reduce the influence of moral hazard on people's demand for medical care. So he made sure that when people received medical care, they would be responsible for enough of the cost of that care to scrutinize the necessity of whatever interventions their doctors were recommending.[16] Today, David Goldhill wants to reduce the impact of moral hazard on the U.S. healthcare system, transforming what it means to have healthcare insurance in America. In particular, he wants to turn Americans away from first-dollar insurance plans, toward ones that cover only the cost of catastrophes.

Catastrophic Coverage

It is rarely a good sign when water drips through the ceiling onto your dining room table. When that happened to our house, it cost several thousand dollars to repair the ceiling and the second-floor shower that had caused the water damage. That wasn't the only expensive surprise our house has sprung upon us. We once had electrical problems that I (wisely) chose not to repair on my own. Another time, our back porch demanded resurfacing, after it began thrusting splinters into the unsuspecting feet of barefoot guests. And our toolshed engaged in an earnest impersonation of the Leaning Tower of Pisa, making me wonder—how do they close the doors on that place?

My wife and I have homeowners insurance, but we didn't turn to it for any of these expenses. That's because we bought insurance to cover the cost of unexpected catastrophes. If we suffer a calamitous fire or have our roof ripped off by a hurricane, our insurance will keep us whole. We pay out of pocket for more modest repairs. As a result, when things break down, we scour the internet for repair services that offer low prices and high customer satisfaction.

David Goldhill wants health insurance in the United States to work more like my homeowners policy. He wants to replace overly generous health insurance plans, ones that pay for every minor expense, with catastrophic coverage plans that pay only when people incur extremely high healthcare costs.[17] If you have catastrophic insurance, you will pay for annual checkups and blood pressure pills. You might even bear much of the cost of arthroscopic surgery to clean out that ratty cartilage in your right knee. But if you need a $400,000 liver transplant, your insurance will cover the vast majority of your expenses.

Many conservatives share Goldhill's enthusiasm for catastrophic coverage. Avik Roy, a senior fellow at the Manhattan Institute, contends the United States should adopt "a free market for the 70+% of healthcare where market forces can most directly apply," in which people have the time and ability to comparison shop and use "universal catastrophic insurance for those situations where market forces work less well."[18] Benjamin Domenech, publisher of *The Federalist*, endorses catastrophic coverage as an affordable "backstop against medical bankruptcy."[19] Nobel laureate Milton Friedman endorsed catastrophic coverage in a 2001 essay, stating it would protect people from "events that are highly unlikely to occur but that involve large losses if they do occur."[20] He endorsed a system like Singapore's, for which people put money into health savings accounts, paired with health plans that carry high out-of-pocket expenses, often in the form of high deductibles. (A deductible is the amount a person must pay for health care before insurance begins covering part of their costs.)[21] Politicians like Paul Ryan and Tom Price have endorsed similar agendas, although they have rebranded high-deductible health plans as "consumer-directed health plans."[22]

In recent years, an increasing number of Americans have chosen insurance plans that resemble catastrophic coverage. In 2006, 10 percent of American workers chose plans that carried deductibles of $1,000 or more. That number rose to greater than 50 percent by 2016.[23] The growth in high out-of-pocket health insurance in part reflects efforts by employers to reduce the cost of employee benefits. The days of American companies dominating the world's economy are long gone, meaning they can no longer afford to ignore the high cost of insuring their employees. Private insurance premiums rose more than 58 percent between 2006 and 2016, with family coverage costing more than $18,000 a year.[24] That's a big expense for employers to bear, particularly when trying to compete with companies located in countries that have lower healthcare expenses. American companies have responded by passing an increasing amount of that expense onto their employees through high-deductible health plans. According to a 2018 report from PricewaterhouseCoopers, a quarter of American companies offer only high-deductible health plans to their employees, and another quarter are thinking of following suit.[25]

The turn toward higher out-of-pocket expenses isn't limited to employer-sponsored insurance. Out-of-pocket costs have been rising for Medicare patients, too. In 2016, one in four Medicare beneficiaries spent more than 10 percent of their income covering copays and other out-of-pocket expenses.[26] That proportion rose to almost one in two among people with cognitive or physical limitations, like patients who had suffered strokes or had advanced Parkinson's. Under Medicare, there's not even a ceiling on people's annual out-of-pocket expenses. As a result, almost one in five elderly Americans report having a hard time paying for medical care.[27] By contrast, only 3 percent of senior citizens in France have such problems.[28]

The move toward high out-of-pocket health plans isn't driven only by stingy employers and heartless Medicare administrators. It also reflects the preferences of many individual consumers. In 2011, for example, Bob Shah chose a plan with a $5,000 deductible when the monthly premium of his previous plan shot up several hundred dollars a month.[29] "Every year they [the insurance premiums] go up," the fifty-year-old food mart owner said, "even if I never go to the doctor." He bought a high-deductible plan, figuring it would save him money while still protecting him from the costs of serious illness.

It is these consumer-based choices that excite market enthusiasts, who hope many more Americans will join Bob Shah in choosing insurance plans that cover catastrophic costs, while leaving them responsible for other healthcare costs. In theory, such coverage will cause patients to scrutinize the cost and quality of their medical care, like patients do in Singapore. Fans of high out-of-pocket insurance plans believe Americans will be able to shop their way to more affordable care. But is that realistic? What exactly happens to patients' decisions when they pay out of pocket for medical care? To begin exploring the limits of healthcare consumerism, let's see what happened to Chris Howard after a shocking trip to the restroom.

An Alarming Experience

There is no better color to signal an emergency than red. Red is the color in your rearview mirror when a fire truck rushes up behind you, heading to a blaze. It is the color of the flag NASCAR officials wave when signaling drivers to stop because of an immediate threat to driver safety. It was the color the Bush administration chose after the September 11,

2001, terror attacks to signal the highest risk of a subsequent attack. And, it was the color of the toilet water one day after Chris Howard passed stool.

Howard figured it was probably just a hemorrhoid, or maybe stress-related ulcers from the seventy-five hours a week he spent managing a trucking company in North Carolina. That's why he was shocked when a colonoscopy test uncovered cancer in his rectum—stage three: a cancer that had already begun invading the wall of his intestinal tissue. Any more advanced, and he would have a stage-four tumor, a metastatic cancer spreading to different body sites. And so, at the ripe young age of thirty-eight, Howard found himself face to face with a life-threatening illness.

After going online to research local cancer centers, he arranged for an appointment with Yousuf Zafar, an oncologist at Duke University who specializes in the care of people with tumors that arise from the stomach, pancreas, colon, and rectum. Zafar is blessed with a quick wit and an optimistic demeanor, important attributes in his chosen profession because advanced gastrointestinal cancers are often incurable. Fortunately, in recent years new treatments have come to market that hold promise for slowing down some of these cancers. According to Zafar, "a decade or two ago, patients like Howard would have received months of traditional chemotherapy, with vomiting, diarrhea, and hair loss," all for an average survival time of about two years. Those treatments are still around today, but patients also have the option of newer, more tolerable treatments, including biologic drugs and immunotherapies that have more than doubled survival time. In fact, according to Zafar, almost half of all stage-three colon cancers were curable at the time of Howard's diagnosis in early 2014. Howard had reason to hope that, by discovering the cancer when he did, he had dodged a bullet.

In hopes of shrinking Howard's tumor prior to having the cancer surgically removed, Zafar prescribed a chemotherapeutic drug called capecitabine (Xeloda), approved by the Food and Drug Administration (FDA) in 2005 for treatment of advanced colon and rectal cancer.[30] Howard's body tolerated the therapy without incident and, even better, follow-up scans showed his tumor shrinking. Delighted by this good news, Howard went ahead with the surgery, expecting to come out on the other side completely cancer-free. However, upon returning to the clinic after his operation, Howard received shocking news. His cancer had spread to his liver, a spread that hadn't shown up on any of his imaging tests. Rather than being cured by the surgery, Howard's cancer had progressed to stage four. He wasn't cured; he was terminally ill. He wasn't finished with treatments; he was only beginning.

Fighting back tears, Zafar tried to provide reassurance, explaining that Howard could slow down the cancer by going back on chemo. Now it was Zafar's turn to be shocked. Touched by his doctor's empathy, Howard told him, "I can't go back on the medicines." When Zafar responded with befuddlement, Howard explained, "I don't have enough money to pay for the chemo." You see, even with insurance covering the majority of his expenses, Howard had been responsible to pay $400 a week out of his own pocket for the capecitabine, which at the time was available only as a brand-name drug, Xeloda, in the weeks preceding his operation. (That might sound like stingy coverage, but capecitabine cost more than $4,000 a week at the time of Howard's treatment, meaning insurance was still covering 90 percent of the price.) He had also been responsible for hefty copays for the computed tomography (CT) and MRI scans Zafar had ordered to monitor his tumor, and for the operation he underwent to remove the cancer. As a result, by the time of his surgery, he had depleted his bank account. If that operation had cured his cancer, as expected, he'd have been able to go back to work and replenish his financial stores. But with no more savings to deplete, further treatment was out of reach.

Zafar was despondent. Mostly, he was distressed that Howard's tumor was incurable. In addition, he was upset that he hadn't recognized that Howard had paid so much out of pocket for his chemo. Zafar was especially troubled about this oversight because he could have treated Howard's cancer with an older therapy, an intravenous chemotherapy that would have been just as likely to shrink Howard's tumor as capecitabine, but with little or no out-of-pocket expense. By some fluke of the American health-care system, insurance companies often pay most of the cost of IV chemotherapies, considering such treatments to be hospital expenses worthy of generous coverage. By contrast, insurance companies categorize chemotherapy pills as medication expenses, which they don't cover as generously.[31] "I thought I was improving Chris's quality of life by prescribing him pills, and relieving him of the need to come to my office for IV treatment,"

Zafar told me. "If I had checked on his out-of-pocket costs, this never would have happened."

Chris Howard bought the kind of high-deductible health plan that enthusiasts like David Goldhill believe will empower American healthcare consumers. In Goldhill's defense, Howard's insurance plan should have contributed more generously to his healthcare costs once he had paid off his deductible. Nevertheless, Howard's story illustrates the dangerous naïveté of viewing patients (and their physicians) as rational decision makers, scanning the horizons for the best combination of cost and efficiency among people's healthcare alternatives.

We *do* have a healthcare spending problem in the United States, and overly generous healthcare coverage *does* contribute to that problem. But we have to be careful about rushing too quickly from diagnosis ("overly generous insurance reduces consumer motivation") to treatment ("the threat of incurring out-of-pocket expenses will turn patients into savvy consumers").

If we want to understand the role of consumer markets in curbing healthcare spending, we need to understand how doctors and patients make medical decisions. Before we create laws designed to empower patients, we need to explore what such empowerment means in exam rooms and hospital beds. We need to put healthcare markets in their place— empowering people like Chris Howard to make informed healthcare choices among affordable alternatives while also regulating groups like doctors, hospitals, and pharmaceutical companies so they can provide people with healthcare goods and services without bankrupting them.

In Part II of this book, I will describe what smarter healthcare markets look like. But before we can see our way to smarter markets, we need to understand how we got into this mess in the first place. That will be a job for the rest of Part I.

2

SHOPPING IN THE DARK

It makes no sense to promote healthcare policies that ask people to pay out of pocket for their medical care if patients cannot figure out the cost of that care before receiving it. The promise of healthcare markets depends in large part on patients learning about the costs of proposed healthcare interventions before receiving them. It also depends on people understanding, when they purchase health insurance, how much their plan expects them to pay out of pocket for their healthcare. Unfortunately, such learned understanding is not the norm in the United States, as illustrated by what happened to Andrea Polk when she experienced a concerning symptom.

It started as a vague sensation in her right ear. Something wasn't quite right, but the symptom wasn't severe enough to require immediate attention. Over the next few days, the sensation progressed—it felt like she was on an airplane that had changed altitude too quickly. Polk needed to see a doctor.

At the time, Polk was a busy undergraduate at Duke University. A daughter of two social workers, she could afford to attend that expensive university only thanks to hefty doses of financial aid. Fortunately, Polk could afford to see a doctor, because she had signed up for student health insurance. So she went to student health, where a primary care physician looked into her ears, probably making sure her symptoms weren't merely the result of a buildup of earwax. Unsure of what was causing her symptoms, Polk's primary care physician referred her to the ear, nose, and throat

(ENT) clinic. Several days later, Polk showed up at that clinic, surprised to discover she had to pay before seeing the doctor: "I thought the appointment would be covered by my insurance, but I had to swipe my credit card before they would see me." She had never heard the word copay before, but with little choice in the matter, she swiped her card and waited for the nurse to call her name. Eventually, she saw the ENT physician, who examined her and then sent her down the hall to an audiology testing room, where she donned headphones and raised her hand when she heard beeping sounds in either ear. At the end of the appointment, the doctor told Polk her "symptoms will probably resolve shortly." She returned to campus, reassured.

A couple of weeks later, Polk received a bill from the ENT clinic for $800. Not a bill as in, "We sent an $800 claim to your insurance company and just wanted you to know we are waiting for their payment," but, instead, a document stating that her audiology test was "not covered by her insurance" and therefore she owed the clinic $800—by the end of the month.

Polk was stunned. She had already spent thousands of dollars on insurance—money she and her parents had scrounged together—and now the insurance company wouldn't pay for the test? Polk called the insurance company to question the bill. A clerk explained that her plan "doesn't pay for routine hearing tests." "But my test wasn't routine," Polk stated incredulously. "Your test result was normal," the clerk said. "We only pay for the test when it is related to an illness or a problem, not when it is routine screening." "But I had a problem. That's why they ran the test!" Polk clarified. "I'm sorry, but the test wasn't *indicated*, so we can't pay for it."

Polk received medical care without any idea of what that care would cost. Although she found out about the copay for her ENT visit before seeing that doctor, she learned about the copay only after arriving at the clinic. This left her no time to decide whether she should give her ears more time to recover on their own before spending that kind of money. Worse, when Polk went to the ENT clinic, the cost of her audiology examination was completely hidden. She didn't have an opportunity to check online for the price of audiology testing at other local clinics, or to contemplate whether she needed the test at all. In normal consumer markets, people learn and compare the price of goods and services before purchasing them.

Polk learned that in healthcare markets, patients are often forced to shop in the dark.

In this chapter, I'll illuminate the opaque world of healthcare prices in the United States. I'll show that Polk is far from alone in having difficulty figuring out what she will have to pay for medical care in time to decide whether to receive that care. I'll briefly explain *why* healthcare prices are so often hidden from patients. And I'll explore the psychological forces that dissuade many people from even trying to find out the price of their healthcare. But first, I'll start with a price that's right out in the open, for all to see, but that nevertheless leaves most people mystified about how much they'll pay once they decide what to buy.

I'll start by showing what happens when people purchase healthcare insurance.

Insurance Inscrutability

The last time you bought a car, you probably knew whether it had cruise control or four-wheel drive. You didn't have to read a complicated manual to know whether it had a sun roof or third row seating. Contrast that with the last time you bought health insurance. How well did you understand your coverage? Any idea how many physical therapy appointments your insurance company promised to pay for if you strained your back? Did you know whether your plan would pay for chemotherapy pills and, if so, how much of that cost it would require you to bear?

Choosing insurance is often terribly confusing. It starts with inscrutable terminology, like *copay, coinsurance,* and *deductible.*[1] Mary Politi, a medical decision-making expert at Washington University, led a research study in St. Louis in which her team interviewed people in low-income neighborhoods to understand how they chose insurance plans. One of the people she interviewed explained that "the language [of insurance] isn't necessarily built for understanding." He couldn't remember the difference between a premium and a copay; "I kept messing up in my head. I was 'okay, which is which?' It was really confusing."[2] Other people Politi interviewed were confused about the word *deductible*. In normal consumer contexts, the word suggests a bargain, like the seller is reducing the price of a good. All else equal, wouldn't you rather buy a shirt where the store deducts $20 from the price rather than one where they only deduct $10? In insurance contexts, however, *deductible* has an upside-down meaning—a $5,000 deductible means your insurance will not cover *any* of your expenses until you've spent $5,000 out of pocket on medical care.[3] Because of this upside-down connotation—with bigger deductibles being worse than small ones—only 22 percent of the people Politi surveyed understood the term, even after reading a definition.[4] To make matters even more confusing, under the Affordable Care Act (ACA), insurance companies are forbidden from charging patients for essential services, such as screening colonoscopies for people age fifty and older.[5] That means a person can enroll in a high-deductible insurance plan—confused about what a deductible is—receive a colonoscopy for free, and then, after getting an X-ray for an ankle sprain, wonder why he or she has to pay the full cost of the test.

Consider another insurance term: *coinsurance*. It signifies the percentage of medical expenses a patient is responsible for; for example, a 10 percent coinsurance rate means when you receive $10,000 of medical care, you'll be responsible for $1,000 of that cost.[6] The word *coinsurance* confused many people in Politi's study, with one person telling the research team he thought coinsurance referred to people who have "two separate insurances." After hearing the actual definition, he was exasperated: "The language, it's very convoluted. . . . It assumes that the average person has a reading skill and a knowledge set that most people don't have, that college graduates don't have."

Because of jargon alone, many people have difficulty understanding their health insurance choices.[7] To make matters worse, even when they understand the details of available plans, they often get overwhelmed by the bewildering array of plans vying for their business.

Consider websites where people shop for insurance under the Affordable Care Act. On a typical website, the options are listed in rows, with information spilling down across a half-dozen or so columns. One column might list the deductible and another the monthly premium, while other columns lay out the copays required for primary care and subspecialty appointments, emergency room visits, and hospital stays. One column might list the price of generic versus non-generic drugs, while yet another column indicates the maximum out-of-pocket expense a patient can incur in a given year. Some plans charge lower premiums but higher out-of-pocket costs.

With all these facts laid out in crisp, clean detail, informed consumers presumably have all the information needed to make a choice. But are they up to the challenge of processing all that information and choosing plans that fit their preferences and health needs?

When researchers have given people this kind of health insurance information, they've discovered that many make bad choices, choosing plans that are demonstrably worse than other plans offered.[8] For example, suppose two plans are identical—same copays, same out-of-pocket maximum, same deductible, and so on—except for one difference: Plan A costs more per month than Plan B. In such a situation, no one in their right mind would choose Plan A.[9] Nevertheless, when behavioral economists have studied health insurance choices among employees of large companies, they've discovered that a third to a half choose plans guaranteed to cost them more money than available plans they don't choose.[10] For example, one company offered its employees a plan carrying a $1,000 deductible and a relatively low monthly premium. It offered another plan carrying a $750 deductible with a premium costing $44 more per month. Many employees chose that second plan, presumably to lower the size of their deductibles. But let's look at the math of that choice. People who chose that second plan were required to pay $528 more in premiums over the course of the year, $44 per month times twelve months.[11] I wasn't a math major in college, but paying $528 to lower your deductible by $250 doesn't add up!

One of the problems with insurance choices is that good choices often depend upon a person's ability to do complicated math. Even when people are fully informed about the choices they face as consumers, the sheer complexity of this math can undermine their decisions. Herbert Simon referred to these decision-making problems as "bounded rationality."[12] Simon was a Nobel Prize–winning economist at Carnegie Mellon University whose ideas helped establish the field of behavioral economics. In his work, Simon challenged the assumption of rationality predominant in economic theories of the early and mid-twentieth century. He pointed out that lack of knowledge can cause people to make irrational choices, ones that go against their best interests. For example, suppose a person wants to maximize her chance of surviving a life-threatening illness; she will have a hard time doing so if she isn't aware of a treatment option known to maximize her odds of survival.

But Simon didn't see knowledge as the only barrier to rational choice. In addition, when decisions become too complex, he contended that people sometimes lack the "computational capacity" to identify the right choice.[13] For example, when I play chess, I have a clear goal: to win the game. And I have full knowledge of the rules, aware of how each piece moves and the like. But when I consider all the moves available to me, I'm quickly overwhelmed; I can't figure out which move or moves maximize my chance of coming out victorious.

For many people, health insurance is like chess—it's too complicated for them to figure out what choice to make. For example, people with ongoing health problems often face predictable expenses they should ideally factor into their insurance choices. A person with rheumatoid arthritis might be taking medicines costing $10,000 a year; he should realize that a high-deductible health plan, despite having relatively low monthly premiums, will cost more in the long run than other plans because of high out-of-pocket expenses. Nevertheless, due to the complexity of insurance choices, around 40 percent of people with chronic illness choose plans that end up *predictably* costing them more than alternative plans would have cost.[14]

Insurance choices are also undermined by the sheer number of plans some people choose among, a phenomenon behavioral scientists call choice overload.[15] Many behavioral economic studies have shown that too much choice can be demotivating. As Columbia professor Sheena Iyengar famously demonstrated, people are more likely to purchase jams from supermarket tasting booths displaying six flavors than from ones displaying twenty-four.[16] When contemplating an overwhelming number of flavors, people disengage from the decision; it's simply too much to think about. They worry they'll purchase strawberry rhubarb jam and later regret they didn't buy apricot. To avoid regret, they decide not to decide.[17]

But of course, health insurance differs in important ways from supermarket jams. When it comes to purchasing health insurance, people often don't have the option to not decide. Under the first eight years of the ACA, people paid a tax penalty if they failed to purchase health insurance.[18] Forced to make a choice, people perused their options. In some locations, that meant choosing from almost fifty plans.[19] Faced with the prerequisite of making a choice, information overload takes its toll.[20] Consider a woman

Politi interviewed: "I'm concerned that I make this decision to help me today, [and then] maybe my diabetes, maybe my gout if that's flared up, . . . then I'm afraid that my choice [of an insurance plan] may eliminate my dental [coverage] in the future." This woman was stressed, because she knew the importance of this decision: "Once I make it, it's done . . . until next year."[21]

Frequently, when people are overwhelmed by choice, they give up and pick whatever they can find a reason to pick ("I like the name of that plan") or whatever comes easily to mind.[22] They resort to simple decision rules, even if that means ignoring important information relevant to making the best choice. For example, people might base their choices on a single attribute—monthly premium, say, or lowest maximum out-of-pocket cost—without paying attention to other important attributes, such as whether their plan covers experimental treatments or mental health.[23] Sometimes the devil is in the details, but instead, people anchor on one data point instead of wading through the muck.[24] One study showed that when Medicare enrollees chose insurance plans to cover their medication expenses, only 20 percent chose ones that optimized their out-of-pocket coverage.[25] Similarly, a study of 18,000 health insurance enrollees found that almost a quarter didn't know whether they had chosen a traditional insurance plan or a managed healthcare plan (called an HMO, at the time).[26] That's like leaving the car dealer without knowing whether you bought a Honda or a Lamborghini.

Some health policy experts have tried to overcome the problems caused by information overload. For example, when the state of Massachusetts created an insurance exchange as part of its healthcare plan (dubbed "Romneycare" after Mitt Romney, governor of Massachusetts when the plan was enacted), folks designing the website simplified the information by dividing the plans into three groups.[27] Instead of, say, showing people eighteen insurance plans available in their neighborhood, the website explained they should first choose from three categories of insurance plans: bronze plans, with low premiums and high out-of-pocket costs; silver plans, with medium premiums and medium out-of-pocket costs; or gold plans, with high premiums and low out-of-pocket costs.

But research I conducted with David Comerford, a behavioral economist at the University of Stirling, showed that this well-intentioned effort to simplify insurance choice—with bronze, silver, and gold plans—could unwittingly influence people's decisions. Members of our research team rode buses in Durham, North Carolina, one afternoon, and handed commuters a one-page brochure describing bronze, silver, and gold plans, followed by a short survey asking them which type of plan they'd be interested in if they were shopping for insurance. The twist in our study was that, for a random half of commuters, we switched the description of bronze and gold plans: for one group, we described gold plans as having "higher monthly costs, but lower costs when you receive care," and for the other, we described them as having "lower monthly costs, but higher costs when you receive care." We discovered that people preferred gold plans over bronze plans, *no matter which type of plan was described as gold*.[28] The connotations of Olympic medals—where gold is better than bronze—overwhelmed the information we gave them about their health insurance choices. In another study, my collaborators and I presented people with a set of insurance plans, ordered top to bottom from lowest to highest monthly premiums.[29] We presented them with actual plans available on Healthcare.gov as part of Obamacare. Here's the twist—for half the people, we reversed the order of the plans, from highest to lowest monthly premiums. This reordering of the same five plans led to a dramatic shift in people's choices. For example, one insurance plan (which happened to have the second lowest monthly premium) was chosen by almost one in three people when we presented plans the way Healthcare.gov presents them: from lowest to highest monthly premium. But when we flipped the order of plans, only one out of sixteen people chose that plan. In a sea of complex information, people unwittingly allowed the mere ordering of plans to influence their decisions.

So far, I've laid out a few behavioral economic phenomena that undermine people's insurance choices ranging from knowledge deficiencies to information overload. Presumably, we could overcome some of these problems by simplifying people's choices, an approach I'll discuss in Part II. But that would still leave us with another important challenge for healthcare consumers: recognizing that the difference in price across insurance plans doesn't merely reflect the difference in deductibles and premiums, but also reflects hidden differences in the way insurance companies decide whether to reimburse patients for the care they receive. In one of our studies, a woman with breast cancer complained that her insurance company refused to pay for her new chemotherapy pill. Her oncologist was perplexed: "They said 'no'? . . . That is a big surprise because you have all the reasons to be on it." He explained that the medicine was FDA-approved for her cancer. They talked about appealing the decision, but with no confidence they'd succeed.

This conversation highlights perhaps the most inscrutable part of insurance decisions—figuring out what services competing insurance plans will pay for, in time to inform your choices. Some insurance plans are significantly more likely to deny payment for treatments they consider experimental. Some insurers are more likely to conclude a procedure is "not indicated." Some are more aggressive about establishing barriers to dissuade doctors from ordering expensive tests and treatments, thus reducing the chance patients will get those interventions. But when people purchase insurance, they have no way of figuring out which plans are more and which less aggressive about denying care.

Free markets have a hard time promoting societal well-being when people don't understand what they are buying. Insurance choice is beset by specialized terminology, choices that are tough to compare, and information that's hard to pinpoint when it's time to pull the trigger. In that kind of decision context, markets don't pan out. And we haven't even gotten beyond insurance choices to the more consequential choices Americans face when they get sick—figuring out what medical care they should receive. In fact, after people choose insurance plans, the shopping isn't over. For many people, it has just begun.

What's This Going to Cost Me?

Even imaginary grandmothers deserve to know the price of their medical care. That was the inspiration behind a study led by Pete Cram, a physician at the University of Toronto. Cram recruited a group of students to call hospitals around the United States to get estimates of the cost of hip replacement surgery.[30] Cram's team explained they were helping their sixty-two-year-old grandmother, who needed a new hip but didn't have health insurance. How much, they asked, would the procedure cost?

Getting a satisfactory answer to this question was teeth-gnashingly difficult. For starters, most hospital websites didn't publish phone numbers patients could call to receive price estimates. Finding the right person to talk to, who could answer this question, often required patience that would test a seasoned diplomat. Compounding this difficulty, when Cram's shoppers got lucky enough to find hospital employees able to give them price estimates, those estimates were often limited to hospital charges, leaving the team in the dark about how much the surgeon would charge for the procedure. You see, when patients get hip replacements, hospitals charge them for the cost of the operating rooms, the antibiotics, the artificial joints, and the anesthesia drugs, but they don't usually bill them for the time and effort of their surgeons. Those bills come separately, from surgeons' offices. That means Cram's research assistants, to determine the full price of their imaginary grandma's hip replacement, needed to call not only the hospitals where the procedure would take place, but also the offices of surgeons who would perform the procedures. When making these calls, they often encountered an additional slew of "let-me-transfer-you-to's." The result of all this superhuman effort? Cram's team got complete price information only 10 percent of the time.

Why was it so difficult to get this price information? The difficulty didn't occur because Cram's team shopped for an obscure medical procedure. According to the Centers for Disease Control and Prevention (CDC), over 300,000 people receive hip replacement surgery each year in the United States.[31] The difficulty also didn't occur because people lack the time or motivation to shop for this kind of procedure. Hip replacement surgeries are rarely urgent, meaning most patients have plenty of time to research their alternatives. Moreover, hip replacements are expensive, meaning lots of patients have an incentive to scrutinize the cost of available providers.

So, why is shopping for the price of hip replacements so difficult? The difficulty arises in part from the many goods and services included in the hip replacement surgery. Hospitals typically charge patients for the use of the operating room (OR) and for the labor provided by OR nurses and technicians. They also charge patients for the cost of the medicines used during the procedure—like antibiotics, sedatives, and painkillers—and for the equipment used during the procedure—like scalpels, bandages, and the artificial joint.

A discerning bargain hunter could ask about the cost of each component of the procedure, and search for a less expensive antibiotic or metal implant. But it is almost impossible for patients to find out the cost of their antibiotics or their metallic implants. In fact, even their surgeons can't produce that information. A research team led by Kanu Okike, himself an orthopedic surgeon, asked American orthopedic surgeons to estimate the cost of the devices they use in their procedures; the vast majority didn't have a clue. When asked about the cost of relatively inexpensive accoutrements, like surgical clips or staples, most surgeons significantly overestimated the price. When asked about expensive devices, like hip joints, they significantly underestimated the price.[32] Ask a doctor how much something costs, and you are unlikely to get an accurate answer. American physicians practice largely unaware of the cost of the services they provide.

I don't blame doctors for being unfamiliar with all their prices. In medical school, we are not trained to understand the economics of healthcare, our schedules bursting with courses on diagnosing and treating illness. Moreover, it doesn't make sense for orthopedic surgeons to know the cost of specific devices, when those costs will be folded into hospital bills that, at least until recently, were largely covered by people's insurance plans.

Price opacity is not unique to hip replacements but, instead, is the norm for most medical care in the United States. When researchers tried to find out prices for gallbladder surgery, hysterectomy, and screening colonoscopy in California, they succeeded less than a third of the time.[33] When another group of researchers called Philadelphia-area hospitals to find out the price of electrocardiograms, they succeeded only three out of twenty times.[34]

This price opacity might not be a big deal, if healthcare prices in the United States showed little variation. If every hip replacement procedure cost around the same amount, there wouldn't be much reason for people to shop around. But that's not the case. Some hospitals charge as little as $10,000 for a hip replacement, while others quote prices greater than $80,000.

Healthcare prices in the United States often vary dramatically across hospitals and providers. Carpal tunnel surgery can cost as little as $3,000 or as much as $15,000; an MRI of the brain for as little as $624 or as much as $7,106. In normal markets, such price variation would cause consumers to flock to lower-priced providers, as long as they offered decent-quality care. But price information is often so difficult to ascertain that people cannot direct their business to affordable providers.

In most parts of the economy, price variation is a sign of a healthy market. Such variation allows customers to pressure manufacturers to either lower their prices or raise the quality of their offerings enough to justify higher prices. If Apple wants to charge more for its cell phones than Samsung, it needs to manufacture superior products. But in healthcare, such variation often arises from the bewildering complexity of the United States healthcare system, which often leads hospitals to charge different amounts to different patients for the same procedure. A hip replacement at Des Moines General Hospital might cost one patient $450 (the copay), another $3,000 (the 10 percent coinsurance charge), and yet another $30,000 (if he or she doesn't have insurance). Maybe one patient hasn't incurred any previous healthcare expenses this year and must fork over the first $2,000 of her deductible before insurance kicks in. Maybe another patient is in the same situation but faces a smaller deductible. Maybe another patient has reached her deductible but faces different copay obligations, or a different coinsurance rate. Oh, yes, and depending on which company carries their insurance policy, the hospital will probably have negotiated a different price for the procedure.[35]

To make matters even more confusing, the amount any patient pays out of pocket depends critically not just on what insurance plan they have purchased, but also on whether that plan decides the service was "indicated." Andrea Polk ran into that word when she discovered her insurance company was not inclined to pay for her $800 audiology test. In my research on physician–patient cost conversations, I have come across scores of physicians and patients fretting about whether insurance will cover services the physician wants to order.[36] One physician we studied was trying to order an echocardiogram for his patient, who was taking chemotherapy that might affect her heart function. The physician explained that because it had been a while since she'd had an echo, she should be eligible, but then added that "insurance companies are getting kind of funny about these things." He could not suppress his frustration. "I think there are ulterior motives [behind their decisions]. It is a harmless test. The only toxicity is financial toxicity."

Sometimes even when people get price estimates for medical interventions, those turn out to be wrong, because some of the people involved in providing the care aren't covered by the patient's insurance company. Consider a screening colonoscopy Laurence LaRose received, one he planned on undergoing without anesthesia. When he arrived for the test, his doctor told him anesthesia was routine for the procedure. LaRose relented, but only after receiving assurance that "anesthesiology would be covered." Unfortunately, the anesthesiologist working in the clinic that day was not under contract with LaRose's insurance company; he was "out of network," leaving LaRose with a bill for $1,012.[37]

Surprise bills are surprisingly common in the United States. When researchers from the Federal Trade Commission analyzed patients admitted to American hospitals in 2014—specifically, those admitted through emergency rooms—they discovered one in five incurred bills for "out-of-network services." In Florida and New York, that number was closer to one in three.[38]

Sometimes, patients receive surprise bills because their medical care goes in unexpected directions. Under Obamacare, for example, patients are not supposed to pay anything out of pocket for screening colonoscopies, to encourage people to receive these important, lifesaving tests. But sometimes physicians see polyps during screening colonoscopies and remove them; it is those polyp removals, after all, that prevent polyps from turning into deadly cancer. Unfortunately, until the regulation was revised, removal of the polyp transformed the free screening test into a cancer treatment, and Obamacare didn't make such treatments free.[39] As a result, some patients woke up from their colonoscopies to find out they had to pay hundreds of dollars for what they thought was a free screening test.

We have a healthcare shopping problem in the United States. When shopping for health insurance, many people find the experience incomprehensible, overwhelming, and misleading. Once they've got insurance, they can't easily figure out what specific healthcare interventions will cost them, and too often receive surprise bills with outrageous price tags.

Why are healthcare prices in the United States so inscrutable? Price opacity doesn't just roll up to thousands of insurance plans and tens of thousands of arcane reimbursement rules. For more than three decades, it was the law of the land.

Too Much Money to Bring Out of the Dark

Would you like the federal government to publish your name, address, and details of your personal income for everyone to see? In 1977 American physicians detested the idea. Joseph Califano, who oversaw Medicare as Secretary of Health Education and Welfare, had just published the names of every physician or physician group billing Medicare for at least $100,000 worth of services the previous year. Now Califano wanted to go further, and publish names, addresses, and Medicare billing data for every physician caring for Medicare patients, regardless of how few patients they'd seen; he hoped such data would make it easier for third parties to identify physicians engaging in Medicare fraud.[40] Physicians were enraged, accusing the government of violating their privacy. Determined to halt Califano, the Florida Medical System filed suit.[41] The Fifth Circuit of Appeals sided with the physicians.

So far, I've laid out a host of factors that make it hard for Americans to determine the price of medical care. Physicians aren't taught to pay attention to healthcare prices. Insurance is so complex that no single healthcare service has a single price. And the healthcare system is so disconnected that a single procedure, like a hip replacement, can generate a bevy of bills—one from the hospital, another from the surgeon, and (surprise!) another from the out-of-network anesthesiologist who helped with the case. Now I turn to another crucial factor that leads to opaque healthcare prices in the United States: payers and providers are determined to keep those prices in the shadows.

Why so much secrecy? Consider what happened in the late 1990s, when my wife, Paula, was director of managed care at Temple University Healthcare System in Philadelphia. In her job, she helped Temple negotiate reimbursement rates with local insurance companies. Each negotiation was unique. One insurance company played hardball over the cost of bypass surgery, and another over the price of a hip replacement. As a result, Temple did not have one price for bypass surgery. It had a Medicare price, a Medicaid price, a price for insurance company A, and another for insurance companies B and C. Then two local insurance companies merged, the two companies now having access to the prices each had negotiated for Temple's services. The newly merged insurance company quickly realized one company had negotiated a better price for bypass surgery than the other, and vice versa for the cost of hip replacement. The newly formed company demanded Temple lower its prices to match whichever of the two companies had negotiated a lower rate for any given service.

This is all to say: there is a reason healthcare providers like to keep their prices secret. Advertise the results of negotiations and everyone will demand your best offer. It has long been customary for hospitals and insurers to adopt gag clauses after they negotiate prices with each other, to keep those prices confidential.[42] As a result, your local hospital knows what it charges Aetna for bypass surgery, and of course Aetna knows what it's going to pay your local hospital for that service, but you can't know that information—it is confidential.[43]

Such secrecy partly explains the high price of healthcare in the United States. When patients are forced to shop in the dark, it is easier for healthcare providers to raise their prices. But secrecy alone cannot be the explanation for America's price problem. After all, insurance companies know the price of people's medical care, and seemingly have every reason to push for better prices from doctors, hospitals, drug companies, and the like. So why are prices so high?

The answer is: eighty-two.

Power and Prices

Bismarck passed his revolutionary sickness fund bill in 1883. The U.S. government didn't get seriously involved with healthcare payment until 1965—eighty-two years after Bismarck's legislation, when President Johnson signed Medicare and Medicaid into law, providing healthcare coverage to elderly and low-income Americans, respectively. By the time Medicare and Medicaid were established, healthcare providers had had more than eight decades to gain power and prestige. With all that power and prestige came the ability for doctors and hospitals to set the prices of their services. It was because of all this power that Johnson agreed to have Medicare reimburse physicians at the seventy-fifth percentile of customary charges; such generosity was the price the president had to pay to keep providers from opposing his legislation.

Insurance companies were no better than Medicare at combating rising healthcare prices. In theory, insurance companies in the 1950s and 1960s should have been working to restrain healthcare spending. But for the most part, they didn't. Doctors and hospitals billed them for services, and the insurance companies paid, with few questions asked. In part, insurance companies were relatively passive because both Blue Cross and Blue Shield owed their existence to hospitals and doctors, respectively, who had funded the original plans that became those networks.[44] In effect, the private healthcare insurance industry in the United States was less a competitor with providers than it was a partner.

Insurance companies had another reason not to fret about high healthcare prices. They knew if they could raise premiums enough to match rising expenses, they would make more than enough money to cover the rise in prices. Over the long run, healthcare inflation is good for health insurance companies. Suppose health insurance companies price their premiums to achieve a 4 percent margin at the end of the year. It's better to take home 4 percent of $100 million than 4 percent of $80 million. High healthcare spending is good for the insurance industry.

We have a healthcare shopping problem in the United States because of a collision of factors. We have high prices because we have powerful providers. We have a history of protecting patients from those prices through generous insurance coverage. And even when coverage is less generous, patients often don't understand the basics of that coverage, and have a hard time finding out the cost of medical alternatives in time to inform their healthcare choices. I've explored many of the structural forces that have purposefully hidden healthcare prices from most Americans—the secret price negotiations between payers and providers, and the reluctance of government payers to take on these powerful interests.

As a behavioral scientist, however, I see much more than politics and economics at play. I see patients grappling with difficult medical decisions at the same time as they struggle to understand the healthcare system those decisions must be made within. As a result, too many people end up in the situation Andrea Polk found herself in, after receiving that surprise bill for the $800 audiology test. They lose trust in the healthcare system and become reluctant to receive even necessary medical care. Polk's view of American healthcare was permanently altered by that surprise $800 expense.

One year after her ENT appointment, Polk's primary care doctor noticed a lump on her thyroid and recommended an ultrasound. The former Polk, the one from twelve months earlier, would have nodded along passively, doing whatever her doctor recommended. But the new Polk asked him how much it would cost. He didn't know, but he was confident it would be covered by insurance. Besides, he told her, the test was "necessary." She reluctantly agreed.

The ultrasound revealed a tiny mass: "Most likely benign," her doctor told her, "probably nothing but an inactive growth. But you should get a biopsy." More tests? More expenses? All for what would turn out to be "probably nothing." "Is this test really necessary?" Polk asked. "I don't know if it's necessary, but it's a test I think you should get. On the off chance that this is something serious, you don't want it to go untreated for six or twelve months. You want to nip it in the bud."

Polk wasn't keen to nip anything. She wanted to graduate with enough money to put down a deposit on an apartment in Los Angeles, where she planned to launch her career as an actress. So she refused further testing. And that is where her story now stands. She graduated from college and moved to California, where she landed a leading role in a television comedy series. A small mass still sits on the right side of her thyroid. Probably nothing. Hopefully benign. But only time will tell.

With prices hidden in the shadows, American patients have little chance of exerting the kind of consumer savvy needed to reign in U.S. healthcare spending. Patients need help. Time to see whether their doctors are prepared to provide it.

3

WHO'S IN CHARGE? THE SURPRISING TRUTH ABOUT MEDICAL DECISIONS

Her baby was unhappy, whimpering when she squeezed his leg gently. Thinking it was a minor injury, she left her baby at home and headed to the medical school where she worked as a research professor. Her husband got home earlier than she did that afternoon and called to tell her that their baby was still in pain. She rushed home from work and saw that he was no better than when she'd left that morning. Her worry was growing, but the clinic down the street had closed for the day. Should she bring him to an urgent care clinic or wait until morning to schedule an appointment? Not wanting to take any chances, she brought him to urgent care, where they told her everything would be fine and prescribed an over-the-counter anti-inflammatory medication.

As we've seen, a market advocate might look at a story like this and see the hazards of overly generous insurance. Many conservatives argue that overly generous insurance floods emergency rooms (ERs) and urgent care centers with patients who are not emergently ill. Pat McCrory, former governor of North Carolina, once complained that the state's Medicaid program was "broken" for failing to contain the use of expensive ERs.[1] That was also the conclusion of a 1992 report from the inspector general of the Department of Health and Human Services, whose office estimated that as much as 61 percent of ER use by Medicaid patients was inappropriate or marginally appropriate.[2] Concerned about such overuse, many Medicaid programs have begun charging people for unnecessary ER visits.[3]

But how do we know whether exposing patients to higher out-of-pocket costs improves their choices? Critics of generous insurance point to increased ER use after Medicaid expansion under Obamacare.[4] But increased use doesn't necessarily mean increased *inappropriate* use. Take the concerned professor, for example. Was that urgent care visit inappropriate? Even though she worked at a medical center, she herself wasn't a clinician. How was she supposed to know whether her baby could wait another day to receive medical care? Moreover, it wasn't overly generous insurance that caused her to go to urgent care, for the simple reason that she didn't have any insurance coverage for her baby, who happened to be a dog, not a human. When her husband called to tell her the dog was still whimpering, she was overwhelmed with guilt for not seeking medical care earlier. So she panicked. Part of her knew that her dog would make it through the night without veterinary care, but the mother in her was consumed with the possibility that any further delay could have fatal consequences.

The story of the panicked professor is true. (I have hidden her identity to protect her dog's confidentiality.) I tell her story to point out two truths. First, many patients, or parents of patients, don't know how quickly they ought to seek medical care. Second, even when people face out-of-pocket expenses, they might still seek out medical care that expert clinicians would deem to be unnecessary.

Of course, the panicked professor's story is a mere anecdote. People on all sides of the political spectrum can draw upon anecdotes that support their worldviews. Indeed, politicians disagree vehemently about whether higher out-of-pocket expenses will lead patients, on average, to make better or worse decisions than they would have made without the possibility of such expenses. What pundits seem to forget is that the plural of "anecdote" is not "data." Marshalling a slew of stories to back up your worldview doesn't prove that your worldview is 20/20.

That's why, in telling the professor's story, I don't claim to prove anything about the relationship between out-of-pocket expenses and the quality of people's healthcare decisions. Instead, I tell her story to highlight the challenge many people face when told to act as empowered healthcare consumers. Theories of healthcare consumerism hold that when patients have a financial stake in medical choices, they will more carefully explore their healthcare alternatives. I'll start the chapter by showing that this view is *partially* true: out-of-pocket expenses do cause people to think twice about receiving medical care, but not necessarily in ways that improve their decisions.

Not to suggest that empowerment forces people to make decisions on their own. That's why, in the latter part of the chapter, I'll explore ways to improve medical decisions by having patients partner with their doctors to make those choices. Unfortunately, the research I'll present raises fundamental questions about whether doctors are up to that challenge.

Does a Copay a Day Keep the Doctor Away?

Chemists use test tubes and beakers to control the universe within which they run their experiments. If a chemist wants to figure out how temperature influences a particular chemical reaction, she can mix precise quantities of these chemicals while varying the temperature of the solution, and through these carefully controlled methods discover an answer to her question. By contrast, social scientists rarely have such control over the parts of the world they study. This lack of control makes it difficult to figure out how patients' medical decisions are influenced by their out-of-pocket expenses. Copays and deductibles don't fit into a test tube, leaving health policy researchers to analyze messy data from a messier world. For example, when the Affordable Care Act went into effect, millions of people gained access to health insurance. Over the next half-dozen years, healthcare utilization increased significantly.[5] Was Obamacare responsible for such utilization? That's not an easy question to answer. Over that same half-dozen years, Facebook use grew rapidly, too, as did the number of hours people spent binging *Gilmore Girls* episodes on Netflix.

Fortunately, a few decades ago, a group of audacious researchers at the RAND Corporation in Santa Monica, California, decided to treat people's health insurance coverage the way chemists treat the molecules in their test tubes—they ran an experiment.[6] It was the early 1970s, and leaders from both the Republican and Democratic parties agreed that the U.S. government needed to take steps to ensure that all Americans had health insurance but disagreed about whether such insurance should cover 100 percent of people's medical costs. Politicians on the left, led by Ted Kennedy, were advocating for a government-run system that would leave patients with no out-of-pocket costs. Politicians on the right, led by President Nixon, were pushing for insurance through employers that would leave patients to bear some portion of their healthcare costs.[7] Politicians had good reason to disagree with each other over these important issues. Each side had a plausible point of view, and neither side could justify their view with cold hard facts. Even health economists were split on how much influence free medical care would have on people's healthcare decisions.

The time was ripe for an experiment. But how do you cram a healthcare system into a test tube? The RAND team recruited two thousand families, almost six thousand people, from six U.S. cities, ranging from Seattle, Washington, to Charleston, South Carolina, and randomized them to receive one of fifteen insurance plans. Fourteen of these plans were traditional fee-for-service plans in which doctors and hospitals got paid for every service they provided to patients. One of the plans was a health maintenance organization (HMO). (HMOs were new around that time, and the researchers wanted to get a sense of whether such organizations offered different care than other types of insurance plans.)

The fourteen fee-for-service plans differed from one another mainly in terms of the coinsurance rate demanded from enrollees. Some plans provided all healthcare for free. Some plans required people to pay 25 percent of their medical costs, others 50 percent, and others as much as 95 percent. (For readers shocked at the idea of 25 percent coinsurance being modest, keep in mind that healthcare prices were much lower in the 1970s than they are today.) People with coinsurance were required to contribute money toward their medical care until they reached a prespecified limit, an out-of-pocket maximum, at which point the remainder of their care was free. The insurance plans differed from each other not only according to the coinsurance rates, but also according to the out-of-pocket maximum at which the insurance plan would take over people's healthcare costs. Some plans set the limit at 5 percent of a family's annual income, and others as high as 15 percent.[8] The RAND team couldn't control all the conditions of their experiment, the way chemists can control the temperature of their chemicals. But by randomizing people to different insurance plans, they could count on the likelihood that people receiving free medical care would, on average, be much like those facing copays.

Because of the rigor of this randomization, the RAND experiment provides the best evidence to date on how out-of-pocket expenses influence people's healthcare decisions. The RAND results confirmed what many market enthusiasts had long suspected—providing medical care for free significantly increases healthcare utilization. Families with first-dollar coverage—who bore no out-of-pocket healthcare expenses—consumed 25 percent more medical care than other families. They were also significantly more likely to use ERs, especially low-income families. As for families facing out-of-pocket expenses, they reduced healthcare utilization just about the same amount across all thirteen plans regardless of whether they were responsible for 25 percent or 75 percent of their healthcare costs.

The results I've presented so far from the RAND study prove several things. First, when patients face out-of-pocket expenses, they get less medical care. Second, facing super-high out-of-pocket expenses doesn't reduce medical care utilization much more than more modest expenses (although I'd be cautious about generalizing that conclusion to the prices we see in healthcare today). Third, because some of the reduction in medical care relates to the use of the emergency room, patients' decisions play a role in this reduction of medical care; some people, faced with symptoms of illness, forgo trips to the ER to avoid out-of-pocket costs.

No one has run a more recent experiment to see if the RAND study holds up in today's healthcare marketplace.[9] But non-experimental findings confirm much of what the RAND study established. For example, between 2001 and 2006, millions of Americans enrolled in Medicare plans run by private insurance companies. At the beginning of that time, most of those companies charged patients little to nothing out of pocket when they saw primary care physicians. But over that time period, eighteen plans raised copays for such appointments. Outpatient clinic visits dropped dramatically among people enrolled in those plans.[10] In another study, researchers looked at what happened in 2013, when a large software company switched its employees from full coverage plans (with no deductibles or copays) to plans with high out-of-pocket expenses (with an average deductible of $4,000). The number of people getting CT scans dropped more than 15 percent.[11] Similarly, a systematic review showed that high out-of-pocket plans led to a reduction in the number of people who went to ERs for non-emergent problems.[12] The implications seem straightforward:

high-deductible health plans cause people to scrutinize whether they need medical care.

However, as Oscar Wilde once said: "The pure and simple truth is rarely pure and never simple."[13] When people in the RAND study faced out-of-pocket healthcare expenses, they not only avoided going to the ER for non-emergent problems, but also avoided care that was relatively cheap and, yet, critical to their long-term health and well-being. People put off dental appointments and primary care checkups. They walked around with untreated high blood pressure, thus increasing their chance of experiencing strokes or heart attacks.[14]

People's use of ERs reinforces this sense of indiscriminate decision making. The RAND researchers looked closely at ER use and couldn't convince themselves that people in the free care group were overusing the ER. If they had been going to the ER too often, then the RAND group would have expected to see a higher proportion of these patients sent home from the ER without being admitted to the hospital. Yet when people in the free healthcare plan showed up in the ER, their chance of being admitted to the hospital was the same as that of patients whose plans required copays. In other words, some patients who stayed away from the ER because of the financial cost of their care would have been admitted to the hospital if they had chosen to go to the ER. In fact, patients receiving free ER care were just as sick as those paying out-of-pocket for ER services. Admittedly, some people with free care went to the ER even though they weren't sick enough to require hospitalization. Some went even though they probably could have waited a day to see someone in an outpatient clinic. But the same was true of people facing copays—some of them *also* went to the ER despite having non-urgent illnesses. They were like the panicked professor—they weren't sure whether their symptoms, or their baby's symptoms, warranted emergent care, so they erred on the side of caution despite the financial consequences.

We shouldn't be surprised at people's relatively indiscriminate use of ERs. Most people don't know when their symptoms require urgent versus non-urgent care, whether their symptoms are life-threatening or benign. They don't even know when a twisted ankle is sprained (elevate and ice it at home) or broken (get medical attention).

Let's return to the study I told you about earlier, showing that an increase in Medicare copays led to a reduction in outpatient appointments. That same study also showed that people facing higher copays spent more days in the hospital over the following year than those who received outpatient care for free.[15] Those higher copays caused people to forgo outpatient appointments that could have prevented inpatient admissions. Other studies show similar findings. For example, when California added a one-dollar copay to outpatient visits for its Medicaid recipients, it saw a 17 percent increase in the hospitalization of Medicaid enrollees.[16] So did the California public employees union, when it charged people $10 for doctor's appointments.[17]

The threat of out-of-pocket expenses causes people to avoid necessary medical care. Copays even discourage people from receiving important preventive care, such as colonoscopies or mammograms. Sounds crazy, right? To avoid relatively modest expenses, people forgo potentially lifesaving tests. But modesty is often in the eye of the spender. A routine colonoscopy can cost hundreds of dollars, an enormous sum for many Americans, almost half of whom don't have $400 saved for emergency expenses.[18]

It is naïve to assume that exposing people to out-of-pocket expenses empowers them to be savvy healthcare consumers, and it is cruel to expect them to spend their life savings on vital healthcare services. It is also naïve to think that people who get their medical care for free will seek care only when it is necessary and cost-effective. Indeed, it would be reckless to provide everyone with first-dollar insurance coverage, oblivious to the economic consequences of such generosity.

The specter of out-of-pocket costs won't, on its own, make Americans into savvy healthcare consumers. It is too much to expect people to know when they need medical care, much less to comprehend what specific care is best suited to their health problems. But theories of healthcare consumerism don't depend exclusively on laypeople becoming expert medical decision makers. Not when they can turn to health professionals for advice.

Which raises the question: are physicians up to the challenge of helping patients make wise choices?

As we've seen, patients often face complex choices about medical care, and typically lack the specialized knowledge required to make optimal choices. When the majority of people don't understand their insurance plans, or their treatment alternatives, it is naïve to expect them to make wise choices, unless they can turn to experts, to people with specialized skills for whom these decisions are relatively simple—people like the financial adviser who helps my wife and me decide where to invest our savings. We rely on his help because, even though my wife has an MBA from the University of Chicago, we don't have time to master the complexities of the U.S. tax code. Similarly, even though most patients lack the time or aptitude to understand all of their medical choices, we should not abandon the idea of bringing marketplace discipline to healthcare until we see whether physicians are willing and able to guide patients toward better medical choices.

To illustrate what this guidance looks like, I'll start with the story of a man who needed help figuring out the best way to treat his kidney cancer.

An Alarming Situation

Anthony excused himself from the lunch table to go to the restroom, where he discovered that his urine was filled with blood. By the end of the week, he was diagnosed with kidney cancer and found himself in the office of Brant Inman, a urologist at Duke University. Inman showed Anthony a radiologic image of the one-centimeter mass hanging from the bottom of his left kidney. "The kidney mass had nothing to do with your bloody urine," he said. "It's too small and too far away from the center of your kidney." "Then what could have caused me to bleed?" Anthony asked. "Probably a vein in your prostate," he answered. "As you can see," he said, pointing to the CT image, "your prostate is quite large."

Anthony hadn't seen enough CT scans of prostates to appreciate the size of his gland, but he was thankful his own prostate had decided to spill blood when it did. That bleeding, after all, led to the cascade of tests that uncovered his kidney cancer while it was still small enough to cure. Anthony just had to decide what treatment he wanted.

But of course, Anthony didn't have to figure out his treatment choices by himself. Instead, Inman patiently described his alternatives. One treatment was cryotherapy.[19] With this procedure, an interventional radiologist would stick a needle in Anthony's back and inject the tumor with freezing liquid. "The main advantage of cryotherapy is its gentility," Inman explained. "You'll be playing tennis in a week." This was no small consideration for an avid exerciser like Anthony. There were disadvantages, though, too. "They will biopsy the mass before freezing it, but there is no guarantee the biopsy will yield diagnosable tissue, so we might never know whether the lesion they zap is cancerous or benign." There was also a chance that cryotherapy wouldn't kill all of the tumor cells, an 8–10 percent likelihood, in fact, that the tumor would grow back over the next five years and require further treatment. To monitor for such a recurrence, Anthony would need CT or MRI scans of his kidney three, six, nine, and twelve months after the treatment, plus annually for the following four years.

The second alternative was robotic laparoscopic surgery. With this treatment, Inman would make four tiny incisions in Anthony's belly and remove the mass with the help of several thin instruments. "The advantage of surgery," he said, "is that we will remove the entire mass with clean margins. It will be gone, with only a 2 percent chance of recurrence over the next five years." Because the procedure was more definitive, Anthony would only need follow-up at one and five years—two scans instead of eight.

How should Anthony go about making this decision? He was off to a good start, talking to a physician who was willing to lay out the pros and cons of his alternatives. But he also needed to consider the financial costs of the two alternatives. His CT scan had already cost him a $150 copay, and his appointment with Inman cost another $55. So he could do some of the math already. With cryotherapy, for instance, he needed eight more scans; another 8 × 150 equaled $1,200 in out-of-pocket expenses. Plus, he would need to attend follow-up appointments after every scan, at $55 a pop, plus whatever insurance would charge for the procedure. This was starting to add up.

At this point in the story, you might be skeptical that a patient, newly diagnosed with kidney cancer, would bother to calculate the cost of his treatment alternatives. Well, don't be, because this was no typical patient: it was me, Peter Anthony Ubel. Diagnosed with kidney cancer in the midst of researching out-of-pocket healthcare expenses, I wasn't about to decide my own course of care without contemplating my own expenses.

In fact, the cost of cryotherapy turned me away from that option. Not just the financial expense of all those additional CT scans, but also the time cost of having to sit through all those tests and follow-up appointments.

I chose surgery because I wanted to get the diagnosis behind me. That's when I discovered how naïve I was, to think I'd be able to make this decision on my own.

It was two weeks after the surgery, and I was seeing Inman for a follow-up evaluation. He told me my wounds were healing nicely. Then he discussed how we would monitor the state of my cancer. Just to remind you, before the procedure, Inman had told me that surgery required only two follow-up scans (at one and five years), versus the eight scans I'd need if I received cryotherapy. Inman, however, was no longer comfortable with such infrequent follow-up. "In your case," he explained, "you are so much younger and healthier than average, I want to get a follow-up scan in three months, then annually after that for the next five years."

Surprised by this new course of action, I pushed back: "How fast do renal cell cancers grow?" I asked, figuring nothing dangerous could develop quickly enough to warrant such frequent testing. "Usually about 0.6 centimeters per year," he answered. "Then why do we need annual scans?" I asked. (My reading of the medical literature had taught me that kidney cancers smaller than four centimeters almost never metastasize, and my tumor wouldn't reach that size for several years at such a slow growth rate.) Inman explained that recurrent tumors usually grow faster than primary cancers, although it wasn't obvious that they'd grow fast enough to do harm in three months. I told him I didn't see the necessity for such an early scan.

"Look," he said gently, "we can have fewer scans if you want, but I hate to take the chance of missing a treatable recurrence in a young guy like you." I was fifty-one at the time, whereas the average age of someone diagnosed with renal cell cancer is over sixty, often with a long history of cigarette smoking (a risk factor for developing such a cancer).[20] Inman continued, "If you were older, with a bunch of competing health problems, I wouldn't be so worried. Most of my older patients with tumors like yours end up dying of other diseases, like heart problems, so getting frequent scans in them doesn't make sense."

Earlier in the visit, he had remarked upon how little fat he'd seen around my kidneys during the operation and had commented on how quickly I was recovering from the procedure. My relative youth and healthiness were seemingly causing him to push for more aggressive follow-up. He reiterated his recommendation that I receive an MRI in three months. I flashed a skeptical look in his direction, so he quickly elaborated: "I just saw a patient at the three-month follow-up today who already had a recurrence. Now he had a different tumor than yours" (which seems like a pretty relevant fact to me), "but I have seen too many bad cases in my career, patients whose tumors we discovered too late. Better safe than sorry."

It's hard to argue against the logic of "better safe than sorry," but in my case that logic led down a path of potentially unnecessary tests and procedures, all of which cost money—not only to me, the patient forking over a copay, but also to the rest of the healthcare system. And of course, just two weeks earlier I had chosen to have my cancer removed surgically in part to avoid all those follow-up tests.

In most consumer markets, individual consumers decide what products they want to buy at which prices. My experience with kidney cancer reminded me that in medical markets, physicians often play a large role in deciding what tests or procedures individual patients receive, with little regard for the price of such services. In such settings, it defies logic to expect patients to make the kind of discerning choices that maximize market efficiency. Even savvy healthcare patients will have a hard time reining in healthcare spending in the face of caring physicians preaching an ethic of "better safe than sorry."

Then again, I was hardly a typical patient. I was not only younger and healthier than most patients with kidney cancer, I was also more, um, physician-y. And more obsessed with medical decision making. Before launching from my experience to generalizations about medical decision making, writ large, let's look at another cancer diagnosis, one my colleagues and I have had a chance to study in depth. Let's see how urologists help patients decide how to treat their prostate cancer.

What Should I Do, Doc?

Thomas Hellinger was understandably worried. A week earlier, a urologist at his local VA Medical Center had taken twelve pieces out of his prostate gland to see if any of the tissue harbored cancer cells. Hellinger had now arrived at the urology clinic, anxiously awaiting the verdict. The urologist broke the news: "On your biopsy, the results came back positive for prostate cancer in two cores." He quickly reassured Hellinger that "prostate cancer is a slow-growing cancer," with no immediate threat to his life. Men with early-stage prostate cancer face a choice. They can choose one of two "active treatments"—either surgery or radiation—that will eradicate the cancer. Or they can opt for "active surveillance," where the urologist will conduct tests on the cancer at six-month intervals to see if it has grown.[21] If it does progress, the doctors treat the cancer with some combination of surgery, radiation, and medications. If you are wondering why anyone would allow a cancer to reside in their body untreated, it is because surgery and radiation are relatively arduous procedures. Moreover, both surgery and radiation can cause erectile dysfunction and bladder incontinence, and to date, there's no definitive evidence that surgery or radiation reduces the chance that men will die of prostate cancer, given the sometimes halting, often indolent, nature of such tumors.[22] Surveillance doesn't cause side effects like erectile dysfunction or bladder incontinence but leaves men with an untreated cancer inside their bodies, potentially creating anxiety as they fret about whether their cancer is taking a turn for the worse.

Hellinger faced a trade-off: the certainty of cure versus potential avoidance of miserable side effects. If there was ever a place for empowered patients, this was it. With three viable alternatives, Hellinger had every reason to take an active role in making his choice. In such situations, decision-making experts contend that physicians shouldn't tell patients what to do but, instead, should partner with patients to choose the option that best reflects their preferences, a process known as shared decision making.[23] If shared decision making was the norm, we would expect prostate cancer decisions to depend not only on the particulars of a patient's health—the size of his tumor, the odds his health will decline due to other illnesses, and so on—but also on whether he has an active sex life or whether he is anxious about the thought of living with an untreated cancer in his body.

Hellinger was one of several hundred men we audio recorded as they met with doctors to decide on treatment for early-stage prostate cancers. Across these many patients, we discovered several important medical factors that shape treatment choice. All else equal, younger men were more likely than older ones to receive surgery or radiation. With so many more years for the cancer to potentially grow, the benefits of these two "active treatments" loomed relatively large for young men. Similarly, men with intermediate-grade cancers (called "Gleason 7" based on how they look under the microscope) received more aggressive treatment than those with lower-grade tumors (Gleason 6).[24]

Above and beyond these medical factors, however, another factor loomed quite large in people's treatment choices. As empowered patients, you'd expect their attitudes toward treatment side effects like erectile dysfunction to play an important role. Men who hope to continue to have active sex lives should be more likely to choose surveillance than men unconcerned about sexual functioning. By similar logic, men who are more anxious about the thought of living with cancer inside their bodies should be more likely to receive surgery or radiation than men who are less anxious. But our study did not show such patient preferences playing an important role in treatment choices. Instead, patients were strongly influenced by physician recommendations—by which treatment the urologist told them would be best.[25] Further, those recommendations typically did not reflect explicit discussion of patient preferences.

Physicians often made clinical recommendations with little exploration of patients' attitudes toward the pros and cons of their treatment alternatives.[26] These urgings were almost always well intentioned, with doctors persuading younger men to receive active treatment out of concern that if such a tumor is left alone for a long time, it will eventually spread. For example, one patient in our study had a tumor that was a step above the least aggressive form of the cancer. That was enough to concern his physician, who told him: "My bias is that for somebody young and healthy, that I think would tolerate the surgery, and that I think would be around to experience some of those late side effects of radiation, I generally recommend surgery." This patient received surgery. Rarely did doctors in our study frame this choice to patients in terms of a legitimate trade-off—between the chance of tumor progression and the patient's attitudes toward treatment side effects. Instead, physicians often made strong clinical recommendations, as if one or another treatment was not a viable alternative.[27] In Hellinger's case, the surgeon informed him about the pros and cons of his alternatives, trying to stay neutral, but then mentioned that "if you were my dad, I would treat with surgery. At sixty-three years old and no other medical conditions, I would opt to operate." Want to guess what treatment Hellinger chose?

I mention our prostate cancer research to return to the notion of giving patients "skin in the game."[28] Patients don't have to face out-of-pocket expenses to have lots of incentive to actively engage in their healthcare decisions. The VA provided patients in our study with generous healthcare coverage—their out-of-pocket expenses were not dramatically different depending on their choice of surgery, radiation, or surveillance. In other words, the patients didn't have much skin in the game in terms of out-of-pocket expenses. But the patients in our study had *literal* skin in the game—if a man chooses surgery, a physician is going to cut through his skin to remove his prostate. The men had more than skin in the game, too. Those who chose radiation or surgery faced the risk of spending the rest of their life wearing an adult diaper.

Despite having so much incentive to choose treatments that fit their preferences, patients frequently deferred to whatever alternative their physicians recommended. Patients usually come to the doctor's office with much less understanding of their medical alternatives than their doctors have. They might arrive scared or overwhelmed by their situations. In these contexts, patients often don't act like fully empowered consumers. Instead, they depend upon their doctors for advice.[29] The simple notion—that out-of-pocket expenses will empower patients to scrutinize their healthcare choices—doesn't measure up to the complexities of the doctor-patient relationship.

But let's give market enthusiasts their due. Perhaps some of the veterans in our prostate cancer study were lulled into inaction by the generosity of their healthcare coverage—as veterans, many received prostate cancer treatment for little or no out-of-pocket expense. Perhaps when patients face higher out-of-pocket costs than this, they are forced to talk to their doctors about affordable alternatives, thus initiating a more thorough discussion of patients' treatment goals. Is that possible?

There's only one way to find out. Let's see what happens when patients discuss out-of-pocket expenses with their physicians.

4

WHAT PATIENTS AND DOCTORS TALK ABOUT WHEN THEY TALK ABOUT MONEY

Healthcare consumerism often plays out in medical offices, with clinicians conferring with patients about which medications to prescribe and what tests to order, and patients subsequently experiencing the financial consequences of those decisions. The quality of physician-patient communication about healthcare costs often determines the quality of these healthcare choices.

In 2014, Verilogue Inc. gave my research team access to over two thousand outpatient clinic conversations. In conducting market research for healthcare companies, Verilogue had asked physicians and patients for permission to audio-record their interactions in outpatient clinics. The company gave us transcripts of some of these appointments after removing all identifying information. Thus, my team didn't know the names or locations of any of the doctors and patients we studied. But what we did have—word-for-word reproductions of physician-patient conversations— gave us an unprecedented opportunity to discover what doctors and patients talk about when they talk about money.

Prior to our research, the best studies of doctor-patient money talk relied upon self-reports. Researchers would survey patients and ask them how often they discussed out-of-pocket costs with their doctors, and how comfortable they were broaching the topic. Or they'd survey physicians and ask them what barriers made it difficult for them to discuss healthcare costs with their patients. Most of these studies concluded that money talk was rare. In one study, for example, fewer than one in six patients reported having *ever* discussed healthcare expenses with any of their physicians.[1] Cost conversations appeared to be especially rare in oncology settings, if you believe the answers people gave on those surveys.[2]

But I didn't believe the answers. Instead, when I read these studies, I was reminded of research my friend Norbert Schwarz had conducted, revealing some of the hidden ways survey methods bias people's responses.[3] For example, suppose I want to measure the frequency of spousal squabbling. I survey married people and ask them: "How many times did you and your spouse get into a fight last week?" They'll probably reflect on the past couple of days, remember disagreeing about whose turn it was to wash the dishes, recall some harsh words about which parent is too lenient with their children, and estimate a half-dozen arguments per week. But suppose, instead, my survey asked them: "How many times did you and your spouse get into a fight last year?" When thinking over that much longer timeframe, people are going to recall the barn-buster arguments they've had in the past twelve months—maybe a once-in-a-month blowout that leads one or another to sleep on the couch. By asking about fights over the course of a year, I cause people to think about relatively rare and heated disputes. The phrasing of the survey questions dramatically alters people's answers.[4]

The same survey phenomenon could influence answers doctors and patients give about how often they discuss healthcare costs with each other. They may think researchers are asking about prolonged cost conversations about extremely expensive services. They might forget about all the times they had quick conversations about whether insurance covers a specific test or treatment, or whether the doctor can prescribe a generic drug. That's why we were so excited to leave the world of self-report behind and study the *actual* frequency of money talk in doctors' offices.

We studied three groups of patients: people with rheumatoid arthritis, metastatic breast cancer, or major depression. All these people were seeing specialists for follow-up appointments. We chose these three groups partly because they were diverse: a chronic disabling disease, in rheumatoid arthritis; a life-threatening illness, in breast cancer; and a serious mental illness, in depression. But we also chose them because of something they had in common: all three illnesses can be very expensive to treat.

Our first job was to figure out how often patients discussed healthcare costs with their doctors. If surveys were correct, and only one in six patients *ever* discussed this topic with a physician, then we probably weren't going to come across many cost conversations in these single interactions. So, we read through transcripts, flagging anything we thought might qualify as a cost conversation. In addition, we searched the Verilogue database for words that might signify a cost conversation: words like *dollar, expensive,* or *insurance.* Then we looked more closely at the conversations that occurred on either side of those words, to see if they involved discussion of healthcare expenses.

The short version of our findings is this—we found that money conversations were extremely frequent. Now some of these cost conversations didn't pertain to patients' own out-of-pocket expenses. For example, one oncologist told her patient that "the government will save a billion dollars if they discontinue [the medication] Avastin [bevacizumab] for breast cancer." In another appointment, a patient talked about how much money one of her relatives was spending on medical care. We didn't count these conversations as examples of patients discussing their own out-of-pocket expenses with physicians. Yet even after excluding these cases, we discovered that out-of-pocket expenses came up in approximately 20 percent of breast cancer appointments, 30 percent of rheumatology appointments, and almost 40 percent of psychiatry appointments.[5]

Often it was patients who initiated these cost conversations. A doctor might suggest a new medication only for the patient to ask, "How much does it cost?" Or a patient would return to the clinic and complain about the cost of something the doctor had ordered on the previous visit. But physicians frequently initiated cost conversations, too. In particular, psychiatrists often queried patients about a range of life stressors that could be aggravating the symptoms of their depression: "How are things going at work? With your family? With your finances?" With that last question, patients would frequently mention the high cost of their medical care.[6]

To put this into perspective, across the twenty oncology appointments we studied from Singapore, doctors and patients discussed the cost of care eighteen times, refraining from the topic only when patients were still undergoing tests to determine the type and extent of their cancer. So even though cost conversations are surprisingly common in the United States, they are far from universal. Singapore has had an out-of-pocket healthcare system for several decades. The United States is just beginning the transition into becoming such a system. It will take time for cost conversations to become routine.

Nevertheless, those conversations have begun. And they are already beginning to yield benefits.

Consider one of the rheumatology appointments we analyzed. The clinic appointment was almost complete, but the doctor wanted to make sure he had addressed all of his patient's concerns. "Need anything else?" he asked. "The one I take for my ulcer," she replied, "what do you call that?" He proposed several possible medications: "Omeprazole? Zantac [raniti-dine]? Nexium [esomeprazole]?" "Nexium," she replied. "That's expensive though," he pointed out, showing impressive concern for her out-of-pocket expenses. She responded: "Ain't no more expensive than the Micardis [telmisartan] I have to pay for," explaining that this particular blood pres-sure pill cost her $150 a month. The physician wasn't about to burden her with another expensive medicine. Unsure of how much her insurance would require her to pay for Nexium, he told her to "ask the pharmacist which stomach pill is the least expensive and have him call me."

Problem solved.

Cost conversations between doctors and patients can be productive even when it is hard to get good information about the cost of medical care. In the conversations we analyzed, doctors and patients uncovered a wide range of strategies to reduce patients' out-of-pocket expenses, even when they couldn't get a hold of precise cost estimates. Some strategies were straightforward: switching people to generic medications or giving them free drug samples almost always saves money, regardless of the exact price of a brand-name drug. When no generic was available, and patients needed to be on very expensive medications, doctors frequently told patients to look into copay assistance programs that would cover their costs. Some cost-reducing strategies were more involved. Occasionally physicians spent time helping patients and their families identify insurance plans that would better cover their medical expenses.[7] Overall, when the topic of healthcare costs came up during clinic appointments, doctors and patients identified at least one potential way to lower patients' expenses around 40 percent of the time. The opaqueness of U.S. healthcare prices and the inscrutable-ness of American health insurance do not always thwart people from find-ing more affordable healthcare alternatives.

But that doesn't mean cost conversations were anywhere near as productive as they should have been. Instead, our analysis revealed a range of phenomena undermining doctors' and patients' attempts to factor out-of-pocket expenses into medical decisions.

Missed Opportunities to Make Informed Decisions About Healthcare Costs and Benefits

Theories of behavioral science have shown that people sometimes fail to pick up on cues from their environment due to inattentional blindness—a phenomenon in which people are so focused on detecting one kind of cue that they overlook others. In the most cited example of inattentional blindness, participants watch a video of people passing a basketball among their respective teams. When asked to count how many times the white-clothed team passes the ball among themselves, many participants fail to notice a person in a black gorilla suit walk into the middle of the scene, pound on its chest, and walk off camera.[8]

In a similar manner, because most physicians have not been trained to look for signs of financial distress in their patients, they sometimes fail to recognize patients' financial concerns when they arise in clinical encounters.[9] To make matters worse, patients are sometimes embarrassed to bring up financial concerns to their physicians. Perhaps as a result of such embarrassment, patients' expressions of financial distress might be subtle or ambiguous. This combination of inattentional blindness among physicians and hesitancy among patients increases the chances that physicians will not recognize when their patients are burdened by out-of-pocket expenses.

For example, one of the rheumatoid arthritis patients in our study told her doctor the ulcer pills he prescribed were "so expensive." Failing to recognize her financial concerns, he asked her an unrelated question about her arthritis medicines. In one of the oncology visits we observed, the physician appeared to be too distracted by typing into the computer to recognize his patient's financial concerns. She told him she was supposed to be drinking a nutritional supplement because she was losing weight from her cancer, but that the supplement was a little bit expensive. He said, "Uh huh," and kept on typing. She pointed out that she was developing anemia and needed to be eating high-protein food, and he kept saying, "Uh huh, uh huh." When she finished complaining about the cost of her nutritional supplements, he finished typing and said, "Uh, ok. Let me take a look at this spot," seemingly unaware of her financial concerns.

It's hard to address high out-of-pocket expenses when physicians fail to recognize their patients' expression of financial distress. But such inattentional blindness isn't the only behavioral phenomenon undermining the quality of cost conversations. In our analyses of doctor-patient interactions, we also observed times when physicians picked up on patients' financial concerns but, nevertheless, failed to address those concerns adequately.

Sometimes this failure happened for no apparent reason. For example, in one of the breast cancer clinic appointments we observed, a patient said she couldn't handle the $3,000 a month it cost for her cancer treatments. "No," her doctor responded. "Nobody can handle that. Now, do you have pain anywhere? Does your back hurt?" The physician never returned to the topic of these costs—too busy? too unconcerned? too focused on clinical rather than financial matters to discuss her monetary woes?— meaning the patient was still stuck with that $3,000 monthly bill; not a minute of the clinic appointment was utilized to explore whether there was a way to reduce her financial burden. In another clinic appointment, a woman with newly diagnosed breast cancer was concerned about the genetic test the doctor had ordered: "How much does it cost if I have to pay for it?" the patient asked. "Oh, we don't want to talk about that," the doctor responded.[10] Regardless of whether "we" wanted to discuss the cost of the test, she, the patient, wanted to hold that conversation. I expect this clinician was not callously deflecting the cost conversation but, rather, was redirecting the discussion to take the patient's mind off money matters. He was probably trying to imply that they didn't need to discuss the cost of the test because the test would be covered by insurance or, if not covered, was too important to skip. But if that's what the doctor meant to say, he needed to be explicit, so his patient wouldn't feel like her very real financial distress was not an appropriate topic of conversation.

Sometimes cost conversations veer off topic not because physicians purposely redirect the discussion, but because the doctor and patient let their frustration with the American healthcare system get the better of them. In one clinic appointment, for example, a patient asked her doctor about trastuzumab (Herceptin), a medication she was taking for her cancer. "That's the expensive one," the doctor explained, "and the drug companies make the money, not the doctors." "I think it's awful," she replied. The physician went on to explain how the high cost of the drug was burdening his clinic: "Me as a doctor, you know, buying all these drugs is expensive. We [medical clinics], . . . we're not just banks." (Commonly in the United States, medical clinics purchase medications before injecting or infusing them in their patients. They don't get money back to cover the cost of those purchases until they provide the treatment and receive payment from insurance companies.) "There's a limit to how far we can go," the doctor explained. He continued the conversation: "I have another patient whose bill is $120,000." "God," the patient exclaimed. He replied, "And [their insurance company] has not paid for the first seven months." The patient tried to turn the topic back on herself: "Imagine how much my bill is!" But the physician never addressed the patient's concerns, too distracted by his ire at insurance companies to focus on the patient's needs.

Even when patients and clinicians attempt to engage in productive conversations about healthcare costs, their discussions are often too vague to help patients make informed decisions. To illustrate: in one interaction, a patient asked if an expensive new medicine was "covered by insurance." The doctor assured him that it was. Case closed. Except the case was not closed, because the doctor failed to distinguish between *whether* insurance covered the treatment and *how well* it covered it. Many of the cost conversations we observed followed this pattern, of questioning whether a service is covered, but never addressing what the insurance company would expect patients to pay for it. Insurance might pay for that expensive new medicine, but the patient could be responsible for 10 percent of the cost. It might cover the positron emission tomography (PET) scan, but the patient could face a $150 copay. Many physicians have spent most of their careers caring for patients who have robust insurance plans and are consequently slow to recognize that coverage ain't what it used to be.

Once finished with their training, physicians' clinical habits are slow to evolve. Few American physicians were trained in how to discuss out-of-pocket expenses with their patients. Consequently, when they do hold such conversations, the results are often underwhelming. For example, one of the rheumatoid arthritis patients in our study asked about the cost of his methotrexate. "It's very cheap," the doctor responded. "Very cheap?" the patient replied. "Probably," the doctor concluded, and they moved on to another topic. Can you imagine shopping for a new television, only to have the clerk at Best Buy tell you it's "probably cheap"? In another clinic appointment, a man with rheumatoid arthritis asked his doctor whether the medication Arava (leflunomide) was "expensive." The physician responded, "It is more expensive than methotrexate. So, I am not sure your copays will be the same." The physician didn't dig deeper into the issue, a behavior that is completely understandable given the other matters she needed to discuss with the patient and the likelihood that she wouldn't be able to answer the question more accurately than this anyway. But think for a moment about what is happening here. When patients ask doctors about the cost of new medications, there's a good chance that this question is symptomatic of a larger issue. These patients are experiencing enough financial distress that they are willing to disrupt the flow of clinic appointments to bring up the topic. They deserve better answers than "I am not sure" from their doctors.

Finally, sometimes physicians fail to adequately address patients' financial concerns because they forget to discuss less expensive alternatives. For example, one of the breast cancer patients in our study told her oncologist OxyContin (oxycodone) wasn't controlling her pain. In addition, she couldn't afford the brand-name medication. The physician responded by suggesting that she take the OxyContin less frequently, to reduce her costs. This physician was trying to help, but his solution was heartbreakingly inadequate. This patient needed more pain relief, not less. OxyContin is a very expensive, long-acting narcotic. There are several other equally effective medications that are significantly less expensive, such as long-acting morphine.

Suffer Now, Talk About It Later

I have just laid out a series of conscious and unconscious behaviors that undermine physicians' abilities to help patients factor out-of-pocket expenses into their medical decisions. Too often, the result is patients experiencing unnecessary financial distress. Sometimes patients suffer this distress in silence. Other times, they simply skip appointments or stop taking the medicines, to reduce their expenses. And finally, as my research team observed, financial distress can reach a point where patients feel they have no choice but to confront their clinicians.

One of the patients we interviewed was Maria Talverez, who was being treated by an oncologist for breast cancer. Talverez attended dozens of healthcare appointments over the course of her treatment. She discussed her symptoms with doctors and conversed about what treatments were most likely to slow down her malignancy. But she didn't talk about money with them, even when she began experiencing significant financial distress: "With everything going up—gas, everything—I have to pay rent, groceries, food, clothes, and medicine," she told my research team, "and just the Medicare insurance, the supplement, and the drugs. I mean that's almost $300 per month, right there, with nothing else." Talverez had gone from a comfortable and seemingly secure existence to living on the financial edge, scrutinizing every purchase, even fretting over routine expenses. But she didn't want us feeling sorry for her. "There are people living in vehicles, and homeless people; and cold people and hungry people," she explained. "I pray for those all the time. I am very, very grateful that I have a shelter over my head and food to eat." And while it was a struggle to pay for her medicines, she said, "it happens."

But it happened at tremendous personal cost. In the middle of her cancer treatment, her husband's health failed. "We were in debt. I was sick; he was sick." Then he died. "I lost my house, all this stuff." So she finally disclosed her financial problems to the oncology nurse. "I told her that I could not afford to take the Femara [letrozole, a cancer drug], and she said, 'Well, you can apply for help; I'm sure you can get help.' So then I did. I started applying for help with the copay, and I got it."[11]

Talverez suffered unnecessarily. The financial distress she experienced was avoidable—neither she nor her clinicians talked about her out-of-pocket costs up front, when such talk could have saved her money. This silence is all too common in U.S. medical clinics.

Jessica Harris, a former master's degree student at Duke, interviewed women like Talverez who, because of the cost of their breast cancer treatments, were experiencing significant financial distress.[12] Most of these patients told Harris that they brought up money matters with clinicians only after things reached a breaking point. Healthcare costs need to be discussed up front, before doctors and patients make treatment choices, so patients have a chance to figure out whether they can afford the treatments, or whether they need some kind of financial assistance. If Talverez's doctor had mentioned the cost of the Femara up front, or inquired about her general financial situation, Talverez might have been able to receive copay assistance sooner. People should not have to lose their homes before discussing healthcare costs with their clinicians.

In our research on physician-patient interactions, my research team came across many examples of patients who complained to their doctors about the high cost of tests or treatments ordered during previous appointments. Many expressed shock at their out-of-pocket costs, suggesting that such expenses were not discussed in earlier interactions.

Why so little talk, so late?

Imagine you bring your car in for an annual inspection, and the auto mechanic suggests that you receive additional testing to look for unrecognized problems. What questions would you ask before deciding whether to get this testing? Danielle Brick and I posed this question to a group of research volunteers. (Brick is a marketing professor specializing in consumer behavior.) Almost without exception, people said they would ask what the tests were looking for and how much they would cost.[13] This was not a surprising finding; people usually don't receive consumer services without first asking what the services will cost. But consider what happened when Brick surveyed a separate group of people and asked them to imagine that they were seeing their doctor for an annual checkup and the doctor suggested some testing to look for unrecognized problems. When reporting what questions they would ask before deciding on the testing, only a minority mentioned money. Money talk hasn't become routine yet in the U.S. healthcare system. As a result, patients end up receiving medical care only to find out later how much the care costs.

Sometimes patients are hesitant to discuss financial concerns with their doctors because they worry such forthrightness will be socially unacceptable. In one of the clinic visits we observed, a woman with breast cancer was apologetic about bringing up her financial concerns: "I hate to be absolutely obnoxious with money, but, um, I need to figure out what my insurance is going to cover. And if it's something I can't really afford . . . how does that affect treatment?"

Sometimes physicians are hesitant to discuss healthcare costs, believing that such conversations violate their moral duties.[14] In fact, after I published an op-ed in the *New York Times* calling on doctors and patients to discuss healthcare costs, I received an angry email from a practicing physician: "I am sure if, God forbid, you or a family member is ever seriously ill, you would want to try ANY [his emphasis] potential curative or helpful treatment, regardless of price."[15] It is impossible for a marketplace to work efficiently if the people providing services believe it is their moral obligation to hide price information from their patients.

But even lacking such moral objections, physicians have practical reasons to be cautious about discussing healthcare costs with patients during their clinical interactions. For starters, many clinical appointments are quite short, and time spent discussing insurance coverage is time not spent discussing other important matters.[16] In addition, patients' out-of-pocket costs, as we saw in a previous chapter, are often opaque even to physicians. It is unsatisfying for physicians to bring up a topic ("Let's talk about the cost of Femara") without being able to follow through satisfactorily ("Now I don't know how much that medicine will cost you, because it depends on your insurance coverage and where you are in paying off your annual deductible, but, well, just thought I'd let you know that the cost might, ahem, be an issue"). Finally, even when doctors do discuss costs with patients, even when they are well informed about the magnitude of patients' expenses, they sometimes get cost talk backwards. Consider what happened when Yi Ling discussed treatment options with her oncologist.

Getting Cost Talk Backwards

Ling had just received surgery for a newly diagnosed cancer and was now meeting with her medical oncologist. She came to the visit with her daughter, who asked the oncologist to explain her mother's situation. "She needs chemotherapy," the oncologist told Ling's daughter. "Basically, she has what we call nodal disease." "So, it has spread, has it?" her daughter asked. "There is a tumor in these lymph nodes, yes," he responded. Ling sat silently, but her daughter was not ready to accept the chemotherapy recommendation without learning more: "I would also like to know, if we plan for chemotherapy, what is the cost? Because it is really difficult for us to pay."

Ling's story took place in Singapore, where, as we have seen, discussing healthcare costs is routine because the system requires patients to cover a portion of their medical expenses out of pocket. For that reason, even in the face of advanced cancer, patients typically discuss the cost of their healthcare before receiving treatment. That doesn't mean, however, that they factor the cost of care into their treatment decisions. When Ling's daughter raised concerns about the cost of her mother's care, the oncologist tried to reassure her that cost would not be a problem. "I would not worry too much about costs, as they can be deducted from Medisave," he said. "But if there really is a problem, the social worker can come in and help with the finances."

Ling's daughter remained anxious: "Our Medisave account has very little money and we use it to pay for our children's insurance and all that. . . . So if her treatment is expensive, then we won't have insurance for our kids." Many people in Singapore struggle financially because of high healthcare expenses, despite the country's relatively low prices and mandatory healthcare savings. But the oncologist promised to help, pledging to refer her to a social worker, who could help them find financial assistance: "Don't worry too much about the cost. We will sort it out." The oncologist then went on to describe the most serious side effects Ling could expect to experience from the chemo. "Sometimes [patients receiving chemotherapy] can have a little bit of diarrhea; sometimes they can feel a little tired. They can have nausea, but usually it is not so common with the kind [of chemo] that we are going to give her."

He was planning her first round of treatment, which included both a pill and IV medicine, when Ling's daughter brought up another concern: "Every week she comes in for an injection?" The oncologist explained that they would place a long-lasting IV line above her collarbone. Ling's daughter was concerned about that treatment: "I don't know whether she will cooperate." She told the doctor that her mother had a psychological illness that caused her to be "easily agitated" and, on occasion, "depending on her mood," interfered with her ability to understand what was going on. She was worried that her mother would yank out the IV access in a fit of agitation. The oncologist quickly shifted therapeutic gears. Recognizing that the chemo was no longer feasible, he told Ling's family that chemotherapy wasn't necessary, after all. "Surgery alone—70 percent of patients like her, stage three, are cured already. But if we give surgery and chemotherapy, then another 10 percent of patients like her are cured. Do you understand? So, if there are one hundred patients, seventy will be cured by surgery, and if we give chemotherapy, we save another ten."

It is important to understand two things that happened here.

First, once he realized chemo wasn't feasible for Ling, the oncologist shifted into reassurance mode. He did his best to make the family feel good about her treatment, even though she had missed out on a potentially better one. My research team noticed a similar behavior among urologists in our study of prostate cancer decision making. One of the hospitals in our study did not have access to robotic surgical equipment, which distressed some patients who believed that this procedure was superior to non-robotic surgery. The urologists at that hospital often went to great lengths to convince patients that robotic surgery was no better than non-robotic. Their descriptions of the pros and cons of robotic surgery differed significantly from descriptions given by physicians at hospitals that did have robotic technology.[17]

Second, prior to mention of Ling's psychological illness, the oncologist had discussed neither the percent chance that Ling had already been cured by the surgery, nor how chemotherapy would change that percentage. When discussing how much the treatment cost, and whether it would put the family under financial distress, he hadn't thought these numbers to be relevant. But now that it looked like Ling would not be able to receive chemotherapy, the oncologist described the chemotherapy differently—not as standard therapy for Ling's illness, but as a treatment option that patients need to understand well enough to decide whether its benefits outweigh its harms: "There is no right or wrong decision." In Ling's case, the doctor believed that the risk she would become agitated about the IV line outweighed the benefits of the chemo. But notably, he didn't think that the high financial cost of the chemo was enough to cause Ling or her family to forgo the treatment. When Ling's daughter raised important concerns about their ability to afford the chemotherapy, the oncologist hadn't given them information about Ling's survival rate with and without the chemo. He hadn't given them a chance to factor the cost of care into their decisions.

In an ideal world, when patients or loved ones face high out-of-pocket costs for potential medical interventions, they will discuss these costs with their healthcare providers, so they can decide whether these costs, and other potential side effects of the intervention, are worth accepting to receive the benefits of the intervention.

In Singapore, healthcare providers often do a great job of addressing the cost of treatment with patients, so patients can estimate their out-of-pocket costs in advance and seek financial assistance if necessary. They far surpass American physicians in explicitly addressing the cost of care with their patients. Doctors in the United States can learn a lot from their Singaporean colleagues. However, Singaporean physicians do not always take the next step, to embed discussions of the cost of medical care into more general discussions of the risks and benefits of the intervention in question.

Healthcare consumers cannot decide what they think of the costs and benefits of their alternatives if their doctors don't discuss the cost of these alternatives before they've made up their minds. Good decision making needs to happen forwards, not backwards, and decisions need to be made not just by doctors, but by patients, too.

5

THE END OF LIFE AND THE LIMITS OF HEALTHCARE MARKETS

Robyn's curly red hair hung askew as she stiffly tilted her head to the side. Healthy three-year-olds don't usually get neck spasms, so her mother, Bernadette Dornan, brought her to their primary care doctor, who prescribed anti-inflammatory medicines to dampen her pain. Not much later, Robyn began to have difficulty walking.[1] Another few trips to the doctor, and Dornan's worst fears were confirmed—Robyn had a life-threatening cancer, a neuroblastoma that had already spread to her chest, bones, and bone marrow.[2]

Dornan didn't have time to mourn the bad news as she busied herself whisking Robyn to doctors' offices across Ireland. First, there was surgery, to remove whatever parts of the tumor the doctors could get their scalpels on. Then it was off to radiation oncology clinics, to zap what was left of the tumor. Then to medical clinics, where doctors prescribed chemotherapy in hopes of further thwarting Robyn's tumor. For a handful of years, Robyn was cancer-free, running around the playground like a normal child. But then, Dornan noticed a lump on the side of Robyn's face. A CT scan showed that Robyn had a tumor in her jaw. Her cancer was back, and this time, there was no chance it could be cured by surgery, chemotherapy, or radiation. Robyn's only hope was an experimental vaccine, a treatment that would stimulate Robyn's immune system to attack the cancer. That vaccine, however, was available only at Memorial Sloan Kettering Hospital in New York City. To treat her daughter's cancer, Bernadette Dornan would need to cross an ocean.

And one more thing—she'd need $350,000.[3]

How much would you spend to save your child's life? I would deplete my savings and borrow against future earnings. I'd spend every dollar I could get my hands on (an amazing fact given that I'm currently paying a couple of colleges a small fortune to take my children out of my house). But Dornan didn't have enough money saved or enough future income to cover the cost of her daughter's care. What should society do when a little girl's life depends on finding a few hundred thousand dollars?

To answer that question, consider a famous incident from the late 1990s when Kimmy Merrill, a six-year-old girl from Oswega, Pennsylvania, fell into an abandoned well, her cries unnoticed in the remote countryside until her mother, Susan, wandered within earshot of the well. Unable to rescue Kimmy, even with the help of neighbors and local firefighters, Susan pleaded for rescue workers to dig a hole parallel to the well. Desperate townspeople gathered nearby as the evening temperature began to plummet. Nervousness morphed into panic. Sensing that the scene was becoming unruly, the Oswega mayor finally took control of the situation, stepping in front of the news cameras. "After a meeting of the Oswega emergency council," he announced, "we have determined that the cost of digging a parallel hole is prohibitive. We are going to have to let the girl die. Sorry, folks."

Unbelievable, right? Of course it is. I made up Kimmy's story to highlight a fundamental truth about healthcare spending—when it comes to life-or-death decisions, cold-hearted economic thinking rarely applies. Few communities will turn their backs on a dying child for lack of money. No parent will allow a $350,000 price tag to stand in the way of her child's survival. When people are terminally ill—especially young, attractive ones—no one wants to talk about bending the healthcare cost curve.

End-of-life illnesses raise fundamental problems for efforts to control healthcare spending. This is not a new problem. In a 1963 essay, Nobel Prize winner Ken Arrow wrote about how "the concern of individuals for the health of others" turns healthcare into a non-marketable commodity.[4] The existence of universal healthcare coverage in almost every developed country (save the United States) is evidence of most people's unwillingness to allow finances to stand in the way of patients receiving lifesaving medical care. Almost everyone has difficulty saying no to expensive healthcare

at the end of life, from doctors to insurance companies to federal governments, as I will soon discuss. But this being a book about patients as
healthcare consumers, I'll start my exploration of end-of-life healthcare by
seeing what happens when patients with serious illnesses face high out-of-
pocket expenses.

Why Patients Have a Hard Time Scrutinizing
End-of-Life Care

Market discipline depends on consumers having the ability to walk
away from a raw deal. The tactic is easier to deploy in some contexts than
others. When shopping online for fleece jackets, people can easily walk
away, at least figuratively speaking, from sites that don't offer competitive
prices. But in other contexts, it is much more difficult to behave like fru-
gal consumers. Few people, for example, are in the right state of mind to
play hardball with their local funeral directors after a loved one dies; no
one wants to act like grandpa isn't worth the money. Is it any wonder that
the average price of a funeral now runs more than $10,000?[5] Even harder
than negotiating the price of funeral expenses is the thought of shopping
for healthcare discounts at the end of life. When people experience urgent
medical problems, walking away does not feel like an option. Lying on an
emergency room bed with crushing substernal chest pain, no one is going
to negotiate the price of emergent cardiac catheterization. Stricken with
sudden paralysis of the right side of their bodies, few people are going to
question the cost of the CT scan their emergency room doctor orders to
see if they have internal bleeding in their brain. In cases of urgent and
life-threatening healthcare problems, the medical marketplace is sabotaged
by the psychology of nothing to lose, where people have little motivation
to scrutinize the cost, or necessity, of potentially lifesaving interventions.

Consider the case of Sean Recchi, who was determined to get the best
possible care for the rapidly growing lymphoma threatening his life. To
receive that care, he trekked from Ohio to the MD Anderson Cancer
Center in Houston, where his father-in-law had received lifesaving treatment a decade earlier. Enrolled in a bare-bones insurance plan, Recchi had
to deposit almost $50,000 just to begin a course of treatment. Within a
week, MD Anderson asked him for another $35,000.

Steven Brill recounted Recchi's story in *America's Bitter Pill*, a magazine-length exploration of the wallet-busting cost of American healthcare.[6] Brill told Recchi's story in part to introduce readers to the crazy prices charged by hospitals like MD Anderson. For Recchi's care, the hospital charged him $1.50 for a single Tylenol tablet. One hundred such pills on Amazon cost $1.49. The hospital charged Recchi $283 for a standard chest X-ray, which was $260 more than it would have charged a Medicare patient. As for Recchi's chemotherapy, the doctors prescribed rituximab, which cost Recchi $13,702. For a single injection.

These prices are clearly outrageous. But the people at MD Anderson hadn't pulled a fast one on Recchi. They hadn't offered him care and then slapped him with the bill. Instead, in contrast with the purposeful price opacity we explored a few chapters ago, MD Anderson was completely upfront about the cost of Recchi's care. The reason I am telling you Recchi's story is to illustrate that, on the rare occasions patients do get price information before receiving their treatments, those facing life-threatening illnesses may not be in a position to negotiate. With almost $100,000 of expense bearing down on him, Recchi paid—what good would that money do him if he were dead?

In Recchi's case, the treatment at MD Anderson was no guarantee of long life. The same went for Robyn Dornan, the Irish girl whose mom raised money for an experimental vaccine that was in no way guaranteed to stall her tumor. But when it comes to end-of-life treatments, the certainty of success is not what motivates people to spend money they don't have on treatments that might not work. Instead, they are motivated to avoid certain death. As behavioral economists and psychologists have shown, there's no probability that matters more to people than one that changes success rates from 0 percent to anything larger than 0 percent.[7] When I teach behavioral economics, I illustrate this "certainty effect" by polling students early in the semester and asking them how much they would pay, out of pocket, for a chemotherapy that increases their five-year survival rate from 52 percent to 53 percent. They don't spout off large sums. Later in the semester, I ask them what they'd pay for a chemotherapy that increases their survival from 0 percent to 1 percent. They start talking about real money. (Admittedly, it is their parents' money, but you get my point.)

When it comes to risky decisions, all percents are not created equal.[8] If there are three bullets in the chamber of a gun that can hold six, I'd pay a lot of money to remove a bullet before subjecting myself to a round of Russian roulette. But if there were six bullets in the gun, meaning I faced certain death, I'd pay an even more enormous sum to remove one bullet.

It is challenging for patients to act like cost-conscious consumers when they feel their life is on the line. Markets function best when consumers can trade off the cost and quality of goods and services, when they can decide whether they would be happier purchasing something or holding on to their money. But people have a hard time putting a price on potentially lifesaving healthcare treatments. Money and mortality feel incommensurable.[9] That can be true even when people's lives aren't on the line, as long as they *feel* like their lives are at risk. In recent years, for example, controversy has raged over whether women less than fifty years old should receive mammograms, after a leading medical organization concluded such screening causes more harm than good (in women without known risk factors for breast cancer).[10] In some cases, mammography leads to diagnoses like ductal carcinoma in situ, or DCIS, that despite questionable impact on life expectancy, nevertheless lead many women to choose aggressive and harmful treatments.[11] In other cases, mammography leads to false warnings—to worrisome shadows that, when biopsied a couple weeks later, turn out to be benign.[12] The harms of these diagnoses and overdiagnoses are real, but they shrink in relation to people's fear of the harm caused if they miss a cancer that could have been cured. When people worry about the threat of a fatal illness lurking in their bodies, they don't act like savvy consumers.

And it's not because they otherwise lack savviness about consumer decision making. Consider the medical advice Mark Cuban tweeted out to his many followers in April 2015, urging them to "have your blood tested for everything available," even suggesting they should receive such tests quarterly. In a follow-up tweet, he elaborated, "a big failure of medicine = we wait until we are sick to have our blood tested."[13] Cuban is a brilliant man who made a fortune in the software industry; he's now best known for his enthusiastic, bicep-bulging courtside manner at Dallas Mavericks games, an NBA team he owns, and for his eyebrow-flexing performances on *Shark Tank*. But as smart as Cuban is, he's no match for the psychology of certainty. It is scary to realize that a serious illness may be stealthily developing in your body. It's tragic when loved ones become sick from what appear to be preventable causes, from cancers, for instance, that if detected earlier could have been removed.

Cuban's advice is horrible, because such testing would do more harm than good. People would undergo expensive testing that would mainly uncover nonexistent diseases, leading to potentially harmful follow-up tests or procedures.[14] Run a whole-body CT scan on a healthy population of billionaires and you will find lots of nodules and cysts and other "incidentalomas" (as we healthcare types call them), but you'll find very few precancers or other pathologic lesions that, thanks to those unprompted scans, will now be thwarted before they can cause morbidity or mortality.

Unfortunately, the psychology of "life at all costs" is more powerful than statistics about false positive tests. No number of false warnings, or unnecessary treatments for harmless growths, can stand up to the possibility of saving one person's life.[15] No abstract data about the number of people experiencing cancer due to radiation from all of those scans can compete with the thought of people whose cancers are undiscovered for lack of screening.

Most patients don't feel the need to scrutinize the complex harms and benefits of medical interventions—including the financial cost of those interventions—when they believe their lives are on the line. That's why patients are relatively insensitive to the price of cancer drugs. For every 10 percent increase in the price patients pay out of pocket for cancer treatments, their demand for such treatments declines just one-tenth of 1 percent.[16] To put that into perspective, every 10 percent increase in the cost of arthritis drugs reduces demand 2.1 percent, a twenty-fold increase in price sensitivity.

There's another reason many patients are insensitive to the price of medical care when they experience serious, potentially life-threatening illnesses. They reach the point where they have spent so much money out of pocket on medical care that insurance companies pick up the rest of their costs. That point is known as the out-of-pocket maximum. Imagine a person gets sick and incurs lots of medical expenses. She will be responsible for her early expenses, until she has paid off her deductible. After that, she'll be responsible only for copays or coinsurance, depending on the specifics of her coverage. But eventually, she'll reach her out-of-pocket maximum for the year and won't be responsible for any more expenses (at least for in-network providers). From that time through the end of the year, she has no incentive to reduce her healthcare expenses.

How common is it for people to reach their out-of-pocket maximums? In research I conducted with Yousuf Zafar (not yet published), we found that most patients with serious cancer reached their out-of-pocket maximum by March, almost regardless of what insurance plan they had purchased.

In this section of the book, I've critiqued the idea that patients with financial responsibility for a portion of their healthcare costs will pressure healthcare providers to reduce the cost and improve the quality of care they provide. Remember, such consumerism does not depend on turning toward a completely free market healthcare system; it can potentially be accomplished by providing people with catastrophic insurance coverage— in other words, require patients to pay out-of-pocket for predictable, relatively inexpensive medical care like annual checkups and blood pressure pills, but when they get really sick, and reach their out-of-pocket maximum for the year, have insurance cover the rest of their costs. With such coverage, no patient would presumably be forced to decide between financial solvency and potentially lifesaving medical care.

But herein lies the rub. Patients with life-threatening illnesses would have little reason to scrutinize the cost of their care. That $650,000 hospital bill that so incensed David Goldhill?[17] Most of that cost would still have been covered by his father's insurance company, even if he'd had catastrophic coverage. In fact, the power of catastrophic coverage is limited by the huge amount of healthcare expenses consumed by a very small proportion of the population. According to one analysis, more than one-fifth of healthcare spending is attributable to just 1 percent of patients, and half is consumed by 5 percent of patients.[18] Among Medicare and Medicaid recipients, the 5 percent of people consuming the most medical services generated almost $100,000 a year of healthcare spending, accounting for over one-third of all expenditures.[19] That's a huge amount of healthcare spending among a small number of people who, basically, have little reason to scrutinize the cost of their care.

Most people, for most of their lives, won't consume many healthcare services—a colonoscopy here, a few blood pressure medicines there; a bout of gallstones here, a knee replacement there. But then a serious illness strikes, a life-threatening or chronic disease—perhaps a diagnosis of rheumatoid arthritis or multiple sclerosis—with the accompanying cost of high-priced drugs, or a traumatic brain injury that causes serious neurologic impairment with the accompanying nursing home and rehabilitation costs. Their healthcare spending will skyrocket. With nothing to lose, they won't scrutinize that spending.

Catastrophic coverage might have a role to play in controlling healthcare spending and in encouraging patients to scrutinize the cost and quality of their medical care. But like most healthcare interventions, it is not a panacea for our problems. If we want to reduce the cost of end-of-life care and the care of life with serious illness, we need to see whether providers are willing and able to hold down these costs.

Doctors Have a Hard Time Saying No to Expensive Care at the End of Patients' Lives

It is not easy for physicians to acknowledge their patients are going to die. It's often harder for them to think money ought to be the difference between life and death. As a result, many physicians are insensitive to the price of life-prolonging interventions. For example, my colleagues and I asked American oncologists to imagine they were caring for a patient with metastatic cancer who is expected to live twelve months with standard therapy. We told them a new drug is available that costs $50,000 more than standard therapy and asked how much that drug would need to increase life expectancy for them to prescribe it for their patients. On average, they told us they would need to see a six-month increase in survival.[20] Based on that answer, oncologists are willing to spend around $100,000 for a year of life. But $100,000 isn't actually the price oncologists place on a year of life for their patients. I know this because I ran an experiment and switched up the scenario for a random half of the oncologists we surveyed, telling them the new drug was $125,000 more expensive than the standard treatment. When asked about this much more expensive new drug, oncologists *still* stated they would prescribe the drug if it provided a six-month increase in survival; that's a cost of $250,000 for a year of life. In effect, when deciding how much benefit a drug needs to promise to be worthwhile, oncologists were insensitive to price.

Pricing of cancer drugs in the United States depends in part on this price insensitivity. I learned this when I presented results of this study at a press conference in Washington, DC, attended by, among others, a man who ran the oncology division of a major pharmaceutical company. He explained their pricing strategy for cancer drugs was based on this same realization: that oncologists wouldn't blink at a price tag of $100,000 per patient, as long as that drug provided a statistically significant increase in life expectancy.

Is it any wonder eleven of twelve cancer drugs brought to market in 2012 were priced at more than $100,000 per patient?[21] Companies making cancer drugs realize they can demand a premium for their products even when survival benefits are modest. For this reason, the cost-effectiveness of oncology drugs has plummeted in the past few decades. In the mid-1990s, generating an additional year of life with cancer drugs cost an average of about $60,000. By 2014, that average had jumped to more than $200,000.[22]

As if $100,000 per patient isn't enough money, keep in mind most chemotherapies are not prescribed in isolation. For example, a drug called pertuzumab (Perjeta) was approved by the FDA for the treatment of metastatic breast cancer in 2012, coming to market at a price of over $100,000 per patient. For that price, it delayed progression of the disease by six months.[23] Pertuzumab is designed to work in combination with trastuzumab (Herceptin), a drug that costs around $80,000 per patient. That's almost $200,000 just for these two drugs, a price that doesn't capture the cost of other medications, nor of surgery, nor of radiation treatment. Now all of this money might be well spent. But it is also money that is not scrutinized. Most physicians prescribe these treatments regardless of their price and without any attempt to seek less expensive care.

So far, we have seen that patients fearing for their lives are either hesitant to bring up financial concerns with their clinicians or, when faced with the high price of care, feel compelled to pay. Meanwhile, clinicians, earnestly trying to give their patients hope, urge them to undergo treatment, with no concern for cost. Perhaps we need to ask third-party payers to fix this mess.

Insurance Companies Can't Say No to Lifesaving Medical Treatments, Either

Dying is costly. In the last twelve months of life, Americans spend around $80,000 on medical care. Over the last three years, they spend almost $160,000.[24] Those numbers don't account for the nine in ten people who receive substantial, unpaid care from family and friends in their last days of life.[25] Almost half of healthcare spending in the last year of life takes place in hospitals. With so much money at stake, you'd think American insurance companies would have figured out how to curb end-of-life spending. But of course, most of this spending doesn't come from the coffers of private insurers. It comes from Medicare and Medicaid, with the latter program playing a critical role in covering the costs of long-term care.[26] These programs are subject to political pressures from the many people who make money caring for people at the end of life—hospitals and doctors, of course, but also pharmaceutical companies as well as companies who make ventilators and defibrillators and the like. End-of-life spending is good for the healthcare industry!

But private insurers in the United States *do* have a stake in end-of-life care. In 2017, one in three Medicare enrollees—19 million people—received coverage through private insurers in what's known as the Medicare Advantage program.[27] It would seem those companies have every interest in holding down end-of-life spending. More broadly, they have incentive to constrain the cost of caring for the sickest enrollees. Serious illnesses are expensive, regardless of whether people are terminally ill. People can live with metastatic cancer for many years, often taking expensive drugs to slow the progression of their disease. Spending on cancer drugs in the United States ballooned more than 50 percent between 2006 and 2010, to over $1.5 billion.[28] If you laid 1.5 billion dollar bills flat on the ground, you'd cover an area more than four times the size of Central Park. (I'm not sure that puts the dollar figure into any better perspective. But it is a pretty cool image!) Why aren't insurance companies tackling these enormous expenses?

It starts with their historical roots. The private health insurance industry was created in the 1930s and 1940s by hospital and physician groups as a way to guarantee people would be able to pay for their services when they got sick.[29] As a result, in the early days of American health insurance, third-party payers like BlueCross and BlueShield were not particularly concerned about costs, because they were dependent on the financial support of the same hospitals that were billing them for the cost of patient care. In addition, the companies recognized that when expenditures rose, they could pass on the cost of healthcare to patients and employers by raising the price of insurance premiums. In addition, for the first few decades of the private health insurance industry, the American economy was robust enough to absorb rising healthcare expenditures.

Over time, however, insurance companies became less passive about rising healthcare costs. For starters, a wide range of insurance companies entered the market that didn't owe their existence to hospitals. And employers, faced with the rising cost of healthcare benefits, began pressuring insurance companies to restrain healthcare expenditures. Yet it was still difficult for insurers to push back on the rising cost of serious illness.

Consider what happened in the late 1980s and early 1990s, when some insurance companies refused to pay for bone marrow transplants in women with metastatic breast cancer. The companies claimed the treatment was unproven in this population, and thus experimental. In response, patients sued their insurance companies, with several succeeding to the tune of millions of dollars. The industry quickly reversed course and began covering the treatments. In 2000, research showed this aggressive and expensive intervention harmed breast cancer patients more than it helped them.[30] The insurance companies' claims were right after all, but in the meantime, they had been forced to pay for the unproven treatment, by a society unwilling to take hope away from women with breast cancer.

It shouldn't be surprising, then, what an insurance executive told me in 2014, when I asked him why his company was willing to pay $100,000 for cancer drugs that yielded a mere two-month increase in life expectancy. He told me his company would be slaughtered in the marketplace if it denied such a treatment to its enrollees. As long as a cancer drug is "best in its class" and offers patients the greatest odds of survival, insurance companies have little negotiating power. In such situations, pharmaceutical companies set prices knowing that if, say, Aetna refuses to pay the price, patients will complain to the media and the company will get reamed by its competitors. "We need the government to take the lead on these matters," the CEO told me. "If it doesn't set some kind of limit here, we [insurance companies] won't be able to either."

So, is this CEO right, that we should count on the United States government to take the lead in these matters?

Uncle Sam Has a Hard Time Saying No, Too

Some political pundits like to accuse government bureaucrats of undermining the people's will. I can't defend every bureaucratic decision coming out of Washington. But I can report confidently that the many federal employees I've interacted with remain in a near constant state of vigilance about the desires of the American people. Medicare administrators might want to reduce expenditures for people with serious and life-threatening illnesses. But their efforts to curb such expenditures are strongly constrained by political pressures. After all, when the Democrats were crafting the Affordable Care Act, they came under attack for creating what the Republicans branded as "death panels." Republican Sarah Palin used this term in response to a provision written into the ACA that planned to reimburse physicians for their time spent discussing end-of-life treatment goals with patients.[31] Just talking about end-of-life care gets the American government into trouble.

Perhaps public pressure on Medicare administrators explains some of the expensive constraints imposed on the program. For example, federal law requires Medicare to cover anti-cancer chemotherapies any time they are prescribed for medically accepted indications, even if those drugs are outrageously expensive. In addition, insurance companies that contract with Medicare enrollees to provide pharmaceutical coverage are required to cover all drugs for major or life-threatening illnesses, with federal rules specifically mentioning "drugs used in the treatment of cancer."[32] To make matters worse, sometimes the federal government has a hard time saying no even when evidence comes to light showing drugs don't work as well as expected. For example, in 2004, the FDA approved Genentech's drug Avastin (bevacizumab) for the treatment of metastatic colon cancer, a disease for which the drug dramatically improved survival. Four years later, the FDA extended indications for bevacizumab to include breast cancer on the basis of a randomized trial that demonstrated an increase in "cancer-free survival," the length of time patients remain in remission after treatment. Following this new approval, Medicare began paying for bevacizumab for patients with metastatic breast cancer, per its obligation to cover medically indicated care.

Within twelve months of approval for this new indication, however, additional trials showed bevacizumab did not lengthen patient survival for breast cancer patients. Bevacizumab kept the cancers at bay a little bit longer, but once the cancers returned, they were fatal more quickly. Based on that evidence, the FDA withdrew its approval for bevacizumab for the treatment of breast cancer.[33] This withdrawal, however, didn't halt Medicare payment for such treatments. Why? A leading clinical organization, the National Comprehensive Cancer Network, endorsed bevacizumab for breast cancer treatment even in light of these new trials.[34] That put Medicare officials in a bind—if they reversed course and stopped paying for bevacizumab, they could be perceived as refusing to reimburse patients for medically indicated care. Once a medical treatment becomes the standard of care, it is often difficult for physicians to stop offering the treatment, even when evidence suggests the treatment is not benefiting patients.[35] Would you like to be the Medicare official who announces patients will no longer receive a drug that prolongs breast cancer remission? Would you like to be President of the United States when that announcement is made?

I'm not contending that the U.S. government, or any government in the world, will pay whatever it takes to prolong the lives of its citizens. After all, we could reduce highway fatalities in the United States by repairing our decaying infrastructure. But highway fatalities are unpredictable—the lives saved by highway repairs are unidentifiable.[36] In contrast, when a medical treatment might be the difference between whether someone lives or dies, it's hard for the government to say no. In 2015, the U.S. government spent $40 billion treating people with kidney failure (also called ESRD, for end-stage renal disease).[37] That wasn't just because a bunch of people sixty-five and older needed dialysis treatments. It was because anyone in the United States with ESRD, no matter their age, is covered by Medicare for the simple reason that when paying for dialysis became the difference between life and death, the U.S. government sided with life.

When Medicare was established in 1965, it didn't cover the cost of long-term dialysis treatment, in large part because such treatment hadn't yet become routine. But just a few years later, a White House committee concluded that Medicare should cover the cost of dialysis for all Americans with kidney failure.[38] Many politicians were skeptical about whether the young program could afford to take on another expense. Medicare costs had already begun growing almost 30 percent per year as more people enrolled in the program, and as providers ramped up the intensity of medical care they offered to beneficiaries.[39] But Shep Glazer, vice president of the National Association of Patients on Dialysis, believed Medicare ought to find the money. Himself a dialysis patient, he made a passionate appeal before the House Ways and Means Committee on November 4, 1971: "I am 43 years old, married for 20 years, with two children ages 14 and 10. I was a salesman until a couple of months ago, until it became necessary for me to supplement my income to pay for the dialysis supplies. Gentlemen, what should I do? End it all and die? Sell my house and go on welfare? . . . If your kidneys failed tomorrow, wouldn't you want the opportunity to live? Wouldn't you want to see your children grow up?"[40]

Then, against the wishes of his legislative partners, Glazer lay down while a nephrology trainee from Georgetown University began dialyzing him. No senior physicians were willing to administer the dialysis session, out of fear that something would go wrong and they would be blamed for undermining the dialysis advocacy community. Their caution was understandable. Only five minutes into the dialysis session, Glazer's heart began racing and the trainee had to end the demonstration.

Glazer's dialysis session had little apparent effect on legislative maneuvering.[41] Only a handful of legislators witnessed the five-minute treatment. Even supporters were irked by the stunt, one Senate staffer blurting out, "What the fuck is going on here?" at the sight of Glazer's dialysis session. Several months later, legislative drafts out of both the House and Senate contained language extending Medicare to people with disabilities but contained nary a word about dialysis. Then, in a last-minute maneuver, Senator Vance Hartke proposed an amendment to the budget bill. "More than 8,000 Americans will die this year from kidney disease who could have been saved if they had been able to afford an artificial kidney machine," he testified. "We have the opportunity to begin a national program of kidney disease treatment assistance." After only thirty minutes of debate, the Senate approved the amendment, in a 52–3 vote. Almost half the

Senate was absent. With scant deliberation, the United States had committed itself to a new entitlement program.

Dialysis treatments are the medical equivalent of a girl in a well. Fail to intervene, and people with ESRD face imminent death; take action, and most survive. It's hard to deny help to identifiable people—a girl in a well, a person with kidney failure—whose lives depend on public action.[42] For that reason, perhaps, the U.S. government took treatment of kidney failure out of the consumer realm. No one would be denied dialysis anymore because of an inability to pay.

Lifesaving treatments don't easily fit within consumer markets. The fundamental characteristic of a free market is a consumer's ability to decide whether to buy what someone is trying to sell her. When a Barcalounger is too pricey, that consumer can stick with her non-reclining chair. When a patient with kidney failure finds dialysis beyond his means, however, his only choice in a free market is to die. Recognizing the radicalism of leaving dialysis care to the free market, the U.S. government took on the cost.

It's hard for governments to turn their backs on end-of-life needs.

We seem to be at an impasse. Many patients cannot say no to expensive treatments if they believe their lives are on the line. Doctors prescribe desperate treatments, insensitive to cost. And the people covering the cost of this care—private insurers or government programs—feel they have no choice but to pay. It isn't easy to leverage the power of consumer markets in the world of medical care, particularly for lifesaving treatments. That's why, in bringing market discipline to healthcare, we need to create smarter, more compassionate markets—ones designed to mesh with the realities of medical decision making.

Time to see what it will take to improve healthcare markets.

A RECIPE FOR SMARTER
HEALTHCARE MARKETS

6

SHINING A LIGHT ON HEALTHCARE PRICES

There are some medical conditions all of us would be lucky to avoid. Anything that doctors at a tertiary care system call "a fascinating case" is almost always best to avoid. A new diagnosis the doctor asks you to sit down before receiving—that's an illness you don't want to experience. And then there's Susan Kirby's situation, when her doctor looked at the result of one of her blood tests and simply said "wow."

Kirby had been battling rheumatoid arthritis (RA) for more than a decade. Because of the disease, she had swan neck deformities of seven of her fingers, each of the affected digits fixed in permanent undulation like a swan's neck.[1] Her left wrist was twisted sideways, as if every finger was trying to trade places with her pinky. The surface of her eyes felt like sandpaper. On a good day, Kirby awoke with whole-body stiffness that didn't dissipate until noon. Most days were not good days.

Kirby's physician had exclaimed "wow" at the result of her erythrocyte sedimentation rate, which revealed that she was experiencing dramatic levels of inflammation in her blood.[2] The sedimentation rate, rather than hovering around a value of 20 or 25 as it would in a normal person, came in at 87, "sky high," in the words of her rheumatologist. If Kirby's slew of medications had been working as intended, her body would not be so ravaged by inflammation. But the methotrexate pills she took every week and the abatacept (Orencia) she injected every month were, in Kirby's words, as effective as "sugar water." Kirby wasn't ready to give in to her illness. A few years earlier, she had taken two medications that had worked for a while before losing their effectiveness. She knew that battling RA meant switching up her mix of medications once in a while to find a mix that would bring her inflammation back under control. She needed to find the right recipe to calm her inflammation: "Let's see. We did A, B, C," Kirby said. "But we still have D, E, F, G, and H," her doctor replied. "Well, that's why I like you," Kirby quipped. "You know your alphabet!" Kirby's rheumatologist began exploring her available alternatives. He asked her whether, all else equal, she preferred an injectable drug or one that would be given intravenously. "Well, I am a really hard stick for an IV, and I have these itty, bitty baby veins." The rheumatologist explained they could try a drug called Cimzia (certolizumab pegol), which Kirby could inject into her abdomen or thighs.

By now, you can probably guess where this conversation is headed. The rheumatologist will prescribe a new medication, and Kirby will get slammed with an unaffordable copay; or she will ask him about such financial matters, and he will tell her not to worry—her treatment takes priority. Based on the past three chapters, you might expect me to dismiss any notion of giving patients more "skin in the game," to incentivize them to scrutinize the cost and quality of their medical care.

It's true that I am concerned about the naïveté of fixing the U.S. healthcare system solely through consumer markets. Most patients in the throes of illness can't be expected to behave as rational, discerning consumers. Nor can physicians be expected to dismiss millennia of paternalistic practices, of guiding patients to the best medical choices, and instead play a role equivalent to a Best Buy salesperson, pointing out the features of patients' cancer treatment alternatives the same way they might describe the attributes of the HDTVs on display in the home entertainment section. But I'm also concerned about another naïve belief—that consumerism should have no role in healthcare practice. I would go as far as to say that wherever you live right now, and whatever kind of healthcare system you interact with when you are sick, you are ensconced in the world of healthcare consumerism.

For those of you living in the United States, such consumerism is impossible to ignore. Your healthcare system is teeming with insurance plans that require beneficiaries to cover at least some of their healthcare expenses out of pocket. But what about places like the United Kingdom or France, where patients face few copays or deductibles? Healthcare consumerism is relevant to you, too. Even there, consumerism is key to good medical decision making. Consider a Londoner with early-stage prostate cancer who has to decide whether to receive surgery, radiation, or active surveillance; or a Parisian with breast cancer who has to decide between mastectomy versus lumpectomy with radiation.[3] Despite receiving medical care for free, these patients have a huge incentive to be active healthcare consumers; after all, the right choice in those situations depends on a given patient's treatment goals—whether he is willing to put up with the side effects of surgery or radiation to rid himself of the cancer, or whether she is willing to undergo a major surgical procedure to avoid six weeks of radiation. Patients act as healthcare consumers whenever they make an effort to choose medical alternatives that align with their goals.

Moreover, even when medical care is free, it has costs. A Londoner who chooses to treat his prostate cancer with radiation will incur expenses going back and forth to the clinic for those treatments, and one who chooses surgery will face non-healthcare costs related to that treatment—such as the cost of missing work and of asking loved ones to care for him during the recovery.

What about paternalistic healthcare systems, where doctors tell patients what to do and the government covers all their expenses? Even in those systems, we haven't eliminated the need for people, as patients, to behave as healthcare consumers. Even when a paternalistic physician tells a patient to take cholesterol pills, and even when those pills are free, that patient has to decide whether to *actually* take those pills each day as prescribed. After all, those free pills come at a cost—they carry the risk of side effects. Even in a "doctor knows best" healthcare system, it is patients who decide whether to go to the ER or the doctor's office when they experience symptoms, or to simply tough it out.

In short, we too often think of healthcare consumerism as necessarily involving the kind of high out-of-pocket expenses that give patients incentive to scrutinize their care. But even in the absence of out-of-pocket costs, many medical decisions still hinge on patient preferences. That also means that many of the problems I've laid out so far in this book are not limited to out-of-pocket healthcare systems. They are universal. Absent any out-of-pocket healthcare expenses, patients still struggle to make informed consumer choices. They still interact with clinicians who make choices for them without considering their goals and preferences.[4] And in the face of serious or life-threatening illness, they often don't feel like they have any choice. Regardless of the structure of a healthcare system, we have to figure out how we can best empower patients to make healthcare choices that reflect their values, while making healthcare affordable for society as a whole. That's why, in this second part of my book, I'm going to explore better ways to engage patients in their healthcare decisions.

Patients need to be empowered as decision makers regardless of whether they face out-of-pocket expenses. But in the remainder of this book, I will focus mainly on the out-of-pocket side of consumerism. I'm going to endorse giving patients a direct economic stake in some of their healthcare choices. Asking patients to consider the cost of their healthcare alternatives should play a role in improving healthcare systems. Not the kind of blunt out-of-pocket costs favored by most market enthusiasts today, like those high-deductible health plans I critiqued earlier. Instead, I will point toward smarter healthcare markets—with more nuanced insurance designs, and with consumers tackling high healthcare prices with the help of intelligent government interventions.

I want patients to have some exposure to out-of-pocket costs because, absent any such costs, either they will demand overly expensive care or society, to control costs, will need to deny them access to care even in situations where they would be willing to incur high out-of-pocket costs.

More importantly, despite all the problems I discussed in Part I regarding factoring out-of-pocket expenses into medical decisions, it *is* possible for clinicians and patients to make wise decisions about how to spend patients' money. Returning to Susan Kirby, the woman ravaged by inflammation from RA: when her rheumatologist asked whether she preferred injections or infusions, he was embracing consumerism, whether he recognized it or not. He was trying to make sure her treatment choice reflected her views of the relative burdens and benefits of available therapies. In her case, she faced potentially high out-of-pocket expenses depending on which treatment she chose, so her rheumatologist also asked Kirby about her insurance coverage: "I have new prescription insurance this year," Kirby responded. "It's not near as great as before." She described the patchwork of health insurance and pharmaceutical benefits management companies

covering her prescriptions. With this information in hand, her rheumatologist came up with an idea: "The nice thing about Cimzia is that you
can get it one of two ways. You can either get it as a prescription or as a
medical benefit that would go through Medicare Part B." Part B is the
portion of Medicare that covers physician services, the kinds of things you
have to get at a doctor's office. People can take pills at home, for example,
but they can't always get injections or IV infusions. "[The Cimzia] wouldn't
count as a prescription," he continued. "The only difference is you would
have to see me here every month for a shot." He laid out a plan to find
out which alternative would be most affordable for her, and then finished
addressing her other medical concerns.

Kirby's rheumatologist practiced the kind of cost-sensitive medicine that
excites proponents of healthcare consumerism. Kirby's experience reveals
what can happen when patients and physicians engage in robust conversations about healthcare costs. As we have seen, this kind of explicit, cost-
conscious decision making is not currently the norm in American medicine.
Many patients aren't as willing as Kirby to admit when they are concerned
about the cost of their care. And many physicians aren't as facile as Kirby's
doctor at folding cost conversations into the flow of a clinical encounter.
But it is possible for patients and their clinicians to work together—as
consumers and providers—to scrutinize the costs and benefits of medical
interventions so that patients receive the care that fits their goals.[5] In this
section of the book, I'll lay out several ways to improve healthcare consumerism, as well as tell you some healthcare practices and policies that
should not be left for healthcare consumers to enact on their own.

Like Kirby's RA medications, the ideas I'll discuss won't work in per-
petuity. Some might work for a while before becoming as effective as sugar
water. In addition, much the way Kirby found the right combination of
pills, through trial and error, we will need to test recipes—mixtures of
policy "ingredients"—to find out what work best together to improve
healthcare markets. Think of my proposal as a list of ingredients, none of
which suffice on their own as a satisfying meal. Most ingredients, in isolation, aren't delicious. Vanilla extract and table salt on their own taste ter-
rible, but both improve the flavor of many meals. Cinnamon is a challenge
to swallow by itself, but add it to a recipe, and it's often the ingredient
that causes delighted diners to ask, "What's in this entrée?"

In subsequent chapters, I'll discuss ways to address outrageous health-care prices, and I'll explore smarter ways to design insurance plans so they align out-of-pocket expenses with the costs and benefits of medical care. I will even address some exciting ways to empower patients who face serious or life-threatening illnesses. But none of these policy proposals are hearty enough to stand on their own. Instead, they need to be mixed together, in amounts not yet determined, until we find a palatable way to improve healthcare markets.

In this chapter, I'll lay out the first few ingredients of my recipe, by addressing a challenge I laid out early in the book—the difficulty Americans have discovering the cost of care in time to inform their healthcare decisions. I'm going to explore what it will take to bring healthcare prices out of the dark.

Price Transparency Entrepreneurship

In Part I, I explored the long history of price opacity in the U.S. healthcare system, with prices hidden by providers and payers who don't want the public to know the details of their secret negotiations. Many experts are hopeful that the internet can disrupt this secrecy, the way it has disrupted so many other parts of the economy.[6] To get a sense of how such disruption might work, I decided to shop online for cataract surgery during a summer vacation in 2017. I wanted to see how easy or hard it was to get a price estimate. You see, the price shopping studies I discussed in Part I typically involved researchers calling healthcare providers and asking for price quotes. But few people shop that way anymore. Why telephone some poor hospital employee when Google can tell me what I need to know?

So I googled "price of cataract surgery."

The top four links were advertisements for eye centers near where I was vacationing. The first was from Cedar Run Eye Center, which promoted itself as "northern Michigan's first [eye center] to offer Laser Cataract Surgery." I scanned the link for price information but couldn't find any. (I did, however, read their proud claim that "every patient in northern Michigan deserves the best technology available anywhere." God bless America! Try to shop for healthcare prices, and you encounter techno-bragging instead.) The second link was a site informing me that the average cost of a cataract procedure in Traverse City was $2,014, based on "the median of five medical providers who perform cataract procedures" in the area. It listed prices ranging from $1,250 to $3,500, and also pointed out that the price "differs based on your insurance type."

Curious to see whether I could get more precise information, I followed a link to a free quote. It asked me to pick what type of procedure I wanted to price:

66,982—Cataract Surgery
66,983—Cataract Surgery W—lol, 1

Having no idea what "Cataract Surgery W lol" was (a procedure where the anesthesiologist uses laughing gas?), I chose "Cataract Surgery." I continued by informing the site that I had no insurance. It responded by telling me: "Unfortunately, we don't have any partners in our network that can provide you with a quote for that procedure," then provided me with the names and addresses of clinics I could call for price estimates. All the wonders of the internet, and I was left with hours of phone calls just to price out a common medical procedure.

But I wasn't going to conclude, after a single shopping experience in remote Michigan, that the internet had failed to disrupt medical markets. I knew that lots of companies were trying to make a business out of providing people with healthcare price information. For instance, a healthcare price transparency company called Castlight Health had gone public in 2014, valued at over a billion dollars.[7] That valuation was premature, reflecting unrealistic optimism about the company's business model. But the market's enthusiasm for Castlight reflected a strong belief among many investors that there was money to be made in the price transparency business.

To get a broader understanding of healthcare price transparency, I recruited a team of Duke undergraduates to conduct internet searches for healthcare prices in a half-dozen American cities.[8] We tried to get price information for a half-dozen medical tests or treatments. We searched in "incognito" mode, thus yielding results unbiased by our previous search histories. What we found was discouraging. For starters, we were inundated with ads for products unrelated to our searches. Our searches also yielded numerous links to healthcare providers, most of whom didn't provide any price information about the procedures we were searching for. We'd search for "price of hip replacement in St. Louis" and uncover links to various orthopedic offices in the metro area, most of which wouldn't give price estimates unless we provided them with personal information. When we offered up such information to a couple sites, we got inundated with text messages and emails, a pretty off-putting experience for a consumer who is trying to compare the price of more than a few providers. Imagine if you wanted to find out the price of an airline ticket from Boston to St. Louis, and the airlines wouldn't give you a price without getting your phone number and email address so they could hound you about your travel plans. Not exactly what market disruption should look like.

Not to say we didn't get any price information. When we searched for the price of a hip replacement, the websites that came up yielded price information almost 5 percent of the time. Better yet, almost 25 percent of the sites that came up when we searched for "price of cholesterol panel" gave us price estimates for that test. The availability of price information varied across locations. While less than 10 percent of sites in Baltimore revealed price estimates, almost 30 percent of sites in Chicago and Los Angeles provided such information.

Perhaps more importantly, a few sites came up across multiple locations for a wide range of procedures and tests. One such site was NewChoice-Health.com, which states its mission is "to help you make informed decisions about your medical procedures by giving you the tools you need to compare facilities in your area."[9] In fact, New Choice Health was the second link that showed up on my iPad that day when I searched for cataract surgeons in northern Michigan.

New Choice Health is one of dozens of companies in the price transparency business. Another transparency company goes by the name Pricing Healthcare. Through that company's website, I learned that the price of a head CT scan in Los Angeles is $299 (for the scan as well as for a radiologist report on what the scan reveals about my brain).[10] Given all the secrecy surrounding healthcare prices, you might wonder how companies like New Choice Health and Pricing Healthcare get their information. According to CEO Randy Cox, when he started Pricing Healthcare, the company relied almost exclusively on crowdsourcing to gather price information. Patients shared their medical bills with the company, which aggregated the data and made it available, in a user-friendly format, for consumers shopping for similar services. Not long after launch, however, Cox started receiving phone calls from healthcare providers asking him to make the prices of their services available to the public. "A lot of people stutter and stare when I say we're getting prices directly from facilities," Cox told me. "That's supposed to be impossible. Not only are we doing it, but facilities are actually paying us to post their prices. And they're sending us updates so their published prices are current."[11] Providers recognize that many patients who face high out-of-pocket costs are looking for affordable care.

Another company, Healthcare Bluebook, makes money by contracting with medical clinics to offer patients a free app that links to their insurance plan so it can more accurately estimate their out-of-pocket expenses. Providers pay Healthcare Bluebook for access to the app in hopes that when patients know prices up front, they'll be less likely to become delinquent on their medical bills.[12] The patients using the app may benefit more than they realize from discovering the price of their clinic visits; a 2016 study found that when people chose lower-cost primary care doctors, they not only saved $20 or $30 for that appointment, but also went on to save almost $700 more over the course of the year, because those doctors ordered less expensive tests and procedures.[13]

Insurance companies, too, have joined the price transparency business. As an Aetna enrollee, I can go to Aetna's website and not only discover the price of a head CT, but also figure out how much of that price I will be responsible for, based on the specifics of my plan and on how much of my yearly deductible I've already covered. At the time I wrote this book, these efforts were nascent. According to a 2016 study, in the second year the company made out-of-pocket costs available to its customers, only 3 percent of Aetna enrollees logged in to the website to look up prices.[14] In California, when government employees were given access to a price transparency website, only 1 percent of people who underwent expensive imaging tests like CTs and MRIs accessed the site. Some people probably don't price shop because they don't think prices vary much across providers.[15] Many others might simply be unaware that such transparency tools exist. Maybe some simply get put off by the complexity of most tools: "Cataract, lol 1" anyone?

To make matters worse, with current price transparency tools, the vast majority of Americans do not have ready access to price information. Pricing Healthcare, for example, lists colonoscopy prices from many parts of the United States. But when I looked in 2016, the company listed only one price in Philadelphia, a clinic that charged $1,910, and only one in Los Angeles, a clinic that charged $750. In addition, when my team of undergraduates compared competing transparency companies, they discovered bewilderingly inconsistent price estimates. Two transparency companies reported that a hip replacement in Philadelphia should cost around $50,000; two others listed prices of less than $5,000 in that same metropolitan area, a nonsensical finding unless they were reporting people's deductibles and copays as being the total price of the procedure.

The market for price information hasn't matured yet. Thanks in large part to all the secrecy I wrote about in chapter two, transparency companies often have a hard time getting hold of timely and accurate price information for their customers. Could private enterprise use a little help from the government?

Information Through Legislation

Over the past half-dozen years, I've spoken to a score of CEOs of price transparency companies. The leadership teams often seem young enough to still be listed on their parents' health insurance plans. They excitedly tell me about their simple solution to America's healthcare problems—an app with prices on it!—and then they try to figure out how to get access to those prices. As we've seen, they are typically thwarted by the many payers and providers who want to keep those prices hidden. But not in New Hampshire, where consumers know exactly where to find healthcare price information. In 2007, the New Hampshire legislature demanded access to the bills that healthcare providers sent to insurance companies—"claims data," in health policy jargon—and began publishing those prices on a website called NH Health Cost. The result?

Consider a price search I conducted in 2016 for a spinal MRI—a high-resolution picture of my often-aching lower back. For the purposes of my research, I informed the New Hampshire website that I was uninsured. In response to my query, it presented me with a lengthy list of imaging facilities in alphabetical order. At the top was Access Sports Medicine and Orthopedics, with a list price of $2,973 for the procedure. Ouch! Alice Peck Day Memorial Hospital was only slightly less expensive, at a price of $2,835. But the website also informed me that the hospital granted a 35 percent discount to people without insurance, meaning my cost would be (only) $1,842.

I clicked on a dropdown menu and sorted the facilities by "what you will pay," rather than alphabetically. There at the top of the list was Portsmouth Regional Hospital, which offered uninsured patients an 86 percent discount on its list price, for an out-of-pocket cost of only $567.

New Hampshire has taken the initiative to put healthcare price information on a user-friendly "are-you-sure-this-is-a-government" website, one of a handful of states that, by the time I finished this book, were making tangible progress in promoting healthcare price transparency.[16] For example, my state of North Carolina passed legislation in 2013 requiring hospitals and ambulatory surgical centers to publicly disclose what they charge to insurance companies for 140 different services and procedures.[17] In 2017, a law in Colorado came into effect requiring hospitals to post self-pay prices for their fifty most common diagnoses and twenty-five most common procedures. Physicians were also required to post prices for their fifteen most common procedures.[18] Other states have been laboring to assemble all-payer claims databases—huge data files amassing reimbursement rates for all the procedures and services that providers offer, from anyone reimbursing them for those services. As in New Hampshire, North Carolina, and Colorado, these efforts are meant to make it easier for consumers to get hold of price information before receiving surprising healthcare bills.[19]

States are also promoting price transparency in other ways. For example, some hospitals negotiate gag clauses with insurers. Under such a gag clause, St. Opaque Hospital can offer Aetna a discount on bypass surgery fees on the condition that Aetna keep quiet about the price.[20] Some states are crafting legislation to ban these kinds of gag clauses. Other states are taking aim at anti-tiering agreements ("we'll give you a price of $X if you agree not to put our product on a high out-of-pocket tier") and going after "most favored nation clauses" ("we'll pay you $70,000 for bypass surgery if you promise not to charge less to any other insurance company").

These price transparency efforts are beginning to have an impact on healthcare prices. Hospitals and physicians in New Hampshire feel pressured to lower their prices because of the state's website.[21] When people begin realizing how much healthcare prices vary, they will start flocking to affordable providers. In fact, a company called AIM Specialty Health reached out to patients scheduled for expensive MRI tests to tell them about low-cost radiology clinics. As a result, the average cost of people's MRIs dropped.[22]

This last point is an important one. Legislation can play a pivotal role in lowering medical prices, making healthcare markets more transparent. That price pressure, in fact, doesn't have to reflect a massive number of consumers shopping online for healthcare services. The very *existence* of publicly available price information can change how a marketplace functions. For example, some local governments in the United States were early advocates for requiring restaurants to publish calorie information on their menus. Many behavioral scientists have conducted research raising questions about whether this information changes what food people order.[23] But other researchers have discovered that even if the information doesn't change consumer behavior, it changes the behavior of the restaurants, which increased the healthiness of their offerings, so they don't look bad compared with their competitors.[24] By similar logic, a local hospital might be pressured to lower the price of bypass surgery if the lower price of their competitor becomes public.

Smart legislation can improve the way consumer markets function. I can figure out the salt content of my favorite crackers because the FDA requires Nabisco to put that information on the package. Without good laws and wise regulations, consumer markets can't function efficiently. Anyone who wants the United States to embrace a more consumer-friendly healthcare system should also support government efforts to shine a light on healthcare prices.

Unfortunately, state price transparency has remained the exception rather than the rule. A 2016 report on price transparency laws still gave most states a grade of F.[25] The report even scolded Massachusetts, which used to get an A grade, for letting its price transparency website go dark. Worse yet for state transparency efforts, the U.S. Supreme Court ruled in 2016 that state all-payer claims databases couldn't require self-funded employee health plans to submit their data.[26] While the details get technical, involving what are called ERISA plans, the big picture is clear—government efforts to promote price transparency are in their infancy and face a series of political and legal obstacles.

That said, I'm optimistic that we will make progress in bringing healthcare prices out of the dark. Too many Americans, and too many American employers, are being crushed by healthcare expenses for prices to remain hidden. In the not-too-distant future, I expect most Americans will become almost as aware of their out-of-pocket expenses as people in Singapore.

Does that mean our shopping problem is solved? Hardly. For starters, who in their right mind shops based on price alone?

Do Healthcare Consumers Need Help from Yelp?

Price transparency information is not very helpful if people have no idea of the quality of that care. People want to know not only the price of their knee replacement, but also the skill of the surgeon performing the procedure. Consider what has happened to the airline industry in recent decades, due to people's obsessions with prices over quality. When I shop for a flight from Raleigh to Iowa City, most websites order the alternatives from least to most expensive. In fact, until relatively recently, it was hard to find information on leg room, availability of edible food, or even percentage of on-time flights. With nothing to guide their choices other than airfare and departure times, consumers have largely flocked to low price flights, which has (in this traveler's opinion) caused a rapid deterioration in the quality of airline service.

We don't want the same thing to happen in healthcare, with a race to the bottom that threatens people's lives. People need access to information about the quality of their medical care. Imagine what would have happened to Uber and Lyft if people didn't have information on the quality of their drivers. Sure, the convenience of beckoning drivers to obscure locations at reasonable prices would have been appealing, but many potential customers would have been nervous getting into the backseat of a stranger's car, were it not for the many previous customers who gave the driver a five-star rating. The same holds for healthcare, to some degree. Suppose a gastroenterologist on the outskirts of town performs endoscopies for half the price of the gastroenterologist recommended to you by your primary care doctor. You'd want to know something about that other gastroenterologist's background before making an appointment.

Imagining I was choosing a gastroenterologist, I went to the popular website Yelp for patient reviews. I saw that Wake Gastroenterology, in Raleigh, averaged only three out of five stars, while Duke Gastroenterology Clinic at Briar Creek, also in Raleigh, averaged five out of five stars. That sounds good for Duke. However, across both clinics I found a total of only three reviews. The Duke Clinic really impressed its lone reviewer, who "trusted her [the doctor] with my life." The Wake Clinic had one five-star review from a woman who described the doctor as "always friendly," and a one-star review from a man who was quite unhappy about the raspy-voiced nurse (?) or med tech (?) who screwed up his IV.

I'm not confident that these kinds of Yelp reviews will help me pick a doctor. With enough data, I could probably figure out which doctors are chronically late or persistently nasty. But I doubt I'd have a robust sense of which ones provide high-quality care.

Fortunately, there are more systematic and scientific efforts under way to provide quality information to healthcare consumers. The Centers for Medicare and Medicaid Services has a website called Hospital Compare, where people can find out how hospitals in their area stack up according to a wide range of quality measures: structural measures, like whether the hospital has an electronic health record that makes it easier for clinicians to see the results of tests ordered by other clinicians; outcome measures, like the percentage of people getting better vision after cataract operations or the percentage who die after bypass surgery; and even patient satisfaction ratings, akin to Yelp reviews, but collected much more systematically and rigorously.[27] Medicare combines all these measures to rate hospitals, with the best receiving five-star ratings, a seal of approval given to less than 2 percent of U.S. hospitals in 2016. In fact, only 20 percent of hospitals received four-star ratings that year.[28] This is a tough test, with no grade inflation. If I were sick, I'd avoid a two-star hospital if I could.

But is Medicare's scoring system up to snuff? My perusal of local hospitals left me skeptical. When I plugged my Chapel Hill zip code into the site in 2017, it informed me that the highly prestigious University of North

Carolina Hospital garnered a paltry two-star rating. (By contrast, Duke University Hospital received four out of five stars.) As a Duke employee, I like to think we hold our own against UNC, but the two-star score didn't jibe with other ratings of the UNC Health System. At the time that I conducted this query, for instance, the *U.S. News & World Report* ranked UNC as having the number-two hospital in the region, and the number twenty-two medical school in the country, out of hundreds of such schools. How could Medicare rate UNC as a two-star hospital?

Quality report cards are fraught with controversy, in large part because the science of measuring healthcare quality is imprecise.[29] Duke, for example, is well known for neurosurgical treatment of brain tumors—Ted Kennedy came to Duke when he was diagnosed with a glioblastoma, a particularly aggressive form of brain cancer.[30] Yet despite Duke's reputation for treating such cancers, *U.S. News* reported Duke's neurosurgical survival rates as being just "average."[31] This report doesn't strike me as plausible. In reporting surgical mortality rates, does *U.S. News* account for the many patients who come to Duke after treatment at their local centers has failed to halt their illness? Do its measures statistically adjust for the fact that one surgeon's patients are sicker than another's?[32] There are a host of challenges in measuring healthcare quality. For example, some quality report cards fail to account for the small numbers contributing to many of the measures.[33] If a surgeon performs only ten thyroidectomies in a year, that will not yield enough data to provide an accurate estimate of how well she performs that procedure. In addition, report cards sometimes fail to address potential flaws in patient satisfaction measures—the possibility, for example, that one internist has more satisfied patients than another because the second internist cares for a less easily pleased population.[34]

To make matters worse, quality ratings can be manipulated by healthcare providers. For example, surgeons who avoid high-risk minority patients can reduce their post-operative mortality rates and thus improve their quality scores.[35] Cardiologists performing angioplasty—a procedure where they open blocked arteries in the heart through a balloon catheter—can manipulate their quality ratings by declining to perform the procedure on severely ill patients.[36]

Experts have proposed ways to improve quality measurement.[37] But even if we improve quality measures, we have yet to figure out how to communicate such information to consumers in ways they can easily use when making medical choices.[38] Take Medicare's one- to five-star rating system. Are consumers supposed to assume that four stars are twice as good as two? And what does twice as good mean, in terms of healthcare quality? If consumers have access to both price and quality data, odds are good that the price data will be easier for them to comprehend, raising the possibility that price shopping will still dominate consumer choice.

I recognize that I am being frustratingly inconsistent. On the one hand, I'm calling for price and quality transparency. On the other hand, I am bemoaning the challenges of incorporating such information into healthcare choices. To quote about 60 percent of medical journal articles: "more research is needed." And that research will never solve all the problems that quality measurement raises in healthcare settings. It's pretty easy to measure the quality of a lawnmower. We can evaluate its energy efficiency and its reliability, confident that our measures don't result from manufacturers manipulating us. Moreover, *Consumer Reports* can summarize that information in a simple, comprehensible manner that average consumers can use to inform their choices. I don't expect healthcare quality to reach this level of reliability and comprehensibility anytime soon.

Some people might conclude that we should stop providing healthcare quality measures to the public until the measures are more reliable. But that approach ignores the other horses that have already left the barn, like Yelp reviews that increasingly inform consumers' healthcare choices.[39] In fact, Yelp reviews of hospital care provide important information not captured in more traditional quality measures.[40] We need to work, urgently, to improve quality measures, and couple those measures with price information.

It won't be easy to make the price and quality of healthcare and healthcare insurance transparent, or to provide such transparency in ways that improve consumers' choices. But we need to confront these challenges. For the foreseeable future, many Americans are likely to face high out-of-pocket expenses for their medical care. Given the high cost of healthcare, consumers deserve information that will help them make these difficult choices. Armed with that information, they can start pressuring healthcare providers, and the healthcare industry more generally, to offer high-quality services at more affordable prices.

Not to say that consumers, on their own, can rein in high healthcare prices. Transparency is but one ingredient necessary to remake medical markets, and consumers are but one of the chefs necessary to assemble a recipe for smarter healthcare markets. Time, now, to turn to another chef, and explore why we shouldn't ask patients to battle high healthcare prices on their own.

7

PRICING HEALTHCARE TO REFLECT VALUE

Listen to some healthcare experts and you might believe that transparency alone will disrupt the healthcare industry, significantly reducing the price of medical care in the United States while increasing or maintaining its quality.[1] However, economists estimate that price transparency legislation will lead to price reductions only on the magnitude of about 5 percent, not an earth-shattering reduction given the trillions of dollars spent on healthcare.[2] Nevertheless, that is a savings I wouldn't scoff at. In more targeted parts of healthcare, like MRI testing, price transparency could save as much as 30 percent, according to one study.[3]

But in some situations, no amount of price transparency will reduce healthcare spending. Consider Alexandra Ramsey, one of the breast cancer patients in our study of doctor-patient conversations. She wasn't happy about the bill for the bone strengthener her oncologist had prescribed. "It's $15,000 a shot," she exclaimed. "That's crazy," her oncologist replied, "but unfortunately it fits in with the rest of the insanity of all of our healthcare system." Ramsey wanted no part of the insanity: "That's a lot [of money]. I don't think I should get it," referring to the drug. "Oh, you're getting it," the oncologist replied, as they both laughed. The price of this drug was completely transparent to Ramsey, but the doctor made her feel like she had no choice but to keep taking it. Sometimes, patients aren't in a position to say no to high-priced medical care.

In this chapter, I will make the case that we shouldn't leave it up to patients, on their own, to combat high healthcare prices. Specifically, I'll

explain why government healthcare programs and private insurance companies should demand that healthcare prices more closely reflect the value
of healthcare interventions. Then, in the next chapter, I will bring patients
back into the fold, exploring ways to empower them to make choices that
promote healthcare value, without denying them affordable access to
necessary medical care.

What Is "Value" in Healthcare?

One of the (many) jokes my children have heard me make too
often plays off the universal desire for approval. I will be at a checkout
counter purchasing groceries or sports equipment when the credit card
reader finally flashes the word "approved," and I react with an undue sense
of glee, exclaiming to the clerk how rarely I get any signs of approval from
whatever child is unlucky enough to be waiting in line with me. With no
pause for comedic effect, my child flashes a look of stern disapproval, and
we head out to the car.

Approval can be hard to come by, not just from teenage children or
stingy creditors, but also from the experts at the FDA who are in charge
of determining whether new medications will be allowed on the U.S.
market. The manufacturers of anakinra (Kineret) spent hundreds of millions of dollars developing the drug, including conducting three costly
clinical trials. Those trials had proven that the drug calmed the fires of
rheumatoid arthritis, or RA, reducing inflammation and pain in patients
whose diseases were not responding well to older medications. But that
wasn't enough for the FDA, which told the company it needed proof that
the drugs were not only effective in treating the disease, but also safe. So,
the company conducted a fourth trial, in almost 1,500 patients, many of
whom were sicker than the patients in the first three trials; they were sick
because they had a wide range of other illnesses, and thus were potentially
more likely to experience side effects from the drug. Fortunately for the
manufacturer, the fourth trial proved that the product was safe even in
these sicker patients.[4] In late 2001, anakinra was approved by the FDA to
be used in the United States.

But the company didn't have the same luck on the other side of the
pond. The United Kingdom has its own criteria for deciding which drugs

are worthy of being covered by the country's National Health System. Like the FDA, the NHS convened a panel of experts to review evidence on the drug's safety and effectiveness; as in the United States, the panel concluded that the drug worked, with health benefits that significantly outweighed its risks. Nevertheless, the panel decided that the NHS should not pay for the drug. They rejected anakinra because the price of the brand-name Kineret exceeded its value.[5]

As I've discussed before, in most consumer markets, governments don't convene expert panels to determine which products are overpriced. Instead, consumers make those judgments, one purchase at a time. Bring a jogging stroller to market for $999, and you'll soon find yourself out of the jogging stroller business, unless you bring a whole lot of value to potential customers. (For that price, the stroller would need to make smoothies for mom or dad at the end of their run!) But in healthcare, as we have seen, consumers aren't always able to judge whether interventions are overpriced. Their physician recommends a treatment and the patient assumes it is the right course of action. In some cases, in fact—intensive care for patients with respiratory failure; liver transplant for someone with end-stage cirrhosis—that treatment might be the only way to avoid imminent death. Patients in need of intensive care or liver transplants aren't in a position to negotiate healthcare prices. For these reasons, it doesn't make sense to leave healthcare pricing solely in the invisible hands of the free market. But if the laws of supply and demand aren't going to set prices, how should governments go about doing that?

One answer gaining popularity right now is: value.

In 2010, Harvard business professor Michael Porter published an essay in the *New England Journal of Medicine* calling for healthcare leaders to refocus their efforts on value promotion.[6] He contended that insurance companies should prosper only if they improve the health of their beneficiaries and that healthcare providers, too, should be paid in relation to the impact they have on patient outcomes. Remember, fee-for-service rewards healthcare providers and healthcare manufacturers for providing *more* care to patients regardless of whether that care improves people's health. Under fee-for-service, a spine surgeon makes more money by performing more spinal surgeries, even if many of the patients are unlikely to benefit from those operations. Porter argued that reimbursement should more closely parallel the value of healthcare interventions, which he defined as the health benefit brought per dollar spent. Since Porter's essay, healthcare experts have increasingly called for American medical care to shift "from volume to value," urging healthcare payers to shift from fee-for-service to alternative models that reward quality and frugality.[7]

Value, of course, is exactly what consumer markets typically promote. High quality and low cost are what discerning shoppers demand. But Porter didn't push for more consumerism to promote healthcare value. Instead, he urged leaders to change how they pay for healthcare, with many of these payment reforms being out of consumers' hands. Specifically, since Porter's influential article, third-party payers have begun turning away from strict fee-for-service in place of payments that simultaneously incentivize providers to restrain the amount of care they provide while improving the quality of that care.[8] For example, under Obamacare, Medicare created a shared savings program for some healthcare providers—organized into what are called accountable care organizations—in which Medicare administrators tracked the expenditures of all patients within the provider network.[9] If those expenses were less than expected, Medicare agreed to give some of that money back to the healthcare organization as a reward, but only if the quality of care they provided was up to snuff. In theory, the shared savings program promotes value by constraining costs while maintaining quality. But notably, the program doesn't actually measure healthcare value; it never quantifies health benefits yielded per dollar spent.

In fact, many current payment reforms promote value without measuring it. For example, Medicare penalizes hospitals whose patients are readmitted more frequently than expected.[10] The program promotes quality by incentivizing hospitals to do a better job of keeping patients healthy after they leave the hospital. Under traditional fee-for-service, hospitals would have potentially made more money by providing poor follow-up care, if that caused patients to decompensate and come back to the hospital (thus allowing the hospital to get paid for another admission). In response to the Medicare readmission penalty, however, hospitals now have an incentive to arrange for nurses to visit patients at home after they've been discharged, to detect signs that their illnesses are decompensating. The Medicare readmission penalty promotes value by incentivizing quality while reducing payment for hospital readmissions. But the program doesn't attempt to measure the value of hospital care.

The shared savings program and the readmissions program are what I call managerial pursuits of value. The programs don't quantify value the way Porter defined it: as health outcomes gained per dollar spent. Instead, they give providers an incentive to trim the cost of care while maintaining or improving quality. These managerial pursuits of value leave it up to providers to decide how they want to manage healthcare delivery, to avoid penalties or obtain rewards. Some might wonder how these programs can be called value-based payments if they never measure value. The answer is simple: if providers find ways to offer the same quality of care more efficiently, they are by definition increasing the value of the care they provide.[11]

But there are downsides to these managerial efforts to promote healthcare value. First, because they don't precisely quantify the health outcomes achieved per dollar spent, we don't know if we've achieved decent value in our healthcare system. Suppose that a new payment model reduced the average cost of a knee replacement, while maintaining the quality of those procedures. We still wouldn't know how much healthcare benefit we were bringing for all the money we spent on knee replacements. We might not even know how many of those procedures were even necessary.[12]

Second, these managerial efforts are often so broad that we have no guidance in deciding how to evaluate innovative healthcare interventions. For example, suppose a medication comes to market targeting metastatic colon cancer. The drug increases life expectancy but also increases healthcare costs. In deciding whether to offer this new drug to patients, we could leave it up to healthcare providers to make the decision; perhaps providers ensconced in accountable care organizations would decide whether the additional expense of the chemotherapy was worthwhile. But if we incentivize those providers to reduce healthcare costs, they will potentially be punished for prescribing that drug, even if the drug is good value.

Fortunately, not all efforts to promote healthcare value are limited to managerial approaches. It is these other efforts that I will focus on in the rest of the chapter, efforts that directly address healthcare prices and that quantify value in a way that will allow patients, as consumers, to be empowered to make choices that reflect healthcare value.

Penny-Wise, Pound-Wiser?

Once the FDA became convinced that anakinra was safe and effective, the company was free to sell it on the U.S. market, at whatever price the company thought the market could bear. But being safe and effective is not the same as being cost-effective. When the United Kingdom's National Health System evaluated the amount of health benefit brought by anakinra versus its cost, it didn't think the drug was cost-effective.[13] The United Kingdom has been making cost-effectiveness judgments since 1999, when the British government created the National Institute for Health and Care Excellence (NICE) to help determine treatment guidelines for the nation's public health system.[14] The United Kingdom is largely a socialized healthcare system, with around 95 percent of healthcare spending coming from the government. That means legislators have a strong incentive to make sure healthcare money is spent wisely. As part of its mission, NICE sets thresholds for how much value new treatments need to bring before the government agrees to pay for them. Specifically, if an intervention doesn't provide a year of good health—a QALY, which stands for a quality-adjusted life year—at a cost of £30,000 or less, the NHS probably won't pay for the product.[15]

When NICE requires that new treatments provide a QALY for £30,000 or less, it is using a threshold approach to promoting healthcare value.[16] Prove that your good or service provides enough benefit for the money it costs, and the NHS will pay for it. The strength of this threshold approach is its explicitness. Anyone developing a new healthcare intervention knows what kind of value they need to create to enter the market. By setting a cost-effectiveness threshold, NICE helps the government avoid busting its budget with slightly effective but very expensive treatments. If you want to charge $100,000 for a treatment in the United Kingdom, your treatment better have an enormous impact on patients' lives. In the United States, as we've seen, pharmaceutical companies routinely charge $100,000 or more for new chemotherapy treatments, even when they extend lifespan by just a few months.[17] That pricing, for that amount of benefit, would not pass muster with NICE.

Importantly for our purposes, NICE's cost-effectiveness requirement amounts to an indirect way of regulating healthcare prices. The British don't tell any manufacturer what to charge for its drugs or devices. Instead, by setting cost-effectiveness targets, they allow manufacturers to estimate the maximum price they can charge for their products and still receive NHS reimbursement. You see, companies can't change the benefits brought by their products—if a chemotherapy extends life by four months, that benefit is fixed. But companies can dramatically alter the cost-effectiveness of their products by lowering their prices. For four months of perfect health, a drug would need to cost £10,000 or less—because £10,000 for a third of a year is equivalent to the NICE threshold of £30,000 for a QALY. In response to some NICE rejections, a number of companies have lowered prices to bring their products under the cost-effectiveness threshold.[18]

NICE's cost-effectiveness threshold policy contrasts sharply with managerial efforts to promote healthcare value. It doesn't take existing healthcare operations and incentivize managers to provide that care more efficiently. Instead, NICE's policy signals what price groups like pharmaceutical companies need to charge for their products to fall under the cost-effectiveness threshold. If the United States wants to adopt value-based pricing, it could follow NICE's lead and set a cost-effectiveness threshold for Medicare reimbursement. (If the government adopted this approach, private insurers would likely follow its lead with, perhaps, a more generous threshold.) For example, Medicare could require proof of cost-effectiveness before agreeing to pay for new drugs, devices, or medical procedures. In theory, it could even apply this cost-effectiveness criterion to interventions that have been around a long time. If a new study showed, for example, that annual checkups in healthy seventy-year-olds are not cost-effective, Medicare could stop paying for such appointments.[19]

Despite all the enthusiasm for promoting healthcare value, I don't expect the United States to embrace NICE-like cost-effectiveness thresholds anytime soon. For starters, even if long-standing practices such as annual exams are not cost-effective, it is politically and psychologically difficult for people to stop doing what they've gotten used to doing.[20] Once healthcare practices become established, it is hard to disestablish them, even when new evidence suggests they are not cost-effective. Patients would understandably complain about losing coverage for the annual exams the medical community has been urging them to schedule. And primary care physicians would saturate the media with criticisms of the government's "dangerously stingy" policies.

There is another reason the United States is nowhere close to adopting a NICE-like cost-effectiveness threshold: the law forbids Medicare from using cost or cost-effectiveness in its coverage decisions.[21] That means the Centers for Medicare and Medicaid Services cannot draft new regulations adopting cost-effectiveness thresholds until Congress gives it that authority. When the program proposed such a plan in 1989, the ensuing controversy caused it to reverse course.[22]

But psychology and law notwithstanding, I am hesitant to embrace the NICE approach as the primary way of controlling healthcare costs, for two reasons. First, it is an all-or-none approach, leaving little or no room for individual patients to spend their own money pursuing what they deem to be of value. As I said earlier, it is this objection I'll address in the next chapter. But I have a second concern: Even if Medicare adopted a cost-effectiveness threshold, we might still find our wallets emptied by expensive medical care. That's because being priced to reflect value is different from being affordable.

When Value Breaks the Bank

Not long after he took up the hobby, other beekeepers told John he should take precautions in case of an allergic reaction to bee stings. But he procrastinated, having suffered at the slings and stingers of more than a few of his beloved pets without any type of allergic reaction. Then one afternoon, driving back from attending to his hives, John began feeling tightness in his chest and a strong sensation that he was about to pass out. He raced to the nearest emergency room, where he spoke several unintelligible words before collapsing. He was in the throes of anaphylactic shock. However, John doesn't have to fear death by bee sting anymore. Through a series of allergy shots, he desensitized his body to bee stings. Just as importantly, he keeps an EpiPen by his side at all times, confident that the device will save his life should he again find his immune system attacking his body in response to an invasion of bee antigens.

EpiPens save lives every day, more efficiently than almost any chemotherapy. A dose of chemotherapy can cost $10,000, with only a small chance of benefiting its recipient. A shot from an EpiPen can save a person's life for just $300. Under almost any definition of healthcare value, EpiPens are a bargain.

Yet I expect that most of you know about the cost of an EpiPen not because you heard people praising its manufacturer for pricing the product at value, but instead because you encountered media reports vehemently criticizing Heather Bresch, CEO of Mylan Pharmaceuticals, for jacking up the price of the device more than fourfold between 2007 and 2016. To put that in perspective, over that same time period, overall inflation in the economy ran at only 15.8 percent.[23] Mylan raised the price of the EpiPen even though the drug it delivers, epinephrine, has been around for decades, so long that it no longer has patent protection. The price hike was possible only because of the patent on the device itself, which makes it easy to deliver epinephrine into people's bodies. The patent left Mylan with enough market power to set prices without fear of competition. In fact, that power enabled Bresch to increase her take-home pay 671 percent, to almost $19 million per year, before people took notice and began questioning her company's outrageous pricing practices.[24]

Not that everyone thought that Bresch deserved criticism. One business leader defended Bresch, saying "important medications should be expensive because they're valuable," even arguing that EpiPen's price was "actually too low."[25] That CEO was Martin Shkreli, the infamous "pharma bro" who was convicted of securities fraud in 2018.[26] Before that conviction, Shkreli was vilified in the media for raising the price of Daraprim (pyrimethamine), a medicine critical in treating some AIDS-related infections, from $13.50 a pill to $750.[27]

I share the public's disgust at the greed of these two individuals. Those price hikes were cruel, and they better not become usual. But it is important to note that even after those price hikes, both EpiPens and Daraprim probably reflect good value. In other words: value isn't the only thing that should determine healthcare prices. An emergency appendectomy can save a person's life, but that doesn't mean the surgeon should be able to charge $100,000 for performing the procedure, even if that price is cost-effective. I've lanced boils that were practically making my patients suicidal. If I charged $2,000 for that five-minute procedure, that might qualify as good value, but it would be an awful price.

Value-based pricing cannot assure affordability. Consider what such pricing would mean for Sovaldi (sofosbuvir), a hepatitis C drug that came to market in 2014 with a $90,000 price tag. Even at that price, Sovaldi is relatively cost-effective for patients with certain hepatitis C genotypes, well below the NICE threshold. Sovaldi is cost-effective in part because it is so effective, curing 90 percent of patients.[28] In addition, it is cost-effective because, by curing people's hepatitis, it reduces the expense of taking care of subsequent liver failure, a disease that sometimes leads to $300,000 liver transplants. But even priced at value, the drug is a budget buster. In its first year on the market, sales exceeded $1 billion.[29] That is money that patients and insurance companies and government programs spent then, with monetary savings typically not following until many years later. Hepatitis C, you see, undermines people's health over the course of years, even decades. Give someone Sovaldi now, and you can quickly eradicate hepatitis C from their system. But absent Sovaldi, that virus might not have caused a person to experience health problems for another ten or fifteen years, and might not have created the need for expensive transplants or cancer treatments for another handful of years after that.

The VA system in the United States quickly confronted this now-versus-later spending problem. When Sovaldi came to market, many military veterans, people cared for within the VA, were infected with hepatitis C. With its budget set by Congress, the VA suddenly found itself in a quandary. It could provide Sovaldi to every hepatitis C–positive veteran, but in doing so it would have to take money away from other deserving programs. While Sovaldi treatments would reduce future expenses for things like liver transplants, those expenses had nothing to do with this year's budget. The American prison system also came under financial stress, with 10 percent of prisoners infected with the virus.[30] Treat all those people with Sovaldi, and we would blow through prison budgets by February.

The Sovaldi example illustrates a limitation of value-based pricing in the form used by programs like NICE. Such programs limit expenditures by denying payment for low-value services, but they don't set a hard limit on how much we spend on healthcare.[31] In theory, even with NICE's threshold in place, the U.K. healthcare system could be inundated with new interventions next year, each one priced at less than £30,000 per QALY. Since each of these interventions would cost the system money, it is theoretically possible for the entire GDP of the United Kingdom to be spent on healthcare while falling under the NICE threshold. In pricing healthcare services, we need to consider not only the value of those services, but also the affordability.

But who, exactly, should be determining affordability? In the United Kingdom, which has a socialized healthcare system, it makes sense for the government to determine both value and affordability. But in the United States, with its much more privatized system, many people would argue that it is the marketplace that should make these judgments. Private insurers should decide what healthcare services they can afford to offer their beneficiaries. Private citizens should decide which insurance companies offer the right coverage at the right price, and which healthcare services yield enough benefits to justify the accompanying out-of-pocket expenses.

These "leave it to the market" arguments overlook the many ways that healthcare goods and services depend on the government for their very existence. In exploring how we should tackle healthcare prices, I will explain why I think governments deserve to play a critical role. My explanation begins in the thin air of the Andes.

Chasing an Enzyme

Most people perceive the sparse oxygen available on the crest of a mountain pass as a burden. Francois-Gilbert Viault saw it as an opportunity. It was 1890, and he was leading a team of hikers through the heights of the Andes. Periodically drawing blood during the hike, Viault discovered that the longer he and his companions lived at high altitude, the more red blood cells they had circulating in their veins. By the twenty-third day of his hike, Viault's own RBC count had risen 60 percent.[32] Something in their bodies—most likely an enzyme—was revving up production of those oxygen-carrying cells. A century later, that enzyme—now sold as a drug called EPO—helped Lance Armstrong pedal up French mountain passes in what we now know to be superhuman time. EPO is an amazing drug, one that has dramatically increased the quality of life of people with kidney failure. I'm going to briefly tell you the story of how EPO went from mystery enzyme to miracle medicine, because the story raises important questions about how much money companies should make from pharmaceuticals discovered and developed, in substantive part, with help from federal funders.

EPO came to market after decades of scientific research funded by the U.S. government. Chief among recipients of those grants was Eugene Goldwasser, a researcher at the University of Chicago who began trying to isolate the enzyme in 1955 at the behest of a mentor. The project took him twenty-two years.

Goldwasser first set out to establish where in the body the enzyme is made. To do so, he injected rats with cobalt chloride, a chemical that revs up production of red blood cells, then took plasma from the rats—plasma being the fluid left after removing all the cells from their blood—and infused that into other rats.[33] In response to these injections, the infused rats experienced an increase in red blood cell production, proving that something in the plasma was signaling their bodies to make more such cells. To figure out what parts of their bodies were manufacturing the enzyme, Goldwasser repeated these steps again, but only after removing, say, the initial rat's pancreas. When the second rat still experienced an increase in red blood cell production, Goldwasser would conclude that the pancreas wasn't critical in producing the mysterious enzyme. Then it was on to the next organ. Eventually Goldwasser figured out that whenever he removed the first rat's kidneys, the plasma didn't stimulate the second rat to make red blood cells. The conclusion was clear: kidneys play a critical role in red blood cell production.

But Goldwasser still hadn't found the enzyme. He knew the substance circulated in the plasma of his rats but could not get enough plasma from them to run the necessary chemical tests. The entire volume of blood in a decent-sized rat is less than four teaspoons, and that includes blood cells in addition to plasma.[34] It would take a lot of rats to get enough plasma for Goldwasser's needs. So he decided to draw blood from a more sizable animal—sheep. He had access to such animals because his office was less than an hour away from some of the largest slaughterhouses in the nation. What Goldwasser didn't know at the time was that a lifetime supply of EPO for a sheep, or a human being for that matter, could fit into a contact lens case. So even with sheep-sized amounts of plasma, and a decade and a half of trudging back and forth to the slaughterhouses, Goldwasser hadn't collected enough hormone to isolate it.[35]

For all the Hollywood tales of lone scientific geniuses, science is usually a group effort. Goldwasser was a brilliant and determined researcher, but he would have failed in his quest if it weren't for the help of Takaji Miyake, a Japanese scientist who collected hundreds of gallons of urine from people with aplastic anemia, dried it to the size of a toaster oven, and sent five hundred grams to Goldwasser. In 1977, Goldwasser was able to use this brick of urine to isolate eight milligrams of EPO, a sample barely the size of three snowflakes.[36]

If I stopped this story right now, the moral of that story would be pretty straightforward. I'd create the impression that it was government money and stubborn academic researchers who deserve all the credit for bringing EPO to market. As a result, it would be almost tautological to conclude that EPO should be a public resource, provided to patients at cost. However, it was no simple matter to take three snowflakes and turn them into a product. Despite the critical role that government funding played in enabling Goldwasser to isolate EPO, it would take private funding to turn EPO into a useful medication.

Goldwasser needed more EPO than he could collect from dehydrated Japanese urine. He needed to partner with someone who could figure out how to produce the enzyme. Thus, he began looking for companies that would partner with him. For a while he worked with Parke-Davis, but when early efforts didn't yield quick results, the company lost interest. Goldwasser next approached Abbott Laboratories, but company leaders had no interest in the project, perceiving it to be too risky. Companies spend money only when they believe they will get a good return on their investment. Finally, around 1981, he connected with a clunkily named startup company, Applied Molecular Genetics, that was focused on using recombinant DNA technology to manufacture new drugs. The company began working with the scientists, believing that EPO could potentially come to market faster than other treatments in its scientific pipeline.

But faster didn't mean fast. Taking EPO from snowflake-sized to mass production was no simple process. First, Amgen, as the company later called itself, needed to isolate the gene that produced the protein, a process that, in 1981, was painstakingly difficult, with more than 30,000 as-yet largely unidentified human genes to sort through. Kuen Lin, the scientist leading Amgen's efforts, worked on the project for two years, the company almost abandoning its EPO efforts on multiple occasions as a drain on the company's finances. Lin eventually isolated the gene, and in 1984, the company filed a patent on the process for producing recombinant EPO. They were finally ready to manufacture the drug.

But would the drug work? To answer that question, Amgen needed to conduct clinical trials. Those trials were predicted to cost more money than Amgen had on hand. So, the company sold Japanese distribution rights of EPO to another company for $24 million. Throughout all these efforts—identifying the gene, cloning the gene, and testing the molecule in patients—Amgen spent lots of money, funds that would not have been forthcoming if Amgen's board and Amgen's investors didn't have hope for substantial profits should the drug come to market. Government funding enabled Eugene Goldwasser to isolate EPO. Profit-seeking investors enabled Amgen to turn EPO into a product.

Profit is not evil. Money can motivate people to do good. While I like to think that I became a physician to help people, I could have helped people by becoming a social worker or a grade school teacher, perhaps a public defender. I became a doctor because I wanted to help people while making a good living. Is it so awful to do well by doing good? The people working at Amgen can feel proud about making products that have helped millions of people. And they shouldn't be ashamed that by helping people, they take home a decent paycheck. As for the people who invested in Amgen—some might have cared primarily about the fate of people with kidney failure, but others also invested in Amgen to maximize the return on their investment. We have lots of smart people developing drugs (and applying to medical school) because they want to do well by doing good. If we take financial rewards out of the healthcare industry, we'll have many fewer people pursuing these careers.

Amgen and its investors spent a lot of money trying to turn EPO from a few snowflakes to a viable product. They deserved to profit substantially from their investment. But how substantially? And at what cost to U.S. taxpayers?

When Government Healthcare Spending Generates Private Profits

When Congress established the End-Stage Renal Disease Act in 1972, congressional staffers told legislators that dialysis currently cost $25,000 per year for each patient in the program, a cost they were confident would decline over time as the treatment became more efficient. They didn't account for the possibility that a genetically manufactured enzyme would one day become a mainstay of ESRD treatment. Erythropoietin (EPO) came to market in 1989. Within one year, the majority of dialysis patients were receiving EPO treatment, at an annual cost of more than $6,000 per patient.[37] By 1997, Medicare's annual expenditures on EPO approached $1 billion; by 2001, Amgen's annual profits for EPO exceeded $1 billion, the majority of its revenue coming from the coffers of the U.S. government.[38]

In a free market, the price of a drug like EPO would be determined by supply and demand. But patients with kidney failure are not in a position to shop for bargain EPO. Indeed, many have been financially ruined by their kidney disease and thus depend on government assistance to pay for their medical care. Moreover, most of us would not be morally comfortable letting patients suffer from severe anemia simply because they can't afford EPO. Which leaves us with the question of what a fair price is for a drug like EPO, given the role the U.S. government played in funding the basic science research critical to development of the drug, and the fact that once EPO came to market, it was paid for almost exclusively by the federal government (Lance Armstrong and his buddies being exceptions).

Most companies selling healthcare products and services in the United States receive substantial revenue from state and federal governments. When pharmaceutical companies price new products, they aren't testing what price the market will bear; they are entering a "market" where their biggest customer, Medicare, might be obligated to pay for their product. In other words, Amgen is far from alone, among pharmaceutical companies, in receiving huge amounts of money from the U.S. government.

Nor is Amgen unique in benefiting from federal funding for basic science research. Most pharmaceutical products are built on discoveries funded by governments. Aaron Kesselheim, a Harvard physician, studied the development of transformative drugs, or drug classes, approved by the FDA between 1984 and 2009. He discovered that it was federally funded researchers who identified mechanisms of disease and treatment and often demonstrated proof that a drug works against the disease in question before industry collaborators developed the product and finished clinical testing.[39] For example, the blockbuster leukemia drug imatinib mesylate (Gleevec) came to market after four decades of research funded by the National Institutes of Health (NIH) exploring the biological mechanisms of chronic myelogenous leukemia. Similarly, development of bevacizumab (Avastin), another tremendously expensive cancer drug, began in an NIH-funded Harvard laboratory in the early 1970s.

It's not just pharmaceutical companies that benefit from government research funding. In 2015, General Electric's Healthcare Businesses made almost $1 billion of profit, a substantial part of that from selling high-powered imaging machines like MRI scanners, which can cost upwards of $1 million each.[40] But it wasn't General Electric that came up with the idea of using MRI technology to image the human body. The science for developing MRI machines was built on government-funded research going back to at least the 1940s. In fact, several Nobel Prizes were awarded to researchers from Europe and North America for developing the scientific underpinnings of the technology. It wasn't even high-tech companies like GE that developed the first MRI machine. That honor goes to John Mallard, who built a whole-body MRI scanner at the University of Aberdeen in the 1970s, without a dollar of industry funding.[41]

But GE *did* invest a lot of money, and human capital, to take all those scientific advances and industrialize them. It built the first truly high-powered MRI machine in 1980, a machine that generated vastly sharper images than its predecessors.[42] The company deserves credit (and even reasonable profits) for increasing the quality of MRI technology. But it doesn't deserve all the credit (or limitless financial rewards). When healthcare companies like GE manufacture healthcare products, they almost always do so by standing on the shoulders of giants.

It's not just governments that help healthcare companies develop their products. Venture philanthropy plays a role, too. For example, some diseases are so rare that it is difficult for companies to recruit patients into clinical trials. In recognition of this problem, philanthropic foundations have spent money developing clinical networks for rare diseases, through which pharmaceutical companies can conduct clinical trials.[43] Whenever treatments come out of such trials, they owe their existence in part to those charitable foundations. The companies making those treatments profit thanks to the largesse of philanthropists.

I don't want to leave the topic of public money before addressing some of the many ways healthcare providers benefit from government and philanthropic funds, too, beyond what Medicare and Medicaid spend on direct patient care. For instance, hospitals that train medical and dental residents in the United States receive billions of dollars a year from Medicare to support their teaching efforts.[44] Medicare pumps even more money into teaching hospitals by increasing the amount it reimburses them for the care they provide. One analysis estimated that for each physician they train, Medicare gives hospitals over $100,000 to cover the cost of their education.[45] In addition, most nonprofit hospitals receive substantial revenue from charitable donors, such as grateful patients or community members who chip in to support their clinical operations.

Healthcare is a public good, straight and simple. Parts of a given healthcare system will be more or less public than others. But every wealthy country invests heavily in healthcare research and delivery. And hospitals around the globe appeal to philanthropists to support their noble aims. Healthcare will never operate purely as a private consumer marketplace.

But even though healthcare is a public good, this doesn't mean that people working in healthcare should be forced to receive minimum wage. Public investment in healthcare research and training shouldn't preclude capitalists from investing in healthcare companies, in hopes of profiting. In fact, no profits mean no products. It is the unlikelihood of profits that explains why so few pharmaceutical companies have brought new antibiotics to market in recent years.[46] The profitability of antibiotics is low because when a patient develops a bad bacterial infection, the infection is usually gone in a couple of weeks. Contrast that with conditions like high cholesterol or diabetes, for which millions of people take pills for the rest of their lives.

Here's the conundrum: if we let the free market set healthcare prices, we will need to be comfortable letting people die when they are unable to pay for life-prolonging treatments. We would also need to stop subsidizing medical education, giving tax breaks to nonprofit hospitals, and funding basic science research with tax money. For these reasons, no wealthy country that I know of leaves healthcare pricing solely to the laws of supply and demand. They take active measures to regulate healthcare prices. Even the United States regulates prices when it sets Medicare and Medicaid reimbursement schedules.

The question isn't whether the public deserves a healthcare system that reins in healthcare prices. It is: How do we rationalize healthcare pricing in the United States? Which brings us back to value, and how experts in the United States have been trying to align the price of healthcare with the benefits produced by that care.

Value-Based Pricing in the United States

To see what value-based pricing could look like in the United States, let's examine an expensive new class of cholesterol-lowering drugs. According to Gregory Curfman, a physician at Harvard Medical School, PCSK9 inhibitors are "rewriting the script" for treating high cholesterol.[47] Introduced in 2015, PCSK9 inhibitors inactivate a protein in the liver, thereby reducing the amount of harmful LDL cholesterol circulating in the blood. They cut LDL levels by more than half, even in people already taking more familiar cholesterol medications like statins, thus helping thwart heart attacks and strokes.[48] But unlike statins, which cost pennies a day, a year's worth of a PCSK9 inhibitor costs more than $10,000. In the United Kingdom, the government requested economic and clinical data from manufacturers to determine whether the drugs, at those prices, reflected good value. The companies presented them with these data, making lots of generous assumptions about how the drugs would reduce morbidity and mortality from heart attacks and strokes.[49] They also reduced their prices dramatically.[50] The result was that the country approved payment for the drugs in patients whose cholesterol levels were resistant to standard therapies.[51] (Time will tell whether the United Kingdom continues to pay for the drugs, which have failed in clinical trials so far to reduce the chance that people will die of cardiovascular disease.)[52]

But what about the United States? How have we dealt with the value, or lack of value, of these drugs? Unlike the United Kingdom, we don't have an official agency to determine whether the drugs are cost-effective. Thus, companies haven't had to lower their prices in the United States to gain regulatory approval. But PCSK9 manufacturers have had to pay attention to value anyway. The high price of their drugs, for a condition that was previously treated on the cheap, created lots of bad publicity. It's not good when your new product gets a "but" headline in *USA Today*: "Cholesterol drug prevents heart attacks—but costs $14,000 per year."[53]

In response to criticism of high prices, drug companies have come up with a plan they contend will more closely map the cost of their products to value—they have offered to link reimbursement to how much their drugs improve people's health, on a case-by-case basis. For example, if a PCSK9 inhibitor doesn't lower a person's cholesterol, the company making the drug will give the patient and the patient's insurance company their money back.[54] Other pharmaceutical companies have followed this lead. For some patients, that means that if their multiple myeloma doesn't respond to chemotherapy, the drug company will rebate the cost of its medication.[55] These money-back guarantees are still relatively rare but growing in popularity.

These rebates trouble me because they don't guarantee value. Suppose a multiple myeloma drug costs $100,000 per patient and provides a year of healthy life at a cost of $600,000, well beyond what most experts would say reflects the value of the drug. If one out of six patients gets a rebate for this drug because their cancer didn't respond, it would still take about $500,000 to produce an extra year of healthy life. That still wouldn't meet most experts' criteria for good value. Rebates could simply be a smart PR move by pharmaceutical companies—"Yes, our cholesterol drug is insanely expensive, but at least we don't charge you for it if it doesn't work!" Better to skip rebates and lower the price for everybody, to bring price into alignment with benefit.

Peter Bach, a physician at Memorial Sloan Kettering, thinks drug companies should vary the price of their products across patients, depending on the likelihood that their drugs will be of benefit.[56] He argues that if a cancer drug extends life by an average of six months in patients with, say, lung cancer, and three months in those with colon cancer, that same drug should be priced lower for colon cancer patients than for those with lung cancer. Writing with Steven Pearson, Bach contends that medications are particularly in need of value-based pricing, because they are "the only major category of healthcare services for which the producer is able to exercise relatively unrestrained pricing power."[57] Both Bach and Pearson have developed systems for estimating what price drugs will need to be to reflect value. They urge private insurers to negotiate contracts with pharmaceutical companies based in part on value.

Easier said than done. Armed with cost-effectiveness data, an insurer can demand lower prices from a drug company, but if that company refuses, the insurer's customers may lose access to the best treatment for their illness. When Sovaldi was far and away the best treatment for hepatitis C, insurers had little negotiating power. It took competition to bring down the price of the drug.[58] Many expensive new drugs don't face such competition, leaving insurers little choice but to pay what pharmaceutical companies demand.

When companies have monopoly power, they can demand high prices. Governments usually combat such power by breaking up the monopoly. But in the case of many drugs, those monopolies are endorsed by the federal government, which issues patents explicitly designed to stifle competition, thereby incentivizing drug companies to develop new products. When drug companies price their patented products reasonably, the system works well: companies make tidy profits, and the general public gets access to excellent medicines at reasonable prices. When companies get too greedy, however, governments need to step in.

In the case of Medicare, it is often difficult to step in and demand concessions from pharmaceutical companies, because the law forbids the program from regulating prices.[59] With the federal government's hands tied, state governments have begun stepping into the regulatory void. For example, in 2017, the State of New York passed a law giving authority to a review board to push for rebates from drug companies whose products aren't priced to reflect value, or risk having the state tell insurance companies that they no longer will be required to offer the drugs to their Medicaid customers.[60] Massachusetts is planning to develop a closed formulary for its Medicaid recipients to help control escalating drug costs.[61]

Nongovernmental organizations have also begun calling on drug companies to adopt value-based pricing. While these organizations lack market power or regulatory authority, they can leverage what behavioral scientists recognize as a surprisingly powerful force: peer pressure.[62] For example, one organization, the Institute for Clinical and Economic Review, has been called "America's NICE" by health policy experts.[63] The institute, which goes by the name ICER, is a nonprofit, nongovernmental analysis factory that measures the value of new healthcare goods and services. Unlike NICE, it has no authority to make reimbursement decisions. But its cost-effectiveness analyses nevertheless influence healthcare prices and practices. For example, when an ICER analysis determined that PCSK9 inhibitors were priced three times higher than they should be, manufacturers lowered their prices (although not enough to achieve good value).[64]

ICER's way of assessing value closely aligns with cost-effectiveness analysis. However, ICER also accounts for the budgetary impact of healthcare interventions.[65] Those high-priced hepatitis C drugs, for instance, are cost-effective even at those prices. But as we've seen, the costs are borne now, and the benefits (and accompanying reduction of healthcare costs) often happen many years later. ICER's reports lay out these budgetary impacts, so decision makers like insurance companies can account for that in deciding whether, and for whom, to reimburse for the medications.

The Bottom Line

Healthcare markets aren't up to the task of bringing prices into alignment with value. Governments need to play a role in restraining healthcare prices. But that doesn't mean we need to embrace full-on, top-down price regulation. Instead, we can turn toward policies that, at least for some types of medical care, give patients a role in deciding whether healthcare interventions bring enough benefit to justify their prices. It's time for another ingredient in our recipe for improving healthcare markets. Time to see how healthcare coverage can be redesigned so that high-value medical care is affordable for patients, and so patients can decide whether they want to pay, out of their own pocket, for low-value care.

8

COVERAGE FOR WHAT COUNTS

Earl Hunter's sore throat had lingered longer than usual. But he didn't give it much thought until the morning he noticed a lump on his neck. A week later, Hunter was diagnosed with stage-four squamous cell carcinoma of his throat, an aggressive cancer that would soon end his life unless he received chemotherapy and hefty doses of radiation.

Just fifty-seven years old at the time of his diagnosis, Hunter thought he was as ready as anyone could be to withstand such arduous interventions. "I was a bit overweight when I got sick," he said, "but I was strong and in good shape, as healthy as I had been in my lifetime; I was even training for a hundred-mile bike ride." Despite his physical strength, the treatment hit him like a category-one climb. "It was hell. I was nauseated by the chemo, really, really sick." To make matters worse, the radiation wreaked havoc on Hunter's gums. Even a soft toothbrush felt like steel wool. As a result of treatment, Hunter's mouth became riddled with painful sores, making every gulp of food feel like hot coals running down his throat. The radiation also damaged his salivary glands, meaning the food particles that remained in his mouth after he swallowed settled next to his teeth, undissolved by saliva—a virtual come-hither to cavity-causing bacteria. The result was a perfect storm crashing down on Hunter's teeth, which began to rot, one by one.

Hunter's illness, and the side effects of his treatments, wreaked havoc on his bank account, too. First, there was the cost of his dental care. Hunter had purchased healthcare insurance through his job, but he hadn't bought dental insurance, figuring he could pay out of pocket for any oral surprises, like cavities or root canals. He hadn't anticipated what would happen if he was diagnosed with throat cancer and every tooth in his mouth began crying out for urgent attention. He underwent one tooth extraction, then another, each one costing a surprising amount of money. But Hunter couldn't see an alternative. His tooth pain was making life almost unlivable. What's more, he'd lost over one hundred pounds since diagnosis, leaving only 115 pounds of flesh to his name. Without healthy teeth, he'd have an even harder time keeping up with his nutritional needs. He called his health insurance company to see if they would cover his dental expenses. "It was my cancer treatment that caused my problems, so I thought they'd pay for it. But the guy on the phone laughed, saying, 'You don't need teeth anyway. People can live without teeth.' " So, Hunter paid out of pocket, his dental bills alone costing him $10,000.

Then his medical bills started catching up with him. His radiation doctors, you see, switched practices partway through treatment, and their new office didn't have contracts with Hunter's insurance company. That resulted in another bill for $10,000, which he received after treatment was complete. He also had to pay out of pocket for a drug called filgrastim (Neupogen) to stimulate his white blood cells, which were being ravaged by the chemo; that medication cost $2,000 per cycle, 20 percent of which was his responsibility to pay. He also paid out of pocket for nutritional supplements infused into his body through a feeding tube. Eventually, he hit the $500,000 lifetime maximum from his insurance company, leaving him on his own to pay for the rest of his treatments.

Hunter might have been able to keep up with all these expenses if he'd been able to stay employed. He worked as an IT consultant at a catfish company. But the cancer and the treatment side effects left him too weak to work.

Why am I telling you Earl Hunter's story? Hunter's story reveals the inadequacies of the solutions I've discussed so far in this section of the book. Hunter's financial woes wouldn't have been solved by price transparency legislation. At almost every step of the way, he knew what his treatments would cost. Indeed, Hunter scrutinized those costs—he figured out whether he could afford the cost of each tooth extraction before receiving it—but was compelled by circumstances to exhaust his life savings on that care. It was either live in poverty or die in misery.

Nor would Hunter's problems have been solved by value-based pricing reforms. Many of the treatments Hunter received were, no doubt, higher priced than they needed to be. As we have seen, chemotherapy and radiation treatments are significantly more expensive in the United States than in other developed countries. But those treatments also bring substantial benefits to patients like Hunter. Even if value-based pricing efforts brought the cost of Hunter's care down by 30 or 40 percent, Hunter would still have been financially crippled by out-of-pocket expenses.

The problem for Hunter wasn't the expense of his care. It was that he was on the hook for so much of that expense. The goal of healthcare markets—of asking patients to be healthcare consumers—is to encourage people like Hunter to figure out whether the benefits of proposed care justify their costs. With such financial encouragement, they will walk away from unnecessary care, or unnecessarily expensive care.

But what if, as in Hunter's case, care is both necessary and necessarily expensive? As I discussed in earlier chapters, people like Hunter deserve to know how much they will be required to pay for their medical care. And that care needs to be priced to reflect value. But when healthcare brings substantial benefit and is priced accordingly, we shouldn't ask people to be on the hook for too much of that price. For healthcare markets to fulfill their promise, we need to give people coverage for what counts. Patients' expenses need to be aligned with value so people like Hunter, with urgent and unassailable medical needs, aren't priced out of the only treatments that give them a chance to thrive.

But how do we do that?

Copay Assistance for Expensive Medical Care

Not long ago, a diagnosis of multiple sclerosis (MS) led, almost inevitably, to severe disability, often within a decade of onset.[1] People affected by MS would experience progressive damage to white and gray matter, under attack from their own immune system. Then, a miracle happened. No, that's not the right way to put it—science happened! A slew of new treatments came to market that, in many people, dramatically slowed the progression of their disease.[2] Thanks to medications like glatiramer acetate (Copaxone) and dalfampridine (Ampyra), people with MS can realistically hope to stave off disability for many years.[3]

But those medications often carry crippling out-of-pocket expenses.[4] Many MS drugs cost more than $85,000 a year, meaning a patient responsible for 20 percent of her medication costs will pay $17,000 a year to treat her disease.[5] That's more than many people can afford. In fact, when annual out-of-pocket expenses exceed $16,000, the majority of people with MS stop taking their drugs.[6] Goodbye medications, hello wheelchair.

When treatments benefit patients as much as MS drugs do, people shouldn't have to forgo those treatments because of cost. In part, we can address the affordability of MS medications by pressuring drug companies to lower their prices. That's because at their current prices, most MS drugs do not provide great value.[7] But even priced at value, those drugs would be quite expensive, as would patients' accompanying out-of-pocket costs.

Fortunately for patients, there is a way to dramatically reduce the amount they have to pay for these drugs. It is called copay assistance. Patients can go to the National Multiple Sclerosis Society website and find a link to financial assistance programs (from many of the companies producing MS drugs) that can cover the cost of their copays.[8] The manufacturer of Ampyra, for example, reassures people that if they can't afford the drug, "our patient assistance team will work with you to see if you are eligible to receive Ampyra at no cost."[9]

Things are a bit more complicated for Medicare beneficiaries, because the program forbids companies from covering people's copays. That means a sixty-seven-year-old with MS can't go to ampyra.com and get help paying for her medication. However, she can look to see if there is a nonprofit foundation that would cover those costs. One such group, the HealthWell Foundation, has given away almost a billion dollars in copay assistance, covering the cost of treatments for diseases like hepatitis C, multiple myeloma, and, of course, MS.[10]

Sounds like we have a system that solves the problem I've laid out so far in this chapter, of helping people pay for the expensive interventions they rely upon to live long and well.

As a physician, if I was caring for a patient who couldn't afford her MS medications, I wouldn't hesitate to refer her to a copay assistance foundation. But as a U.S. citizen concerned about healthcare costs, I strongly oppose copay assistance; I don't think it's a good way to reduce the financial toxicity of medical care.[11] For starters, such assistance distorts insurance markets. Suppose I purchase a high-deductible health plan to lower my monthly premiums, and I do so fully cognizant of what I'm buying. My insurance company can afford to charge me a low monthly premium because it knows that my relatively high out-of-pocket expenses will reduce my demand for medical care. But that pricing rationale will be thrown completely out of whack if I can count on charitable foundations to cover my copays when I get sick. With copay assistance in hand, I'll demand more medical care. In response, the insurance company will have no choice but to raise the cost of monthly premiums for its high-deductible plans, making such plans more expensive for healthy people looking for affordable insurance.[12]

Copay assistance further distorts insurance markets by pulling a switcharoo on how insurance companies determine whether people have reached their out-of-pocket maxima for the year. Under most insurance plans, once a patient contributes enough in copays, coinsurance, and deductibles, she'll reach her out-of-pocket maximum and the rest of her healthcare costs will be covered by the insurer. But often, when patients receive copay assistance, the insurance company bills the patient for the copay and counts the copay toward the patient's yearly maximum, unaware that the patient has been reimbursed for that copay. As a result, later in the year, the insurance company stops charging the patient for any of her copays—thinking they've reached the maximum—and the patient gets everything for free, not just the rest of her medications, but also the costs of MRIs, doctor's appointments, and hospital stays.

To be clear, this end run around out-of-pocket maxima is good for individual patients' finances. But the result is higher costs for everyone else and less pressure on drug companies to reduce their prices. Copay assistance also distorts pharmaceutical markets by allowing drug companies to raise their prices without experiencing public backlash.[13] If patients didn't receive assistance and were forced to pay $1,000 a month for their MS drugs, they'd raise a ruckus with the media or with their favorite politicians. But when patients receive copay assistance, they have less reason to complain about the price of their treatments. That's why drug companies are the main organizations funding charitable organizations like the HealthWell

Foundation, knowing they can donate money to cover patients' copays and still profit handsomely—the 80 to 90 percent of the price paid by insurance companies will more than make up for the cost of providing copay assistance; 80 percent of an outrageous price is still a pretty good payment.[14]

Consider the cost of Duexis, a pain pill that is gentler on the stomach than many over-the-counter pills. Duexis is a combination of two over-the-counter drugs: ibuprofen, a pain medicine, and famotidine (Pepcid), a pill that reduces stomach acid. Both medications are available in generic formulations, with a monthly supply of each costing less than $20. Yet Duexis costs more than $2,000 a month. Who in their right mind would pay an extra couple grand a month just to have two medications placed together into one tablet? The answer: just about any sane consumer, because the manufacturer of Duexis covers 98 percent of patients' out-of-pocket expenses when they receive the pill. That leaves insurance companies to pay this exorbitant cost, which they do presumably because they are afraid of negative publicity for denying medications to their beneficiaries.[15]

If I'm right that copay assistance leads to price inflation, you might think value-based pricing would take care of that problem. But even in such circumstances, copay assistance would be bad policy. For starters, such assistance is often doled out arbitrarily. Consider one of the patients we observed in our cost conversation study, whose left knee was swollen, as were both of her feet, "like loaves of bread," causing "immense pain." Because she was on Medicare, she couldn't get direct copay assistance from a drug company, leaving her responsible to pay $340 a month for her etanercept (Enbrel). "I was on the phone with [the company that makes] Enbrel, crying," she told her doctor, "mad at them. I'm like: 'You guys give free copay assistance to people who have regular insurance.' " Many patients in this situation give up, either paying the $340 or forgoing the medication altogether. This particular patient persisted, however, and found a charitable foundation that covered her copay. "But it was only for a year," she told her rheumatologist, with her assistance disappearing for reasons she couldn't fathom. She was frustrated, unsure whether the medication her doctor prescribed for her unrelenting symptoms would be one she could afford. In well-designed healthcare systems, patients' out-of-pocket expenses aren't this arbitrary.

But the U.S. system is disturbingly arbitrary. Consider one of the breast cancer patients we interviewed, who told us that getting financial assistance "felt like it took an act of Congress. . . . I can't tell you how many times I had to send them copies of stuff." Other breast cancer patients told us the experience was humbling, sometimes to the point of making them feel ashamed. As one patient put it: "They [the assistance foundations] make you call and humble yourself, begging."[16] Compassionate healthcare markets don't require people with cancer to beg for financial assistance. Paying for necessary medical care shouldn't depend on the bureaucratic whims of suspiciously funded charities.

Copay assistance helps many patients, but it leaves too many with unaffordable expenses. We need better ways of aligning out-of-pocket expenses with value.

Value-Based Insurance Design

It's a maddening problem. One of my patients would come into the clinic, his blood sugar reaching for the sky. I'd scan his list of medications on the computer and discover that he had run out of his diabetes pills a month earlier without refilling the prescription. I would start lecturing him on the importance of taking his medications, and he would politely interrupt me: "Dr. Ubel," he'd say, "I can't afford the copay."

Out-of-pocket expenses are one of the leading causes of medication "nonadherence"—patients not taking the pills their physicians prescribe.[17] That's where value-based insurance design, or VBID, comes in.[18] VBID is the brainchild of a physician, Mark Fendrick, who thinks like an economist, and an economist, Mike Chernew, who thinks like a physician. (I wonder which one I am insulting the most with that description!) The idea behind VBID is straightforward. The higher the value of any healthcare intervention, the less people should have to pay out of pocket for it.

To understand VBID, it helps to contrast it with more traditional insurance design, where the more something costs, the more a patient usually must pay for it. A $100 antibiotic might carry a $10 copay, while a $5,000 monthly supply of a pill to treat MS might cost the patient $500 or $1,000. The problem with this type of copay design is that it ignores how much patients would be expected to benefit from the intervention in question.

For instance, that relatively inexpensive antibiotic has no chance of ben-efiting a patient with a viral respiratory illness, while the expensive MS drug might slow the progression of that disabling disease. VBID jettisons the tradition of aligning copays with price in favor of adjusting out-of-pocket expenses depending on how much patients are expected to benefit from specific healthcare expenses. Under VBID, a $100 course of antibiot-ics with little chance of benefiting patients might cost them the full $100. By contrast, a $1,000 pill effective in treating a serious disease might cost them little or nothing.

VBID is a simple idea: High value, low out-of-pocket cost. Low value, higher out-of-pocket cost. Less simple is figuring out what VBID would mean for overall healthcare expenses. In theory, VBID could lower health-care costs by discouraging the use of low-value healthcare. Fewer unneces-sary MRIs means less money spent on MRIs. Some enthusiasts also believe VBID could lower costs by encouraging patients to receive important preventive services.[19] Patients with diabetes, for example, might be more likely to take cholesterol pills and blood sugar medications, thereby staving off strokes and heart attacks and the substantial expense of caring for people with those illnesses.

In practice, however, such savings haven't manifested.[20] In one of the first large trials of VBID, researchers at Harvard identified six thousand patients who had experienced a prior heart attack and tested whether giv-ing them their heart drugs for free would improve their health and thereby lower healthcare costs.[21] The trial showed that patients receiving free medicines were more likely to take those medicines. But they did not experience a reduction in subsequent heart attacks, meaning the cost of providing all these free medications wasn't recouped through a reduction in future healthcare spending.

Why did this ambitious study fail to reduce spending? Mainly because people receiving free medications were only *slightly* more likely to take them. Smarter insurance will only change people's healthcare choices when the cost of care looms large as a reason they do or do not receive such care. Early VBID efforts have focused almost exclusively on lowering the cost of treatment for asymptomatic health conditions.[22] If the only reason you aren't taking your cholesterol drug is the $15 copay, then a VBID program waiving that copay could improve your adherence. But what if you simply hate taking pills? What if the pill causes you to experience muscle aches? What if you simply forget to take it? Your high cholesterol is asymptomatic, after all, and you are only taking the pill to stave off some hypothetical cardiovascular event in what feels like a very distant future. Consider cervical cancer screening. In 1997, the U.S. Medicare program waived copays for pap smears. This policy didn't change the number of women who received those lifesaving tests.[23] People avoid uncomfortable and scary tests for many reasons other than cost.

By contrast, suppose there is a pill that would significantly reduce the amount of pain people experience from inflammatory bowel disease, with no significant side effects, but many people don't take the pill because it is too expensive. Get rid of that copay, and you will probably see a big increase in the number of people taking the pill.[24]

There is another reason smarter insurance designs haven't yet reduced healthcare spending. Most such designs are only half smart. To date, VBID efforts have focused almost exclusively on reducing out-of-pocket medication costs—all carrots and no sticks. For example, Blue Cross Blue Shield of North Carolina adopted a VBID system in 2008, eliminating or reducing copays for generic medications.[25] Medication adherence increased around 3 percent, a pretty typical response to VBID programs.[26] But the insurer lost money in the process—it spent more money giving people free medicines than it saved downstream from the health benefits of those medications.

If insurers hope to reduce healthcare costs through VBID programs, they not only have to lower copays for high-value services, but also need to raise them for low-value ones. Unfortunately, the federal government is making it difficult for private insurers to use both carrots and sticks. In 2017, the Centers for Medicare and Medicaid Services (CMS) began testing VBID among people enrolled in Medicare Advantage plans (private insurance companies that offer Medicare coverage). In testing VBID, however, it allowed insurance companies to reduce out-of-pocket costs for high-value care but forbade these plans from increasing out-of-pocket costs for low-value care. CMS went so far as to redefine VBID, stating that value-based insurance design "generally refers to health insurers' efforts to . . . encourage enrollees to consume high value services."[27] Notably absent from this definition is any thought of discouraging people from consuming low-value services.

Typical government bureaucrats, right? Ignoring the best interests of the American population. But Medicare regulators can't be blamed for lopping off half the definition of VBID, because Congress had required the program to do so. As the House bill put it: "In no case may any Medicare advantage plan . . . increase for any plan year for which the plan is participating, the amount of copays or coinsurance for any item or service covered under such plans for purposes of discouraging the use of such item or service."[28] Under this asymmetrical proposal, third-party payers are expected to provide generous coverage for high-value services, with little opportunity to reduce other healthcare expenditures.

In pursuing healthcare value, the path of least political resistance is to increase the use of high-value care by reducing copays for such services. Such an asymmetrical pursuit makes patients happy by helping them obtain affordable access to important healthcare services. It makes pharmaceutical companies happy because they see an increase in business thanks to more patients being able to afford their products. But it burdens the country with higher healthcare expenditures while doing nothing to reduce the use of low-value services. To curb healthcare spending and to help people afford high-value but costly treatments, we need to redesign insurance coverage to achieve a more balanced pursuit of value.[29] For VBID to lower healthcare expenditures, copay programs need to be more balanced, making high-value interventions more affordable while at the same time increasing the price patients pay for more questionable services.

VBID is a compassionate way to redesign health insurance coverage, to empower patients to make healthcare choices. Traditional high-deductible insurance plans require people to pay out of pocket not only for questionably indicated tests and services, but also for lifesaving chemotherapy. Those plans don't discriminate between necessary and unnecessary care, a fact that goes a long way toward explaining what we learned earlier: that people enrolling in those plans forgo necessary and unnecessary medical care in relatively equal measure.[30] Under VBID, the out-of-pocket cost of people's medical alternatives would rise and fall according to the benefits brought by those services, and their healthcare choices would presumably follow suit.

Now, VBID isn't a cure-all. Its success would depend on many of the policy ingredients I described above. It would require price and quality transparency, for starters, as well as a concerted effort to measure healthcare value. In addition, VBID, as it has been typically characterized, wouldn't address the wide variation in healthcare prices we see in the U.S. healthcare system. At $40,000, for example, a hip replacement is probably priced to reflect value for many patients, as it dramatically reduces pain and increases function. But what if another surgeon would perform the procedure for $30,000? Under VBID, patients would presumably be responsible for modest copays regardless of which surgeon performs their procedure.

VBID can't easily handle that kind of price variation. But another approach can.

Smarter Shopping—with Reference Pricing

The state of California recognized that it was spending a lot of money on unnecessarily expensive hip replacements. A state employee would undergo the procedure, responsible perhaps for a $450 copay, or maybe for a $1,000 deductible, leaving the state on the hook for the rest of the cost. But as we saw earlier, the price of hip replacements varies to a staggering degree; the state might pay $30,000 for one person's hip replacement and $60,000 for another, depending on which physician performed the procedure in which hospital. To avoid paying $60,000 for the procedure, the state could have decided to strictly regulate the price of hip replacements, perhaps establishing a fixed price of $30,000 for the procedure. There is precedent for such an approach. Medicare sets fee schedules for procedures like hip replacements.[31] And the German government sets healthcare prices in its system, even though payments are handled by private insurers.[32] But California chose a different approach, one more aligned with the notion of patients as empowered consumers.

It turned to reference pricing.[33] The state informed employees that they would receive a maximum of $30,000 for the procedure. With knowledge of that reference price in mind, people had an incentive to find out how much money specific surgeons charge for the procedure. If their local hospital charges $40,000, they'd have 10,000 reasons to see if they could find a good surgeon who charges $30,000 or less.

The results of this reference pricing strategy were immediate.[34] High-cost providers began losing business, as state employees turned to lower-priced competitors. Some providers responded by lowering their prices. Others resisted such discounts, probably out of concern that they'd be pressured to offer similar discounts to patients who weren't state employees.

Encouraged by the success of its joint replacement program, California expanded the use of reference pricing to include surgical procedures performed in ambulatory centers.[35] Take cataract surgery, for example. This procedure can be performed in hospitals or in ambulatory surgical centers. From a patient's perspective, it is the same procedure regardless of where it is performed. And yet, it might cost twice as much to have your cataract removed in a hospital operating room than in an ambulatory surgical center, even when it is the same ophthalmologist at both locations, because the hospital will tack on what's called a "facility fee."[36]

To address this bizarre pricing disparity, California set a reference price of $2,000 for cataract removal. It chose that amount because the price was more than enough to cover almost every ambulatory surgical center in the state. Nevertheless, only three hospitals in California came in under that price at the time the policy went into effect. It's not that hospitals charged just a little bit more than $2,000 for the procedure. The tenth cheapest hospital in California charged over $4,000 for cataract removal. The twentieth cheapest charged $6,000, triple the price of most ambulatory surgical centers. With the $2,000 reference price in place, California state employees shifted their business to ambulatory centers. Because of this shift, the state experienced an almost 40 percent decline in the cost of paying for cataract surgeries.

It is not just state governments that are experimenting with reference pricing. In 2013, a consortium of fifty-five Catholic organizations decided to redesign their employee healthcare benefits. Before 2013, a person employed by one of these organizations might pay $10 a month for generic drugs, $25 a month for brand-name drugs, and $100 or more per month for expensive specialty drugs and biologics. This kind of tiered formula is designed to motivate patients to choose less expensive medications. But such formularies are blunt motivational instruments. They might convince a patient to choose a generic medication rather than a brand-name cholesterol pill, but the patient will have no further incentive to choose the least expensive generic medication. Similarly, a patient with rheumatoid arthritis will face a significant copay for a biological therapy, but that copay won't change from one biologic drug to another, even if those drugs have very different price tags.

That's where reference pricing comes in. Drawing upon an idea long used by European countries, the Catholic organizations got together and looked at different categories of medications, and decided how much they would pay for drugs within each category, with the understanding that patients would pick up the rest of the tab.[37] For example, at the time the organizations instituted their reference pricing plan, medications for stomach reflux ranged in price from $26 a month to almost $300; so, the employers promised to cover $26 of the cost of whichever reflux medications patients chose to take, and required employees to pay anything above that amount. Similarly, employees could choose to take $400 nasal inhalers for their allergies, but their employer would only cover $34 of that price, given that an equally effective inhaler was available at that price. The reference pricing plan was influential. The percent of patients choosing the least expensive drug in any particular category of medication rose from 60 percent to 70 percent.[38]

One company—SmartShopper—takes the idea of reference pricing in a different direction. Instead of charging people more for receiving expensive medical care, it pays them to pursue less expensive care.[39] For example, a patient might need some blood work done. Maybe her insurance covers the test, free of charge, or with a modest copay. That means it won't matter to that person whether she receives the test at a lab that charges her insurer $75 or one that charges it $300, so she'll probably go to the lab closest to her home or work. Unless she gets a call from SmartShopper. Working to hold down the insurer's costs, SmartShopper might offer her $50 to go to a less expensive testing site. That $50 incentive is dwarfed by the money the insurance company saves by avoiding the more expensive laboratory.[40]

There's yet another approach similar in philosophy to reference pricing that's becoming increasingly common in the United States—incentivizing patients to receive medical care from what their employer or insurance company deems to be "centers of excellence."[41] For example, California offered its employees a range of insurance plans to choose among. As we discussed earlier, some plans held down the cost of knee and hip replacements through reference pricing, covering up to $30,000 of the expense no matter where people went for such procedures. But other plans agreed to cover the costs of these procedures only if patients went to preapproved centers of excellence. If patients covered by those plans decided to go to other hospitals or clinics, they would be responsible for the entire cost of the procedure. Not surprisingly, use of hospitals not deemed to be centers of excellence plummeted after the program went into effect.[42]

At some point, the practice of reference pricing becomes hard to distinguish from a much more traditional insurance practice, of charging patients very different amounts of money for care received in- and out-of-network.[43] All these practices incentivize patients to be price sensitive when seeking medical care. Just as importantly, these practices give insurance companies leverage when negotiating reimbursement rates with providers; an orthopedic group that demands too much money from an insurance company risks having its potential patients redirected to more affordable surgeons.

Currently, reference pricing differs from more traditional insurance practices by being applied on a condition-by-condition basis. Reference pricing might apply to cataract surgery or hip replacement procedures, without declaring an entire hospital to be "out-of-network" for every possible procedure. In fact, payers can utilize reference pricing without negotiating prices with any providers. They can suss out a marketplace, determine a reasonable price for a procedure, and leave it up to patients to decide where to go.

Healthcare marketplaces really are strange creatures. People providing goods and services don't just lay out their prices, see how many customers come their way, and adjust their prices accordingly. Instead, they negotiate prices with intermediaries—insurance companies—often hiding the results of those negotiations from the broader public. Insurance companies, in turn, offer to pay most of the cost of those services if their customers— patients—receive care from the providers who have contracted with the insurance company. Reference pricing and its close cousins turn little slivers of the marketplace into something much more closely resembling traditional consumer marketplaces, enabling patients to choose their providers based, in part, on price. With one huge difference, of course: the insurance companies still give patients a serious chunk of change—$30,000 for a knee replacement!—to cover the cost of their care.

Like VBID, reference pricing tries to cover people for necessary care, while still giving them a financial incentive to curb the cost of that care. I think of both VBID and reference pricing as coverage for what counts, but not coverage that's blind to cost. To illustrate what I mean by that, let's look in more depth at what health policy experts call "essential services," and see what role VBID and reference pricing can play in covering such services while simultaneously holding down the cost of people's medical care.[44]

Covering Essential Services

Under the Affordable Care Act, insurance companies are required to cover essential services at no cost to their beneficiaries. This list of essential services is determined by professional medical organizations expert at evaluating the strength of evidence regarding whether healthcare interventions benefit patients. For example, whenever the United States Preventive Services Task Force concludes that there is what it defines as A- or B-level evidence that a preventive intervention creates more benefit than harm, that intervention is now deemed to be essential.[45] Thanks to the ACA, screening colonoscopies are now free for all Americans old enough to benefit from such testing. That means no patient will forgo a colonoscopy because of a burdensome copay.

But there's a problem with the ACA essential benefits mandate: the law requires insurance companies to pay 100 percent of the price of essential services, without setting corresponding limits on what providers can charge for those services, thus ignoring the near certainty that when you take away people's incentives to shop for affordable providers, the marketplace will respond by hiking prices. For example, treatment for substance abuse was deemed an essential service under the ACA, thereby requiring insurers to cover it at no cost to their beneficiaries.[46] As a result, some treatment centers began charging outrageous amounts for things like urine tests, often ordering such tests daily for many of their patients knowing that insurance companies would be forced to pick up the tab. The practice became so common, addiction centers began referring to urine as "liquid gold."[47]

Which raises a question: could VBID or reference pricing improve the way we cover essential benefits? I don't expect that VBID is up to the task, at least as it is commonly understood. That's because if colonoscopies are high-value tests, then presumably they will carry little or no out-of-pocket expenses, regardless of price. Reference pricing would probably be a better fit for covering essential services without promoting price gouging. That's because under reference pricing, insurers could be required to provide some number of dollars for a colonoscopy, thus incentivizing people to shop for high-quality providers that operate within that price range. Fifty-year-olds shouldn't have to pay out of pocket for essential tests like screening colonoscopies, but insurance companies should be able to give them an incentive to avoid gastrointestinal clinics that inflate their prices. The same goes for other services deemed essential under the Affordable Care Act. People could get full coverage for appropriately priced addiction treatment, but not for centers specializing in panning for liquid gold.

A reasonable reference price for essential services would simultaneously provide coverage for patients while incentivizing healthcare providers to lower their prices. With reference pricing, we can cover what services ought to cost when priced to reflect value, while letting consumers decide if they want to receive care from providers who charge more for those services.

The State of Our Recipe

Let's take quick stock of our recipe for improving healthcare consumerism, so far. It starts with a healthy dollop of price and quality transparency, mixed together with efforts to align price with value. As part of those efforts, both private and public payers (for example, insurance companies and Medicare) should design coverage that *lowers* out-of-pocket costs for high-value services and *raises* them for low-value ones, using some combination of VBID and reference pricing. Sounds like a nice mixture of top-down and bottom-up approaches to improving healthcare markets. But are these ingredients robust enough to stand up to circumstances that push healthcare markets to their limits? Let's look at whether it is possible to empower patients at the end of their lives.

9

EMPOWERING LIFE-AND-DEATH DECISIONS

In Part I, I laid out some of the problems that arise when we assume that exposing patients to high out-of-pocket costs will transform healthcare into a rational consumer market. In the last chapter of that section, I described the special problems that end-of-life decision making creates for healthcare markets. Now that I've spent Part II brainstorming ways to improve healthcare markets, it's only sensible to see if these or any other suggestions will work in the context of life-threatening illness.

Specifically, I'm going to explore how to empower people, as healthcare consumers, when they face either life-threatening illnesses or severe diseases that threaten their most basic functions. I'll start by exploring recent efforts to curb healthcare utilization among the most expensive patients in the healthcare system. Then I will look at what happens when life-threatening illnesses become staggeringly expensive chronic diseases and lay out the challenge of setting limits on what healthcare interventions we make affordable for people whose lives depend on high-priced medical care.

There's Nothing Super About Super-Utilizers

Back in the mid-1980s, when I was in medical school, we called them "frequent flyers": people who were in and out of the hospital so often that there was almost no point removing their wristbands between admissions.[1] A woman with recurrent chest pain due to anxiety who, nevertheless, rushed to the emergency room each time her symptoms recurred, convinced she was experiencing a heart attack—she was a frequent flyer. A man whose liver failure worsened each time he went on a drinking binge—that's another frequent flyer. Patients like this would receive thousands of dollars of care each time they came to the hospital, from clinicians who *knew* that there had to be a better way.

Today, people like this are known in health policy circles by the much less derogatory term "super-utilizers."[2] The 1 percent of patients who account for more than 20 percent of healthcare spending—they are super-utilizers. The 5 percent of patients who account for half of healthcare spending—they are super-utilizers, too.[3] Super-utilizers include people like Jeremy Seals, a middle-aged man who, in 2011, was admitted on eleven separate occasions to the Oregon Health and Science University Hospital with symptoms of chest pain or shortness of breath. Seals racks up healthcare charges in large part because he doesn't always do what his doctors have asked him to do.

It's hard to blame Jeremy Seals for all his medical woes. Seals left his home at age fourteen, for a life that can only be described as hard. A combination of life stressors and genetics caused him, at age thirty-five, to experience his first heart attack. Since that time, Seals's heart has continued to weaken, leaving him with congestive heart failure and unrelenting bouts of chest pain.[4] Atul Gawande vividly described the challenges super-utilizers like Seals pose for the U.S. healthcare system in a 2011 *New Yorker* article, where he recounted the efforts of Jeffrey Brenner, a visionary family physician who was looking for a better way to care for such people.[5]

Notably, for our purposes, Brenner didn't decide to tackle the high cost of care among super-utilizers by leveraging the power of consumer choice. He didn't try to enroll super-utilizers in catastrophic health insurance plans, à la David Goldhill. Nor did he redesign their insurance to incorporate value-based copays or reference pricing. Brenner probably recognized that giving super-utilizers more skin in the game won't stop them from coming to the emergency room when their heart failure or liver disease spins out of control. Instead, his approach addresses the underlying socioeconomic circumstances that cause people to become super-utilizers. Brenner works to give super-utilizers access to round-the-clock primary care and hires case workers to find services that can support their social needs.[6]

Why aren't people like Brenner leveraging healthcare consumerism to persuade super-utilizers to use healthcare services more wisely? One of the super-utilizers Brenner identified in Camden, where he works, was a twenty-five-year-old woman with migraines who had made twenty-nine emergency room visits in a ten-month period, at a cost of more than $50,000. Presumably, if she had had to pay some meaningful portion of those expenses, she would have worked harder to get regular follow-up appointments with the neurologist, who could have searched for a medication regimen that would keep her headaches under control.

But does anyone think a $50 copay or a $5,000 deductible would have reduced this woman's trips to the emergency room? She didn't need to face high out-of-pocket expenses to pay a high price for her migraine disorder; constant headache pain should have been more than enough motivation for her to find a neurologist who would work to control her symptoms. What's more, having incurred $52,000 of healthcare expenditures, she would have maxed out her out-of-pocket costs by mid-March, leaving her no further financial responsibility for additional ER visits, anyway. Her problem wasn't lack of skin in the game; it was a healthcare system that didn't take the time to provide her with regular follow-up care from an expert clinical team.

Making healthcare markets smarter means recognizing when exposing people to higher out-of-pocket costs isn't the right way to control healthcare costs. In cases like Jeffrey Brenner's patient with migraines, the best solutions likely involve improving healthcare delivery: reaching out to those patients whose exorbitant use of hospitals and emergency departments results from the fragmented way we deliver healthcare to people who have lived hard lives. Sometimes we should explore managerial efforts to promote efficient healthcare delivery before turning to healthcare consumerism.

This being a book about healthcare consumerism, however, I won't dwell on managerial efforts to address the cost of caring for super-utilizers, except to say they deserve to play an important role in reducing the cost of caring for people with serious or life-threatening illness. Instead, I'll discuss how to complement these managerial efforts with policies and practices that empower those patients to make healthcare decisions. Perhaps surprisingly, I'll start this exploration of patient empowerment with, of all things, an algorithm.

Empowering Patients at the End of Life

A couple of decades ago, when healthcare experts debated the high cost of end-of-life care at research meetings, the debate would inevitably stall when one of the discussants would declare something to the effect of: "I'll gladly hear your ideas about how to reduce cost of care in the last six months of life as soon as you can tell me when that last six months begins." The audience would reflect on the data they had heard earlier during that day: studies that had calculated the cost of care in the six months before, say, Medicare enrollees died. They would realize that only in hindsight were we able to know who died of cancer, heart failure, or whatever disease the presenter was studying.

The question about "when the last six months begin" highlights the connection between prognostication and spending. When a patient with emphysema spends time on an intensive care unit (ICU) ventilator, that expensive intervention seems wise when the patient recovers and spends three more years babysitting her grandkids. But when that patient gets readmitted to the ICU three more times in the next four months and never regains enough health to walk up a flight of stairs, much less babysit her grandkids before dying during that fourth hospital stay—we wonder why anyone thought it made sense to spend so much money for naught. The problem of course is that physicians don't know, when they admit a person with emphysema to the ICU, whether she will survive three years or three months.

Doctors are notoriously bad at estimating their patients' prognoses, often overestimating how long their patients will live.[7] As a result, they often delay referring patients to hospice or palliative care.[8] Prognostic uncertainty partially explains why, among people dying of cancer, two-thirds don't receive *any* hospice or palliative care.[9] Physicians are bad at prognostication for a host of reasons.[10] They usually know lots about their patients, but rarely have all the data in hand to inform their predictions; more importantly, they don't know how to use all that data to estimate prognoses. To give you a sense of the magnitude of prognostic uncertainty, consider a study I conducted with Theresa Williamson, a neurosurgeon at Duke. Theresa went to a neurosurgery conference and presented her colleagues with a hypothetical patient who came to the emergency room after a traumatic brain injury. In surveying her colleagues, she provided them with the kind of data they should have been able to use to estimate the patient's prognosis: the patient's age, details of the patient's clinical history and exam, and a description of what the patient's head CT revealed. Then she asked the neurosurgeons what chance they thought the patient had of surviving the hospital stay, if they provided the most aggressive care possible. The surgeons' prognostic estimates ranged from 5 percent to 95 percent, with pretty much every guess in between well represented. In effect, the neurosurgeons had *no idea* what this patient's prognosis would be. Perhaps as a result, when asked whether they would recommend surgery to relieve pressure on the patient's brain, most said they would. If you don't know whether aggressive care will keep a patient alive, but you know he or she will die without that aggressive care, it's pretty easy to offer aggressive care. It is hard to reduce the cost of end-of-life care when even physicians don't know when the end begins.

Such prognostic uncertainty may be on the wane soon, as experts begin mining clinical data to develop algorithms that estimate people's chance of living and dying. In fact, if you have private insurance right now, a computer probably knows whether you are likely to die in the next six months. It knows because insurers and other companies have begun mining claims data, all those healthcare bills generated when people receive medical care. The computer runs the claims data and other publicly available information through proprietary algorithms and, voilà, it can identify, with modest certainty, which people face an especially high risk of dying soon.[11]

Why does your insurance company care about your, um, expiration date? Because, as we've discussed, medical expenses often rise dramatically in the last months of people's lives. A woman's cancer spreads, and she finds herself spending an increasing proportion of her time in the hospital getting tested and treated. Sometimes these expenses are the difference between living six years rather than six months. But eventually, those tests and treatments fail to stave off the inevitable; too often, all that poking and prodding, rather than relieving people of the symptoms of their illnesses, simply leaves them feeling poked and prodded.

Grabbing all the data they can get hold of, computer programmers can test what combination of data best predicts mortality, recheck those predictions with other patients, refine their algorithms, and so on, until they have a pretty good idea of who is nearing the end of their lives. By knowing who is terminally ill, insurance companies can focus on ways to reduce the cost of end-of-life care.

Lest you worry that some kind of for-profit death panel is preparing to pull the plug on your sweet old grandma, consider what a company called Vital Decisions does to help insurance companies tackle end-of-life costs. After pulling insurance company data through a proprietary algorithm to identify people nearing the end of their lives, the company connects these people by telephone to trained facilitators, who talk to them about their healthcare goals. According to former CEO Mitchell Daitz, Vital Decisions doesn't make any decisions about which patients deserve to be admitted to the ICU. Instead, it tries to empower people to make those decisions themselves.[12]

Vital Decisions and the insurance companies it partners with are convinced that if patients are empowered at the end of their lives, the vast majority will opt for less aggressive and less expensive care than they otherwise would have received.[13] Many people wrongly believe that if they forgo another round of chemotherapy or another admission to the ICU, they'll be on their own to battle their illnesses. On the contrary, forgoing lifesaving or life-extending treatment is not at all equivalent to forgoing treatment altogether. For example, hospice care is available to people believed to be in the last six months of their lives; it is an active program of care, delivered at home or in a special facility, designed to provide people with comfort in their last days. Palliative care is available regardless of whether people are near the end of their lives and focuses on addressing suffering that people experience from chronic illness. People receiving palliative care don't have to forgo therapies designed to prolong their lives, either; patients receiving chemotherapy can still get palliative care services. That said, when people do receive palliative care, they often become more open to the idea of forgoing aggressive efforts to prolong their lives.[14] Imagine a person desperately short of breath from heart failure. She agrees to a course of IV therapy in the ICU, thinking it is her only hope for easing her symptoms. If, instead, she also receives palliative care and experiences relief of those symptoms, she might be less likely to agree to another stay in the ICU.

When seriously ill patients talk with providers about their treatment goals, the majority choose less aggressive and less expensive care.[15] Similarly, patients who are encouraged to lay out their treatment goals in the medical chart—an activity known as advanced care planning—are more likely to receive hospice or palliative care.[16]

Having good prognostic information can facilitate the process of advanced care planning. For example, one team of physicians used a predictive algorithm to identify ICU patients who faced a 30 percent or greater risk of imminent mortality. They connected those patients and their families to healthcare coaches, who discussed their treatment goals. The communication intervention significantly reduced healthcare spending, even after accounting for the cost of the coaches.

Vital Decisions is just one of many companies partnering with providers to reduce healthcare costs by empowering patients at the end of life. A company called MyDirectives has developed a software program that enables patients' treatment preferences to follow them, electronically, wherever they receive care. That means that even when patients are incapacitated, their healthcare providers know if they want to forgo specific treatment options.[17] One of the largest companies in this line of work, Aspire, provides affordable palliative care services to patients who otherwise might not have ready access to those services given the paucity of palliative care clinicians in the United States.

But the biggest "players" in the space are more familiar than companies like Vital Decisions and Aspire. They are the insurance companies already paying your healthcare bills, and the providers providing you with your healthcare. Many large insurance companies are working with providers to help them recognize the treatment goals of their terminally ill patients. And healthcare providers are increasingly open to such insurance company collaboration, because they are facing financial incentives to reduce the cost of the care they provide to patients.[18] For all the challenges serious illness creates for healthcare consumerism, there comes a point for most people when receiving more healthcare isn't seen as their best alternative anymore.

In the next dozen years, expect to see a lot of innovation in the United States around end-of-life expenses, including many ways of engaging patients in their healthcare choices. With many private insurance companies and for-profit healthcare companies in the United States, there's plenty of incentive to innovate. But I wonder if the United States will ever embrace the kind of radical innovation taking place right now in the United Kingdom, bastion of socialized medicine.

A Radical Market Fix: From a Socialized System

Malcolm Royle began exhibiting signs of dementia in 2005. If he was like many people with dementia, he began forgetting things he wouldn't normally forget: a friend's name, perhaps, or whether he had already gone to the football game with his friends. As his dementia progressed, he might have failed to recognize his son when he saw him. Under normal circumstances, Royle's dementia would have created a caregiving burden beyond the capabilities of his family. In the United States, the burden of caring for Royle would have almost certainly led his family to place him in a nursing home, the fate of three-quarters of people with Alzheimer's living in the states.[19]

But Royle died at home, in no small part because the British healthcare system gave him money to spend any way he and his family saw fit. Royle's family used part of the money to buy a DVR that enabled his son, Colin, to record his favorite television shows. You might be wondering why the NHS let Royle buy a DVR with money from the nation's healthcare budget. According to Colin, watching these shows reduced his dad's anxiety and gave him a sense of control that was otherwise slipping away: "It might seem quite an unusual item to purchase with NHS money, but it was a great success."[20] Things like that DVR enabled Royle to live at home, thereby saving the government the cost of a nursing home.

The United Kingdom has one of the most socialized healthcare systems in the developed world. People not only turn to the government to pay their healthcare bills, but also receive care in government clinics and hospitals. So it's more than a little ironic that, when it comes to addressing the needs of super-utilizers, the United Kingdom takes an approach that gives consumers much more freedom than the same people would get in the United States. Since 2013, the government has been giving cash to people with chronic complex illnesses and letting them and their doctors decide what they want to spend it on. After identifying people with these illnesses, the government provides them with money commensurate with what they are likely to spend on medical care. The average budget is around $15,000, but they have given as much as $450,000 to a single patient. Those patients, working with their healthcare teams, can decide what way of spending that money will most directly impact their health and health-care needs. Some people in the program have used the money to pay for transportation, medical equipment, or help around the house.[21]

Not surprisingly, the program has been controversial. Some Brits are irate about what they perceive as a government handout, "another example of why this country is a complete joke," as one person told the BBC. Others are concerned that "this money is not vetted appropriately."[22] Some influential physicians are bothered, too. Richard Vautrey, deputy chair of the British Medical Association General Practitioners Committee, is concerned that the program will create moral hazard: "While individuals may themselves value a massage or a summer house, others will understandably start to question why they can't also have such things paid for by the state, and that will just fuel demand."[23]

But there's reason to believe this program will improve lives and even save money in the process.[24] Lots of expenditures can improve people's health even though they're not "healthcare" expenses. Let's start with the basics: food and shelter. When people are too poor to meet basic nutritional needs, their health suffers dramatically. When I was practicing in the Ann Arbor Veterans Affairs Medical Center, a patient returned to the clinic one day with declining health from malnutrition. His physician began anonymously sending him modest amounts of money, and when he returned to the clinic, his health had improved dramatically. (For the record, I wasn't that physician, and I'm ashamed the idea didn't occur to me.) The United States provides supplemental funds for food purchases to low-income citizens; that program has been shown to reduce people's healthcare expenses.[25]

Housing problems are also bad for people's health, with housing instability even increasing people's healthcare costs.[26] When states in the United States have instituted programs to stabilize the living situations of people with chronic illness or disability, hospitalization rates have dropped 20 to 45 percent.[27] If we want a healthier population, we might need to be more open minded about what we allow people to spend health insurance dollars on. As part of that approach, we should begin to think more broadly about what constitutes healthcare. For example, I've helped many of my patients get control of low back pain by convincing them to purchase new mattresses or new office chairs. But to my distress, many of my patients can't afford those purchases on their own, and their insurance companies won't cover these costs because they don't qualify as healthcare expenses. To be clear, I don't blame insurance companies for refusing to pay for mattresses and office chairs; any company that took the lead in broadening its coverage in this manner might find itself out of business, unless, like the United Kingdom, they broadened their coverage while simultaneously setting a limit on people's healthcare expenses. The NHS can give flexibility to its super-utilizers because its flexibility is wrapped within a fixed budget— Malcolm Royle's family could spend his allotment on a DVR, or on a home health aide, or on whatever else they and his healthcare providers deemed reasonable, but their total spending couldn't exceed the budget.

The jury is still out on whether the NHS's personal budget program improves health and well-being, and whether it lowers or even maintains overall spending. I don't describe it here as a proven approach but, rather, as another ingredient to keep within our reach while we cook up a way to control healthcare costs while leveraging consumer preferences. As we've seen, high-deductible insurance coverage won't, on its own, do much to control the high cost of caring for people with serious or life-threatening illness. That's why we need to use a combination of other ingredients—the managerial methods I discussed early in this chapter, the decision coaching methods I described later, and the personal budgets being used in the United Kingdom.

But what about all those other ingredients I described in earlier chapters: things like price transparency and value-based insurance design? Should they play a role in constraining the cost of caring for people with serious illness? To answer that question, I'll turn to the more than $200,000 my wife spends on healthcare each year.

The Price of My Wife's Life

In one of my favorite *Far Side* cartoons, a bespectacled woman is perusing a textbook of veterinary medicine. Down the left side of the page, the book lists a series of equine illnesses—broken leg, infected eye, splayed hoof, and the like. Next to each diagnosis, it lists the corresponding treatments, always the same remedy: "shoot."

That cartoon is the basis of the joke my wife, Paula Greeno, made to her surgeon, Will Eward, when he came to the postoperative recovery room to tell her the biopsy he had taken from her right femur revealed a metastasis of her cancer. Paula knew that before becoming an orthopedic surgeon, Eward had practiced as a veterinarian. She also knew the results of her bone biopsy before he came to her bedside, having received the bad news from me an hour earlier. So when Eward broke the news, she looked up at him and asked: "What treatment would you recommend if I were a horse?"

Paula's breast cancer metastasis was discovered two days before she was scheduled for her first appointment at the survivors' clinic at the Duke Cancer Center, in recognition of what everyone thought would mark five years of being cancer-free. Instead of reaching that anniversary and contemplating backing off on the medications she was taking to thwart her tumor, Paula's doctors now prepared to step up her treatments. Metastatic breast cancer is currently incurable, but it is not untreatable. In fact, Paula's oncologist prescribed a slew of medications known to slow the progression of tumors like hers.

But what would the price tag be for her treatments?

Paula takes a pill called palbociclib (Ibrance) three out of every four weeks, at a cost of $10,000 a month. She also receives two monthly injections—fulvestrant (Faslodex), which costs about $5,000 a month, and denosumab (Xgeva), a veritable bargain at only $2,200 a month. Put these three medicines together, and the annual cost of her medications comes in at over $175,000. Now if she were taking these medicines for one year, and would expect to receive five years of benefit from them, the price of those treatments might constitute good value (by all the definitions we discussed several chapters ago). But the oncologist plans for Paula to take all three of those medications indefinitely, until her cancer progresses, at which point she will shift her to other treatments.

To put Paula's treatments into context, remember that most healthcare experts believe that medical interventions should bring a year of high quality of life for $100,000 or less. The United Kingdom, in fact, is hesitant to pay for treatments that cost more than $50,000 for a quality-adjusted life year, or QALY. One of Paula's treatments, her monthly fulvestrant shot, has an estimated cost-effectiveness of $300,000 per QALY.[28] And palbociclib, her chemotherapy pill, comes in at about $800,000 per QALY.[29]

I'm not telling you Paula's story to once again bemoan the bankrupting expenses people in the United States face when they develop serious illness. Paula has generous insurance and ample financial resources: she won't be bankrupt by her cancer. Nor am I telling you her story to enter into some abstract discussion of pharmaceutical pricing and healthcare value. There's nothing abstract about my take on Paula's breast cancer treatments. I am devastated that, just three months after her fiftieth birthday, Paula was left to wonder whether she'd live to celebrate her sixtieth. I wish I'd received the diagnosis rather than her. She's the much better half of our marriage. So when I report the outrageous cost of her cancer care, I cannot be objective. I'm hugely grateful that she's receiving treatments that can slow the progression of her cancer. But I still believe that her medications are too expensive, and that a healthcare system that strives to promote value should not tolerate, or pay for, such outrageously expensive treatments.

I'm telling Paula's story because any attempt to use the power of consumerism to rein in U.S. healthcare costs must figure out what to do with patients like her, who face life-threatening illnesses. In the conclusion of Part I, I wrote about the challenges that serious illnesses and end-of-life decisions raise for healthcare markets. Now that I have spent Part II laying out a set of policies that can improve healthcare markets, I need to see what, if anything, healthcare markets can do to improve the value of care for patients facing life-threatening illness.

When loved ones face life-threatening diseases, most of us are willing to go to any length to help them. And as we have already seen, our healthcare system responds similarly, sparing little expense to stave off terminal illnesses. But that doesn't mean we can't bring consumer discipline to bear upon treatments for things like metastatic breast cancer. That's why it's worth seeing how well Paula's healthcare expenses would be addressed by the reforms I described in earlier chapters.

Let's start with price transparency. States like North Carolina, where Paula lives, could mandate price transparency for cancer treatments, so Paula could comparison shop for her care. Such transparency could potentially reduce the cost of Paula's care. For example, before receiving her quarterly bone scans and PET scans, she could shop for more affordable imaging centers, thus reducing the cost of those tests. However, I don't expect that price transparency alone will do much to reduce the $175,000 Paula spends on medications each year. For starters, all Paula's medications are still protected by patents, meaning she can't shop around for generic alternatives. Transparency is more helpful in situations where patients can choose among higher- and lower-priced alternatives—expensive and less expensive hip surgeons, for example, or brand-name versus generic drugs. In addition, once Paula got her first bill, to cover her portion of the cost of her chemotherapy, price transparency legislation became moot; she quickly learned what the medications cost her out of pocket.

Now, of course, the point of price transparency isn't just to help people find less expensive prices for the exact same services; it's also to help them decide whether to receive those services in the first place. Find out that it will cost $2,000 to Botox your frown lines, and you might forgo that procedure. In Paula's case, however, forgoing cancer treatment does not feel like an option. Without treatment, she probably won't see our children graduate from college. That's unacceptable!

On the other hand, price transparency information could help Paula and me identify alternative treatments that aren't so outrageously priced. But how in the heck would we do that? We would need to search Medline for ways to treat ER+, PR+, Her2– breast cancer. For the purposes of writing this chapter, I tried to do that, and despite my medical background, I was bewildered. I realized it would take months for me to figure out the literature. And, even then, I wouldn't trust myself to understand Paula's options. Now of course I could go to Paula's oncologist and ask whether she knows of less expensive ways to treat my wife's cancer. But what loving husband would do that?!?

The problem with the cost of Paula's cancer care was not the opacity of her healthcare prices. It was the price of that care.

But of course, price transparency isn't a one-ingredient fix for our healthcare spending problems. For such transparency to have an impact on the cost of Paula's care, it needs to be mixed with some other ingredients. For example, Paula's insurance could be redesigned to align copays with value along the lines of the VBID approach discussed earlier. A VBID insurance plan would force patients like Paula to pay a steep price for their chemotherapy. It would leave her responsible for most of the cost of her palbociclib, since that drug's $10,000-per-month price tag is way too high relative to its benefits as well as for the cost of her other medications. In effect, a VBID plan would place these drugs beyond the reach of all but the wealthiest of patients.

Unless . . .

Unless manufacturers lowered their prices, to reflect the modest benefits brought by their products. Let me pause to highlight a couple of points. First, VBID doesn't do much good without price transparency. If people don't know their out-of-pocket expenses before receiving healthcare interventions, then those costs won't have much chance to influence their healthcare choices. Second, even when coupled with price transparency, VBID doesn't change healthcare prices. Instead, it reduces out-of-pocket expenses for high-value services and raises them for low-value ones. In the case of Paula's chemotherapy medications, VBID would push much of the cost of her care from the insurer to Paula and me. We would be forced to decide whether we could afford those medications or whether, instead, to choose less expensive (and presumably less effective) treatments.

But VBID doesn't function in a vacuum. The real power of VBID is that it gives healthcare companies a strong incentive to align prices with value. If most Americans had insurance plans that covered only high-value services, the manufacturer of a drug like palbociclib would have to lower its price so patients could afford their portion of the cost of the drug.

Paula's story reveals a major reason few insurers have fully embraced value-based reimbursement. They'd have to begin denying robust coverage to cancer patients for chemotherapy when it is not cost-effective. I expect the blame for such stingy coverage would fall harder on insurance companies than it would on the drug companies charging exorbitant sums for their products. That's certainly who I'd publicly shame, if Paula and I could no longer afford our portion of her medication expenses. Okay, I'd probably go after the drug companies, too, writing scathing op-eds in local and national newspapers. But I expect it would be her insurance company that would blink first, because it would have a difficult time defending the value of value-based insurance design in the face of such public relations pressure.

Drug companies have the upper hand in debates about covering the cost of expensive chemotherapy. Patients like Paula pay monthly premiums and expect coverage for the standard of care. They've already entered a customer/company relationship with the insurer but haven't begun such a relationship with the drug companies making their chemotherapy medications. So, it's the insurance company they will be mad at.

Moreover, to slow the move toward value-based reimbursement, drug companies can pull out the innovation card, arguing that efforts to promote healthcare value will inevitably reduce the incentive to develop new healthcare products. The promise of $100,000 chemotherapy pills draws a lot more venture capital than the promise of $10,000 treatments.

I never said that redesigning healthcare markets would be easy. The less money people make as physicians, the fewer people will choose to borrow a couple hundred thousand dollars to go to medical school. The more we lower drug prices, the fewer people will invest in pharmaceutical startups. Much of the developed world has been able to regulate healthcare prices without fear of disincentivizing healthcare innovators, because they could count on the United States—land of unrestricted prices—to generate profits for those innovators. If the United States tackled healthcare prices as aggressively as most Western European countries, the pace of innovation in biotech and pharma would plummet. As a society, we need to set a proper balance between providing people with affordable healthcare and providing healthcare innovators with incentive to develop new interventions. I believe we are out of balance now, paying too high a price for too many healthcare interventions.

Don't get me wrong. As a husband, I'm delighted that Paula's insurance company covers her medication so generously. But as a concerned U.S. citizen, I think her insurer should refuse to pay such high prices for her treatments. To me, Paula's life is infinitely valuable. But healthcare policies and practices shouldn't be determined by the feelings of loving spouses. The money spent on Paula's chemo would be much better spent on other healthcare interventions for other people, or on other societal priorities.

We need to pressure drug companies, hospitals, and highly paid physicians to lower their prices. Doing so will require many of the policies and practices I've discussed so far. But it will also require one more ingredient, which I'll explore in the next chapter: we need to radically simplify health insurance choices.

10

SIMPLIFYING INSURANCE CHOICES

Time for a taste test. Simmering on the stove right now is a delicious-looking stew, made up of the ingredients I've introduced so far. The price and quality of healthcare services are now transparent, available to consumers on user-friendly apps and websites. It is also possible to see whether tests, procedures, and drugs are priced to reflect value. A growing number of insurance plans make use of that value information, either to adjust copays or to establish reference prices. Some insurers are even experimenting with the kind of budgetary approach used in the United Kingdom, giving people more flexibility on how to spend their healthcare dollars.

But when you taste the stew, it is missing a critical ingredient. People still aren't making good insurance choices, causing the whole dish to suffer. Some are choosing high-deductible health plans even though they have chronic illnesses, leading to predictable expenses. Others are choosing plans unaware that the plans don't pay for specialists who have been treating them for decades. Smart healthcare markets depend on wise insurance choices. As we saw in Part I, many people make poor insurance choices because they are either bewildered by insurance jargon, overwhelmed by the number of available plans, or incapable of "doing the math" that will direct them to the best available plan.

Fortunately, we can make insurance choices a lot easier. In the first part of this chapter, I'll lay out several ways to improve people's choices. Then I will show why, if people do make wiser choices, the whole insurance system could go into a death spiral. Which will lead me to my final proposal, an admittedly radical one—I will explain why, if we want to improve insurance choice, we need to dramatically limit people's options.

The Rationale for Improving Insurance Choice

In the absence of harm to others, markets are usually best left to their own devices. We don't want the government telling people whether Air Jordans are priced at value. We don't need the government to educate us about the best way to choose television sets or laptops. But when choices have a dramatic impact on people's lives, and those choices are predictably poor, we should consider whether the government should intervene to make it easier for people to make wise choices.

Such intervention rankles libertarians, of course, many of whom believe market flaws will work themselves out if the government stays out of the way. But what if government intervention is compatible with libertarianism? That's a question being asked by many experts in behavioral economics.[1] Before writing their best-selling book *Nudge*, Cass Sunstein and Dick Thaler wrote a law review article titled "Libertarian Paternalism," in which they argued that it is possible to simultaneously improve people's choices while doing nothing to restrict their freedom of choice.[2] As an example of such freedom-preserving paternalism, they described rearranging a cafeteria so that healthy offerings are placed where people are more likely to choose them. The simple rearrangement of foods influences choices without restricting them.

This raises the question of whether we can, or should, nudge people to improve their insurance choices. The stakes are certainly high enough to warrant intervention. Bad choices could force people to choose between important medical care and fiscal solvency. The choices are complicated, too, as we have seen; people choosing insurance are often confused by technical jargon and overwhelmed by the number of available plans (and the amount of information they need to understand about each plan). Because of this decisional complexity, many people make objectively poor choices. When decisions are complicated, and the stakes are high; when we know that many people make poor choices, choices they wouldn't have made in better circumstances—it's reasonable to look for ways to improve those choices.

At a minimum, we should consider ways to help people better understand their choices. I contend that informing consumers about goods and services they might purchase promotes the goals lauded by libertarians—of giving individuals the freedom to choose how to spend their time and money, based on their unique preferences. Free markets don't function well at promoting people's best interests if people don't know what they are buying. If we want health insurance markets to function effectively, we should make it easier for people to understand the plans available to them.

As it turns out, many people in the Obama administration, including the President himself, were eager to leverage behavioral economic insights when designing the health insurance exchanges. That began with significant attention to designing healthcare.gov in a way that made it easier for people to understand insurance terms like "deductible," which were defined in plain language on the website where people peruse their insurance alternatives. Unfortunately, even with a good understanding of those terms, it is very difficult for most people to do the math and figure out what the likely cost will be of available insurance plans. Imagine, for example, a person estimating the cost of an available plan: she would need to multiply the monthly premium by twelve; then estimate her out-of-pocket expenses across each category of medical service—a few primary care visits times the related copay; a couple of cardiology appointments times the subspecialty copay; the coinsurance rate for all her current medications; plus, perhaps, the cost of a hospitalization or procedure, based upon her need for such services in years. Not an easy bit of math for most people to perform. Oh, yes, and she would have to do that math for every available plan.

That's why I have long advocated for giving people more useful information about the true cost of the insurance plans available to them.[3] When shopping for insurance, people need information about the *total expected cost* of available plans—not just the monthly premiums they will pay but also the out-of-pocket expenses they are likely to incur given their medical history. For example, people with chronic illnesses have predictable healthcare expenses—high-priced medications to treat their ailments or a high likelihood of requiring hospitalization in any given year. These people should not be exclusively focused on the price of their monthly premiums, but they should take account of how generously their plan covers these predictable expenses.

This information is also available on healthcare.gov, in the form of a total cost calculator. The calculator provides total cost estimates, based upon whether people expect low, medium, or high use of medical care in the following year. As an example, a medium amount of care would consist of two doctor visits, one lab or diagnostic test, and two prescription drugs; a high amount of care would consist of ten doctor visits, four lab or diagnostic tests, seventeen prescription drugs, and one day in the hospital.[4] These categories—low, medium, and high—are clearly blunt ways to estimate total out-of-pocket costs. Indeed, when my research colleagues interviewed insurance navigators—professionals who help people with their insurance choices—many of them told us that out-of-pocket estimators often don't do a good job of estimating people's out-of-pocket expenses.[5] But at least the calculators begin to do the math for people.

If we want people to make wise insurance choices, that job shouldn't be limited to estimating expected expenses. We also need to help them comprehend the cost of *unexpected* healthcare needs. I think of this as giving people information on best case, worst case, and expected case scenarios.[6] For example, imagine a healthy twenty-seven-year-old purchasing insurance for the first time. He hasn't needed medical care for several years, other than an occasional trip to urgent care for a sprained ankle. He chooses the plan with the lowest monthly premium, hoping he will once again make it through the year without a major medical expense. Unbeknownst to him, however, another plan is available to him for an additional $15 a month, or $180 a year, which has an out-of-pocket maximum that's $900 less than the plan he chose. Later that year, he slams into a tree while skiing in Colorado and begins to incur substantial out-of-pocket expenses. If he had focused not only on his expected medical costs, but also on a worst-case scenario of experiencing this kind of injury, he might have chosen the second plan and saved himself a decent chunk of change.

With information on total expected costs, as well as best- and worst-case scenarios, people will be less likely to focus solely on monthly premiums, and also less likely to spend time futilely trying to understand the difference between copays, coinsurance, and deductibles. Instead, they will look at the overall impact of various insurance plans on their finances, while also getting a feel for that impact should they experience unexpected health problems.

But of course, choosing an insurance plan isn't just about taking account of premiums, deductibles, and copays. It's also about knowing which clinicians and healthcare systems are "in network." Often, the biggest predictor of a person's out-of-pocket expenses won't be what healthcare intervention she receives, but whether the provider delivering that intervention is covered by her insurance plan.[7] Currently, insurance exchange websites often make it difficult to figure out which doctors are in and out of a plan's network. We ought to make it easier for people to figure out who is in network for a given plan. We also need to test ways to present all this information—likely out-of-pocket expenses, best-case/worst-case scenarios, in-network providers—in a manner that promotes good choices. That's why we should also help people get affordable access to insurance navigators—to people who have the expertise to help them make good choices.[8] Ideally, these navigators should not face conflicts of interest that incentivize them to guide people to particular insurance companies or plans.

It won't be easy to make the price and quality of healthcare and healthcare insurance transparent, or to provide such transparency in ways that improve consumers' choices. But we need to confront these challenges. For the foreseeable future, many Americans are likely to face high out-of-pocket expenses for their medical care. And they will have to decide whether to pay more for insurance plans that reduce (but still don't eliminate) such expenses. Given the high cost of healthcare, consumers deserve information that will help them make these difficult choices. Armed with that information, they can start pressuring healthcare providers, and the healthcare industry more generally, to offer high-quality services at more affordable prices.

Unless, that is, the insurance system depends for its very existence on bad choices.

Good Choices and Death Spirals

Health insurance companies stay in business by charging more on average for premiums than they pay out in medical bills. That leaves them with two ways to make money: reduce healthcare expenses or increase premiums. To reduce spending, insurers can either lower price or constrain utilization. To lower prices, insurers typically negotiate with healthcare providers and pharmaceutical companies and the like, leveraging their market power to extract concessions. To reduce utilization, some insurers try to manage medical care, such as by requiring physicians to get permission—"prior authorization"—before providing expensive care to their patients.[9]

Despite these efforts to reduce spending, the success of most insurance companies more often relies upon their ability to figure out how much to charge for their products. To put it simply, insurance companies try to figure out how sick their customers are going to be, and charge accordingly. If company actuaries accurately predict how much healthcare people will utilize over the next twelve months, and how much that care will cost, the company can price plans just enough above this total to promote their bottom line.

Sounds straightforward, but it gets complicated when a company offers a range of plans and has to figure out what kind of people will enroll in which kind of plans. For example, companies know that people with chronic health problems will be more likely to choose relatively expensive plans, with high monthly premiums, to incur fewer out-of-pocket expenses when they, inevitably, require medical care. They also know that healthy people will be more likely to enroll in less expensive plans—ones with lower monthly premiums—even if those plans carry relatively high out-of-pocket costs, in hopes of being healthy enough to avoid those costs.

But just how often will unhealthy and healthy people choose expensive and inexpensive plans, respectively? As we saw in Part I, people frequently make poor choices, enrolling in overly expensive plans based on their underlying health. Insurance companies factor people's choices into their prices. They know through experience, for example, that a certain proportion of healthy people will enroll in gold plans, with high monthly premiums, and that some chronically ill people will choose high-deductible health plans.

But what would happen to insurance premiums if people understood their choices better? Suppose more chronically ill people choose low out-of-pocket plans and more healthy people choose high out-of-pocket plans. In response to this re-sorting of choices, insurance companies will be forced to raise premiums for the low out-of-pocket plans to cover the high cost of all those chronically ill people. At the same time, they'll need to lower the price of high out-of-pocket plans to lure healthy customers away from competitors. Those price changes will lead to a further re-sorting of plan choices. The relatively healthy people who chose low out-of-pocket plans, to lower their exposure to unexpected costs, will be turned off by the increasingly expensive monthly premiums for those plans, and shift toward higher out-of-pocket plans. That shift, in turn, will cause insurance companies to raise premiums even more for low out-of-pocket plans, because the people remaining in those plans will be even sicker than they were before.

And so on. And so on. Welcome to a healthcare insurance death spiral.[10] When insurance plans cause people to sort themselves according to how sick they are, the price differences across respective plans will increase until the price of insurance for the sickest people becomes unaffordable, no longer subsidized by healthy people choosing those plans.

Death spirals got a lot of press when the Affordable Care Act came into law, as people debated the need for an individual health insurance mandate.[11] Without a mandate, experts contended that many healthy people would forgo insurance, leaving insurers with relatively sicker patients to cover.[12] In response, insurers would be forced to raise premiums, and so on and so on. But it's not just the decision to buy or not to buy insurance that can lead to a death spiral. A smaller version of this death spiral exists when people choose among bronze, silver, and gold plans. Those gold plans— high monthly premium, low out-of-pocket—are only affordable for chronically ill patients if a decent number of healthy people also choose to enroll in them.

So, what should we do to prevent the health insurance death spiral? One approach would be to stay away from any interventions that improve insurance choice. If enough people make bad choices, the difference in price between high and low out-of-pocket plans won't become unbearable. But I find that approach to be unacceptable: we can't have a healthcare system whose survival depends on bad decisions. We need a new kind of insurance mandate, not one that forces people to purchase insurance (although we need that mandate too), but one that compels insurance companies to reduce consumer choice. We need to eliminate high out-of-pocket and low out-of-pocket plans and replace them with smart ones.

Smarter Insurance

Traditional insurance plans have so far failed to cover essential healthcare services while giving patients an incentive to shop for affordable care. Instead, they swing back and forth between untenable extremes: on one extreme, they provide full coverage for essential services regardless of price, and on the other they require people to cover huge deductibles, copays, and coinsurance fees even when those services are critical to their health and well-being. Add to that the new problem we've just explored—that insurance plans depend for their very existence on people making poor choices—and the need for smarter insurance becomes hard to ignore. But what would smart insurance look like?

Smart insurance coverage would rely on some combination of VBID, reference pricing, and centers of excellence to incentivize patients to seek out affordable care, while making sure patients won't be on the hook for the cost of that care when their health and well-being are at stake. For example, smart insurance plans would neither ask fifty-year-olds to pay for screening colonoscopies, nor provide colonoscopies for free regardless of price; those plans would give people enough money to get affordable colonoscopies, while incentivizing them to seek out reasonably priced providers.[13] Smart plans would also make it easy for people to determine their out-of-pocket expenses for available interventions. They would even give people feedback about when they are choosing particularly expensive healthcare providers or healthcare interventions and point them toward alternatives.

How will we convince consumers to choose such plans? I've already described the difficulty people have wrapping their heads around concepts like deductibles and copays. Think they'll quickly grasp terms like VBID or reference pricing? Many people would be afraid of such value-based insurance plans, finding them new and scary.

That's why I'm in favor of moving to a radically different kind of insurance marketplace, one where traditional insurance design becomes a historical artifact. In regulating health insurance coverage, we should move away from sorting people into high and low out-of-pocket plans. Instead, we should incentivize people to enroll in plans that provide generous coverage for high-value services, while requiring people to bear a greater portion of the cost of low-value care. It's easy to think in the short term and imagine all the reasons a smarter insurance system would fail. But let's put the short term behind us for a moment and imagine a more distant future. In this future, the only insurance plans available are smart plans that incentivize patients to pursue high-value services while avoiding low-value services (or paying for them out of pocket). This is no utopian future, of course. Insurance plans, providers, and pharmaceutical companies will still argue with each other about what constitutes value, but hopefully nonprofit, government-endorsed entities will be encouraged to measure value and publish their results publicly. Plans and providers will still squabble over prices, but probably less than now, as more services are subject to reference pricing—"You can charge whatever you like, but everything above $X is going to come right from your patients' pockets." People will still be bankrupt by illness, but not so much by the cost of the medical care as by the financial consequences of being, say, too sick to work. Illness-related poverty is a problem that cannot be fixed by the healthcare system alone.

Under these smarter designs, insurance companies will compete for business in much the same way they do now. They will work to negotiate lower prices with providers. They will look to reduce healthcare utilization, sometimes by denying care and other times by incentivizing providers to practice parsimoniously. They will work to gain high consumer satisfaction ratings to attract customers. They will simply compete for business under a new set of rules that better protect patients from the cost of necessary care while exposing them to the cost of unnecessary care.

If history repeats, Medicare will need to take the lead in adopting these smarter insurance designs. That is something Medicare enrollees desperately need, right now. The way the program is currently designed, Medicare enrollees are often exposed to crippling out-of-pocket expenses for critical medical care. Enrollees with advanced cancer face annual out-of-pocket expenses approaching one-fourth of their household income.[14] If Medicare takes the lead in adopting smarter insurance design, the private insurance industry will follow. If Medicare doesn't take the lead, American employers should step into the void. When, say, 3M lets insurers know that it will only partner with a company that offers smart, value-based plans, insurers will work to design and implement such products.

We won't be able to switch to smart insurance coverage overnight. We will need to move toward such coverage systematically and incrementally. Early smart plans won't be smart as much as they will be less stupid. To transition toward smarter insurance plans, we need to make "smartish" plans more attractive, incentivizing employers and insurers to offer such plans to people, and even possibly subsidizing people to enroll in such plans to overcome potential resistance to their "unfamiliar-thus-scary" design.

Smart insurance: that's the final ingredient in our healthcare pantry, available to add to whatever mix of other ingredients we decide to include in our recipe. So far, Americans have largely subsisted on a healthcare system made from two pretty unpalatable ingredients: overly generous insurance coverage and overly stingy high-deductible health plans, neither one designed to simultaneously encourage the use of high-value care while discouraging the use of low-value care. Our healthcare system is malnourished, like people living off nothing but rice, with critical vitamins and minerals absent from our metaphorical diets. I hope this book builds momentum toward a more balanced healthcare system. Such a system could leverage the power of markets—to enable people to decide which goods and services they are willing to spend their hard-earned money on—while also protecting people from the cruelty of completely unregulated healthcare markets, where their ability to obtain necessary services is constrained by their ability to pay.

EPILOGUE

Erica Decker had stage-four breast cancer, which had metastasized to her liver and bone, the latter leaving her with substantial pain. Worse yet, a positron emission tomography (PET) scan she received a week before her clinical appointment showed that the cancer had progressed significantly since her last test. "So we need to think about what to do next," her oncologist explained.

A great statement, the idea of "we"—both doctor and patient—making a medical decision together. That's a paradigm known as shared decision making, and one that in my research I find is rarely achieved.[1] Many doctors *say* they want to partner with patients in making healthcare choices, but most do not know how to accomplish this goal. Instead, they earnestly overwhelm patients with well-intentioned information, at which point patients ask, "What should I do?" The doctors point them toward treatments, even though they have done little to discuss what patients think about the pros and cons of those alternatives.[2]

This oncologist, on the other hand, partnered like a pro. He explained that "the biggest decision we've got to make right now is chemotherapy or not," to try to slow the spread of the cancer. He continued by explaining that "chemo, thankfully, comes in a huge variety. There are probably a dozen drugs that work for breast cancer like yours. And you can use them one at a time. You don't have to use two, three, or four."

He explained the main difference between available treatments—that some treatments were given intravenously, meaning she would have to come into the clinic for treatment, but one treatment, capecitabine (Xeloda), could be taken as a pill. "And it's not less chemo than any other product," he assured her. "If it doesn't work, we have tons of other options you can switch to, but they are intravenous, so you have to come here and get an infusion."

Decker asked a few questions and then told him she wanted to try one of the treatments: "I got to do what I need to do."

The visit was already a primer on shared decision making, with the oncologist clearly and patiently explaining the patient's treatment choices, simplifying the decision to its first branch point—chemo or not chemo—rather than overwhelming her with in-depth information on all her treatment options. Then, when he moved to the next branch of the decision tree, things got even more spectacular. "If we're going to go for chemo, do you have preference for pills or preference for intravenous? That's purely a convenience issue. If it's intravenous, you don't have to count pills. It's all on us. And there are no prescription problems. If your prescription coverage is poor, [if] you have high copays, I would forget the Xeloda now and stay on the IV. If your prescription copays are small and you like pills and you don't want to be stuck [with needles], go with the pills. What's your copay for brand-name drugs?"

"I think it's, like, $25," she replied.

Do you see what happened here? This oncologist recognized that sometimes the right medical choice depends not just on hardcore medical outcomes, like survival rates and side effect profiles, and not just on traditional health-related quality-of-life concerns, like the convenience of home versus in-clinic treatment. It can also depend on how much a given patient is willing to pay out of pocket for such convenience. Hallelujah!

After discussing the potential financial toxicity of her treatment alternatives, the oncologist made sure to remind Decker that whatever treatment she chose, none of the treatments were expected to cure her cancer. "You're going to die from this," he said compassionately. "Why do this, then?" he asked. He explained that the chemotherapy would give her a two in three chance of slowing the growth of the cancer, thereby helping her live substantially longer.

They spoke for a while about the potential side effects of the chemo. Then Decker handed down her decision: "Let's do IV," she said. "That just seems safer." Decker recognized that the IV therapy would help with her adherence to the care. "I am forgetful. I do forget," she explained.

It is tragic that Erica Decker has terminal cancer. But it is great to know that she traveled her cancer path in partnership with an oncologist who knew how to help patients choose healthcare alternatives that align with their life goals.

We should all be so lucky.

I tell Decker's story to revisit the main themes of this book, and imagine what the world will look like for people like Decker under the smarter system I've described, versus alternatives currently popular on the left and right.

Let's start on the left, with generous coverage of all healthcare expenses, subsidized by the federal government. Under that kind of system, Decker would presumably not face different out-of-pocket expenses for IV versus oral therapy. That would be an improvement over our current system, because people should not be given an incentive to choose IV therapy over pills simply because their insurance company makes an arbitrary distinction between whether these therapies count as physician services or drug expenses. In a socialized, low-to-no out-of-pocket healthcare system, Decker wouldn't face this kind of ridiculous choice. On the other hand, a fully socialized system, with low out-of-pocket expenses, would threaten the nation with crippling healthcare debt. Such a system, if it refused to leverage the power of healthcare consumerism, would have to either strongly regulate prices and/or severely constrain people's choices.

Under healthcare systems endorsed by the right, dominated by lightly regulated private insurers, people's out-of-pocket costs would probably still be determined by arbitrary factors like whether they are receiving oral or IV therapies. After all, when people choose insurance plans, few would have the time or know-how to figure out that some plans arbitrarily charge people more for pills than IV therapies (despite pills being so much more convenient), and even fewer would factor that information into their choice of health plan. As a result, insurers would have little incentive to eradicate this kind of plan design.

Which leaves us in the middle, with the smarter plans I have endorsed. In a smarter system, Decker's insurance company wouldn't levy higher out-of-pocket expenses on oral versus IV therapies. Instead, the price of those chemotherapies, and the out-of-pocket expenses associated with those therapies, would be determined by the *value* of the available alternatives. If an oral chemotherapy was priced to reflect value, Decker would be able to receive it with little or no out-of-pocket expenses. The same goes for IV therapies. In a smarter system, the relative cost of oral versus IV therapies would be determined by how much health benefit each brought per dollar spent, and not by whether it was administered at home or in the doctor's office.

Under a smarter system, patients like Decker would still be asked to make important healthcare choices. They might face choices between effective chemotherapies that come at modest out-of-pocket expense versus slightly more effective chemotherapies that carry significantly higher out-of-pocket expenses. Those willing and able to pay the difference could receive the more expensive interventions, empowering consumers to determine how they want to spend their money.

Which brings me back, finally, to Decker's oncologist. Under almost any kind of imaginable healthcare system, it will be incumbent upon clinicians to help patients navigate their healthcare choices, including the financial implications of those choices, the way Decker's oncologist did that day. To clinicians reading this book, I encourage you to do whatever you can to advocate for the kind of healthcare reforms I have promoted. But in the meantime, please also do what you can (in partnership with other members of your healthcare practice) to help people navigate the financial complexities of their medical care.

To patients and caregivers reading this book, remember not to be shy about asking for information about your healthcare expenses. Don't rush into receiving healthcare goods or services when you have the time to research your alternatives, including finding out the costs of those alternatives. If you don't get good answers—from your healthcare providers or your insurance company—keep after them until they give you good answers, or find new providers or insurers who are more forthcoming.

And to policy advocates and experts reading this book, please work across both sides of the aisle to promote policies that will better align patients' out-of-pocket expenses with the value of their medical care. That might seem implausible in our politically polarized times. But keep in mind that the changes I am proposing here won't require a grand redesign—no need for "Trumpcare" or "Democrat-who-replaces-Trump-care." Instead, we can make our system smarter through incremental steps, with legislation and regulation that should be attractive on both sides of the aisle. Do you think the public would hold angry town hall meetings if Republicans and Democrats got together to pass price transparency legislation? Do you think Rachel Maddow or the people on *Fox & Friends* would freak out if private insurers embraced VBID and reference pricing?

And finally, to all of you committed to working on these efforts, let me know how I can help. I have tenure, after all. Nothing is stopping me from working with you to move America toward a smarter healthcare system.

NOTES

Introduction

1. Tara I. Burton, "The Controversy Surrounding the Death of British Toddler Alfie Evans, Explained," *Vox*, April 28, 2018, https://www.vox.com/policy-and-politics/2018/4/27/17286168/alfie-evans-toddler-uk-explained.

2. Dylan Scott, "How the British Health Care Crisis Translates to America," *Vox*, January 5, 2018, https://www.vox.com/policy-and-politics/2018/1/5/16855814/voxcare-british-health-care-crisis.

3. Kailash Chand, "The NHS Is Under Threat. Only a New Model of Care Will Save It," *The Guardian*, January 4, 2018, https://www.theguardian.com/healthcare-network/2018/jan/04/nhs-under-threat-new-model-of-care.

4. Natalie Stechyson, "Canadian Patients and Doctors Are Sharing 'Excruciating' Wait Times on Twitter," *HuffPost*, November 3, 2017, https://www.huffingtonpost.ca/2017/11/03/canada-doctor-patient-wait-times_a_23266026/.

5. Bacchus Barua, "Waiting Your Turn: Wait Times for Health Care in Canada, 2017 Report," The Fraser Institute, 2017, 1–81, https://www.fraserinstitute.org/sites/default/files/waiting-your-turn-2017.pdf.

6. "Health Care Wait Times Hit 20 Weeks in 2016: Report," *CTV News*, November 23, 2016, https://www.ctvnews.ca/health/health-care-wait-times-hit-20-weeks-in-2016-report-1.3171718.

7. Amanda Coletta, "Canada's Health-Care System Is a Point of National Pride. But a Study Shows It Might Be Stalled," *Washington Post*, February 23, 2018, https://www.washingtonpost.com/news/worldviews/wp/2018/02/23/canadas-health-care-system-is-a-point-of-national-pride-but-a-study-shows-it-might-be-stalled/?utm_term=.4801939cb04e.

8. Adam Taylor, "The British Are Surprisingly Satisfied with Their Controversial Socialized Health Care System," *Business Insider*, September 10, 2013, https://www.businessinsider.com/british-satisfied-with-nhs-2013–9.

9. Elisabeth Rosenthal, *An American Sickness: How Healthcare Became Big Business and How You Can Take It Back* (New York: Penguin Random House, 2017).

10. Wendell Potter, *Deadly Spin: An Insurance Company Insider Speaks Out on How Corporate PR Is Killing Health Care and Deceiving Americans* (New York: Bloomsbury Press, 2010).

11. Clare Foran, "Why So Many Democrats Are Embracing Single-Payer Health Care," *The Atlantic*, July 18, 2017, https://www.theatlantic.com/politics/archive/2017/07/healthcare-congress-bernie-sanders-single-payer-obamacare/533595/.

12. Patients' Choice Act, H.R. 2520, 111th Cong.; Medicare Patient Empowerment Act of 2013, H.R. 1310, 113th Cong.

13. Steffie Woolhandler and David U. Himmelstein, "The Deteriorating Administrative Efficiency of the U.S. Health Care System," *New England Journal of Medicine* 324, no. 18 (1991): 1253–58.

14. S. P. Keehan, C. A. Cuckler, A. M. Sisko, A. J. Madison, S. D. Smith, D. A. Stone, J. A. Posal, C. J. Wolfe, and J. M. Lizonitz, "National Health Expenditure Projections, 2014–24: Spending Growth Faster Than Recent Trends," *Health Affairs* 34, no. 8 (2015): 1407–17; Erin Trish, Jianhui Xu, and Geoffrey Joyce, "Medicare Beneficiaries Face Growing Out-of-Pocket Burden for Specialty Drugs While in Catastrophic Coverage Phase," *Health Affairs* 35, no. 9 (2016): 1564–71.

15. Katherine Baicker and Helen Levy, "The Insurance Value of Medicare," *New England Journal of Medicine* 367, no. 19 (2012): 1773–75; Stacie B. Dusetzina, Ethan Basch, and Nathan L. Keating, "For Uninsured Cancer Patients, Outpatient Charges Can Be Costly, Putting Treatments Out of Reach," *Health Affairs* 34, no. 4 (2015): 584–91.

16. Peter A. Ubel, *Critical Decisions: How You and Your Doctor Can Make the Right Medical Choices Together* (New York: HarperOne, 2012).

17. Bradley Sawyer and Cynthia Cox, "How Does Health Spending in the U.S. Compare to Other Countries?," The Henry J. Kaiser Family Foundation, https://www.healthsystemtracker.org/chart-collection/health-spending-u-s-compare-countries/?_sf_s=health+spending#item-start; S. P. Keehan, D. A. Stone, J. A. Poisal, G. A. Cuckler, A. M. Sisko, S. D. Smith, A. J. Madison, C. J. Wolfe, and J. M. Lizonitz, "National Health Expenditure Projections, 2016–25: Price Increases, Aging Push Sector to 20 Percent of Economy," *Health Affairs* 36, no. 3 (2017): 553–63.

18. G. A. Cuckler, A. M. Sisko, J. A. Poisal, S. P. Keehan, S. D. Smith, A. J. Madison, C. J. Wolfe, and J. C. Hardesty, "National Health Expenditure Projections, 2017–26: Despite Uncertainty, Fundamentals Primarily Drive Spending Growth," *Health Affairs* 37, no. 3 (2018): 482–92.

19. Miriam J. Laugesen, *Fixing Medical Prices: How Physicians Are Paid* (Cambridge, MA: Harvard University Press, 2016).

20. Sarah Kliff and Soo Oh, "America's Health Care Prices Are Out of Control. These 11 Charts Prove It," *Vox*, May 10, 2015, https://www.vox.com/a/health-prices.

21. Jon Krawczynski, Brian Bakst, Patrick Condon, and Martiga Lohn, "Hopes Dim in Minneapolis for Survivors," Associated Press, August 2, 2007, http://apnews.myway.com/article/20070802/D8QOTCi80.html.

22. David M. Cutler, "What Is the U.S. Health Spending Problem?," *Health Affairs* 37, no. 3 (2018): 493–97.

23. Daniel Waldo, "National Health Accounts: A Framework for Understanding Health Care Financing," *Health Affairs* 37, no. 3 (2018): 498–503.

24. David U. Himmelstein, Elizabeth Warren, Deborah Thorne, and Steffie Woolhandler, "Illness and Injury as Contributors to Bankruptcy," *Health Affairs* 24, Suppl. 1 (2005); W. Hollingworth, A. Relyea-Chew, B. A. Comstock, J. K. Overstreet, and J. G. Jarvik, "The Risk of Bankruptcy Before and After Brain or Spinal Cord Injury: A Glimpse of the Iceberg's Tip," *Medical Care* 45, no. 8 (2007): 702–11.

25. W. G. Hunter, C. Z. Zhang, A. Hesson, J. K. Davis, C. Kirby, L. D. Williamson, J. A. Barnett, and P. A. Ubel, "What Strategies Do Physicians and Patients Discuss to Reduce Out-of-Pocket Costs? Analysis of Cost-Saving Strategies in 1,755 Outpatient Clinic Visits," *Medical Decision Making* 36, no. 7 (2016): 900–910.

1. Can Americans Shop Their Way to More Affordable Care?

1. W. G. Hunter, A. Hesson, J. K. Davis, C. Kirby, L. D. Williamson, J. A. Barnett, and P. A. Ubel, "Patient-Physician Discussions About Costs: Definitions and Impact on Cost Conversation Incidence Estimates," *BMC Health Services Research* 16 (2016): 108–20.

2. Thomas A. Massaro and Yu-Ning Wong, "Positive Experience with Medical Savings Accounts in Singapore," *Health Affairs* 14, no. 2 (1995): 267–72.

3. Aaron E. Carroll and Austin Frakt, "What Makes Singapore's Health Care So Cheap?," *New York Times*, October 2, 2017, https://www.nytimes.com/2017/10/02/upshot/what-makes-singapores-health-care-so-cheap.html.

4. William A. Haseltine, *Affordable Excellence: The Singapore Healthcare Story* (Washington, DC: Brookings Institution Press, 2013).

5. Avik Roy, "Singapore's Market-Based Health Care System Puts America's to Shame," *Forbes*, March 9, 2012, https://www.forbes.com/sites/theapothecary/2012/03/09/the-myth-of-free-market-american-health-care/#6d5a0ea5a4f0.

6. David Goldhill, "How American Health Care Killed My Father," *The Atlantic*, September 1, 2009, https://www.theatlantic.com/magazine/archive/2009/09/how-american-health-care-killed-my-father/307617/.

7. P. Neuman, J. Cubanski, K. A. Desmond, and T. H. Rice, "How Much 'Skin in the Game' Do Medicare Beneficiaries Have? The Increasing Financial Burden of Health Care Spending, 1997–2003," *Health Affairs* 26, no. 6 (2007): 1692–701.

8. Plato, *The Republic of Plato*, ed. F. M. Cornford (New York: Oxford University Press, 1961).

9. *The Simpsons,* season 13, episode 11, "The Bart Wants What It Wants," created by Matt Groening, written by John Frink and Don Payne, aired February 17, 2002, produced by Gracie Films and 20th Century Fox Television.

10. Richard A. Knox, *Germany: One Nation with Health Care for All* (Washington, DC: Faulkner & Gray's Healthcare Information Center, 1993).

11. E. P. Hennock, *The Origin of the Welfare State in England and Germany, 1850–1914: Social Policies Compared* (Cambridge: Cambridge University Press, 2007).

12. Ibid.

13. Ibid.

14. Mark V. Pauly, "The Economics of Moral Hazard: Comment," *American Economic Review* 58, no. 3 (1968): 531–37.

15. S. B. Barnett and D. Maulik, "Guidelines and Recommendations for Safe Use of Doppler Ultrasound in Perinatal Applications," *Journal of Maternal-Fetal Medicine* 10, no. 2 (2001): 75–84.

16. Haseltine, *Affordable Excellence*.

17. Goldhill, "Health Care Killed My Father."

18. Avik Roy, "Liberals Are Wrong: Free Market Health Care Is Possible," *The Atlantic*, March 12, 2012, https://www.theatlantic.com/business/archive/2012/03/liberals-are-wrong-free-market-health-care-is-possible/254648/.

19. Benjamin Domenech, "How Trump Can Fix Health Care," *New York Times*, March 21, 2017, https://www.nytimes.com/2017/03/21/opinion/how-trump-can-fix-health-care.html.

20. Milton Friedman, "How to Cure Health Care," *Public Interest*, no. 142 (2001): 3–30.

21. "Glossary—Deductible," U.S. Centers for Medicare & Medicaid Services, https://www.healthcare.gov/glossary/deductible/.

22. Laurence C. Baker, Kate Bundorf, and Anne Royalty, *Consumer-Oriented Strategies for Improving Health Benefit Design: An Overview*, Technical Reviews 15 (Rockville, MD: Agency for Healthcare Research and Quality, 2007), 1–45, https://www.ncbi.nlm.nih.gov/books/NBK44061/pdf/Bookshelf_NBK44061.pdf.

23. Gary Claxton, Matthew Rae, Michelle Long, Anthony Damico, Bradley Sawyer, Gregory Foster, Heidi Whitmore, and Lindsey Schapiro, "Employer Health Benefits 2016 Annual Survey," Henry J. Kaiser Family Foundation, Health Research & Educational Trust, 2016, 1–235, http://files.kff.org/attachment/Report-Employer-Health-Benefits-2016-Annual-Survey.

24. "The New Health Economy in the Age of Disruption: Novel Combinations Attempt to Remake the Health System," PwC Health Research Institute, 2018, 1–26, https://www.sciananetwork.org/fileadmin/user_upload/Documents/2010-2019/2018/Session_601/pwc-hri-the-new-health-economy-in-the-age-of-disruption.pdf.

25. Ibid.

26. Cathy Schoen, Karen Davis, and Amber Willink, "Medicare Beneficiaries' High Out-of-Pocket Costs: Cost Burdens by Income and Health Status," The Commonwealth Fund, 2017, 1–13, https://www.commonwealthfund.org/sites/default/files/documents/_media_files_publications_issue_brief_2017_may_schoen_medicare_cost_burden_ib_v2.pdf.

27. Ibid.

28. Robin Osborn and Donald Moulds, "The Commonwealth Fund 2014 International Health Policy Survey of Older Adults in Eleven Countries," The Commonwealth Fund,

2014, 1–31, https://www.commonwealthfund.org/sites/default/files/documents/_media_files_publications_in_the_literature_2014_nov_pdf_1787_commonwealth_fund_2014_intl_survey_chartpack.pdf.

29. Richard Martin, "Supreme Court Ruling Could Bring Relief for Many Floridians, Uncertainty for Others," *Tampa Bay Times*, June 28, 2012, https://www.tampabay.com/news/courts/supreme-court-ruling-could-bring-relief-for-many-floridians-uncertainty/1237687.

30. "Capecitabine," National Cancer Institute, https://www.cancer.gov/about-cancer/treatment/drugs/capecitabine?redirect=true.

31. Bo Wang, Steven Joffe, and Aaron S. Kesselheim, "Chemotherapy Parity Laws a Remedy for High Drug Costs?," *JAMA Internal Medicine* 174, no. 11 (2014): 1721–22.

2. Shopping in the Dark

1. G. Loewenstein, J. Y. Friedman, B. McGill, S. Ahmad, S. Linck, S. Sinkula, et al., "Consumers' Misunderstanding of Health Insurance," *Journal of Health Economics* 32, no. 5 (2013): 850–62.

2. Mary C. Politi, M. D. Kuzemchak, J. Liu, A. R. Barker, E. Peters, P. A. Ubel, et al., "Show Me My Health Plans: Using a Decision Aid to Improve Decisions in the Federal Health Insurance Marketplace," *MDM Policy & Practice* 1, no. 1 (2016): 1–11.

3. James C. Robinson, "Reinvention of Health Insurance in the Consumer Era," *JAMA* 291, no. 15 (2004): 1880–86.

4. Politi et al., "Show Me My Health Plans," 1–11.

5. Howard K. Koh and Kathleen G. Sebelius, "Promoting Prevention Through the Affordable Care Act," *New England Journal of Medicine* 363, no. 14 (2010): 1296–99.

6. "Glossary—Coinsurance," U.S. Centers for Medicare & Medicaid Services, https://www.healthcare.gov/glossary/co-insurance/.

7. Loewenstein et al., "Consumers' Misunderstanding," 850–62.

8. Richard H. Thaler, "Why So Many People Choose the Wrong Health Plans," *New York Times*, November 4, 2017, https://www.nytimes.com/2017/11/04/business/why-choose-wrong-health-plan.html.

9. Saurabh Bhargava, George Loewenstein, and Shlomo Benartzi, "The Costs of Poor Health (Plan Choices) & Prescriptions for Reform," *Behavioral Science & Policy* 3, no. 1 (2017): 1–12.

10. Anna D. Sinaiko and Richard A. Hirth, "Consumers, Health Insurance and Dominated Choices," *Journal of Health Economics* 30, no. 2 (2011): 450–57.

11. Saurabh Bhargava, George Loewenstein, and Justin Sydnor, "Choose to Lose: Health Plan Choices from a Menu with Dominated Options," *Quarterly Journal of Economics* 132, no. 3 (2017): 1319–72.

12. Herbert A. Simon, "Theories of Bounded Rationality," *Decision and Organization* 1, no. 1 (1972): 161–76.

13. Herbert A. Simon, "Bounded Rationality," in *Utility and Probability*, ed. J. Eatwell, M. Milgate, and P. Newman (London: Palgrave Macmillan, 1990), 15–18.

14. Andrew J. Barnes, Yaniv Hanoch, and Tom Rice, "Determinants of Coverage Decisions in Health Insurance Marketplaces: Consumers' Decision-Making Abilities and the Amount of Information in Their Choice Environment," *Health Services Research* 50, no. 1 (2015): 58–80.

15. Y. Hanoch, T. Rice, J. Cummings, and S. Wood, "How Much Choice Is Too Much? The Case of the Medicare Prescription Drug Benefit," *Health Services Research* 44, no. 4 (2009): 1157–68.

16. Sheena Iyengar, *The Art of Choosing* (New York: Twelve, 2010).

17. Barry Schwartz, *The Paradox of Choice: Why More Is Less* (New York: Harper Perennial, 2014).

18. Sara Rosenbaum and Ross Margulies, "Tax-Exempt Hospitals and the Patient Protection and Affordable Care Act: Implications for Public Health Policy and Practice," *Public Health Reports* 126, no. 2 (2011): 283–86.

19. Amy Burke, Arpit Misra, and Steven Sheingold, "Premium Affordability, Competition, and Choice in the Health Insurance Marketplace, 2014," U.S. Department of Health & Human Services, 2014, 1–26, https://aspe.hhs.gov/system/files/pdf/76896/2014MktPlacePremBrf.pdf.

20. Hanoch et al., "How Much Choice Is Too Much?," 1157–68.

21. Politi et al., "Show Me My Health Plans," 1–11.

22. Joffre Swait and Wiktor Adamowicz, "The Influence of Task Complexity on Consumer Choice: A Latent Class Model of Decision Strategy Switching," *Journal of Consumer Research* 28, no. 1 (2001): 135–48.

23. Saurabh Bhargava and George Loewenstein, "Choosing a Health Insurance Plan: Complexity and Consequences," *JAMA* 314, no. 23 (2015): 2505–6.

24. Nicholas Epley and Thomas Gilovich, "The Anchoring-and-Adjustment Heuristic: Why the Adjustments Are Insufficient," *Psychological Science* 17, no. 4 (2006): 311–18.

25. Jason Abaluck and Jonathan Gruber, "Evolving Choice Inconsistencies in Choice of Prescription Drug Insurance," *American Economic Review* 106, no. 8 (2016): 2145–84.

26. Epley and Gilovich, "Anchoring-and-Adjustment Heuristic," 311–18.

27. Keith M. Ericson and Amanda Starc, "How Product Standardization Affects Choice: Evidence from the Massachusetts Health Insurance Exchange," *Journal of Health Economics* 50 (2016): 71–85.

28. Peter A. Ubel, David A. Comerford, and Eric Johnson, "Healthcare.gov 3.0—Behavioral Economics and Insurance Exchanges," *New England Journal of Medicine* 372, no. 8 (2015): 695–98.

29. A. Z. Wang, K. A. Scherr, C. A. Wong, and P. A. Ubel, "Poor Consumer Comprehension and Plan Selection Inconsistencies Under the 2016 HealthCare.gov Choice Architecture," *MDM Policy & Practice* 2, no. 1 (2017): 1–9.

30. Jamie A. Rosenthal, Xin Lu, and Peter Cram, "Availability of Consumer Prices from U.S. Hospitals for a Common Surgical Procedure," *JAMA Internal Medicine* 173, no. 6 (2013): 427–32.

31. Monica L. Wolford, Kathleen Palso, and Anita Bercovitz, "Hospitalization for Total Hip Replacement Among Inpatients Aged 45 and Over: United States, 2000–2010," *NCHS Data Brief*, no. 186 (2015): 1–8.

32. K. Okike, R. V. O'Toole, A. N. Pollak, J. A. Bishop, C. M. McAndrew, S. Mehta, W. W. Cross III, G. E. Garrigues, M. B. Harris, and C. T. Lebrun, "Survey Finds Few Orthopedic Surgeons Know the Costs of the Devices They Implant," *Health Affairs* 33, no. 1 (2014): 103–9.

33. K. S. Farrell, L. J. Finocchio, A. N. Trivedi, and A. Mehrotra, "Does Price Transparency Legislation Allow the Uninsured to Shop for Care?," *Journal of General Internal Medicine* 25, no. 2 (2010): 110–14.

34. Jillian R. Bernstein and Joseph Bernstein, "Availability of Consumer Prices from Philadelphia Area Hospitals for Common Services: Electrocardiograms vs. Parking," *JAMA Internal Medicine* 174, no. 2 (2014): 292–93.

35. Z. Cooper, S. V. Craig, M. Gaynor, and J. Van Reenen, "The Price Ain't Right? Hospital Prices and Health Spending on the Privately Insured," National Bureau of Economic Research Working Paper No. 21815, 2015.

36. W. G. Hunter, C. Z. Zhang, A. Hesson, J. K. Davis, C. Kirby, L. D. Williamson, J. A. Barnett, and P. A. Ubel, "What Strategies Do Physicians and Patients Discuss to Reduce Out-of-Pocket Costs? Analysis of Cost-Saving Strategies in 1,755 Outpatient Clinic Visits," *Medical Decision Making* 36, no. 7 (2016): 900–910.

37. Elisabeth Rosenthal, *An American Sickness: How Healthcare Became Big Business and How You Can Take It Back* (New York: Penguin Random House, 2017).

38. Christopher Garmon and Benjamin Chartock, "One in Five Inpatient Emergency Department Cases May Lead to Surprise Bills," *Health Affairs* 36, no. 1 (2017): 177–81.

39. Jeanne Pinder, "Isn't Every Colonoscopy Free Now? Well, Not Exactly," *Clear Health Costs,* February 14, 2016, https://clearhealthcosts.com/blog/2016/02/free-colonoscopies-theyre-free/.

40. "Wall Street Journal's Motion to Intervene Reopens Court Case That Blocked Public Disclosure of Medicare Claims Data in 1979," *VR Research,* May 19, 2011, https://www.vrresearch.com/blog/1144.

41. *Florida Medical Ass'n v. Dept. of Health, Ed., Etc.,* 479 Federal Supplement (1979).

42. D. Andrew Austin and Jane G. Gravelle, "Does Price Transparency Improve Market Efficiency? Implications of Empirical Evidence in Other Markets for the Health Sector," Congressional Research Service, 2007, 1–45, https://fas.org/sgp/crs/secrecy/RL34101.pdf.

43. Uwe E. Reinhardt, "Health Care Price Transparency and Economic Theory," *JAMA* 312, no. 16 (2014): 1642–43.

44. Robert Cunningham III and Robert M. Cunningham, *The Blues: A History of the Blue Cross and Blue Shield System* (DeKalb: North Illinois University Press, 1997).

3. Who's in Charge?

1. Lynn Bonner, "Part One: For NC Medicaid program, Is 'Broken' a Bad Rap?," *News & Observer*, July 4, 2014, https://www.newsobserver.com/news/special-reports/article10338068.html.

2. "Controlling Emergency Room Use: State Medicaid Reports," U.S. Department of Health and Human Services, Office of the Inspector General, March 1992, 1–24, https://oig.hhs.gov/oei/reports/oei-06-90-00181.pdf.

3. Michael Ollove, "States Strive to Keep Medicaid Patients Out of the Emergency Department," *The Pew Charitable Trusts* (blog), February 24, 2015, https://www.pewtrusts.org/en/research-and-analysis/blogs/stateline/2015/2/24/states-strive-to-keep-medicaid-patients-out-of-the-emergency-department.

4. Laura Ungar and Jayne O'Donnell, "Contrary to Goals, ER Visits Rise Under Obamacare," *USA Today*, May 24, 2015, https://www.usatoday.com/story/news/nation/2015/05/04/emergency-room-visits-rise-under-affordable-care-act/26625571/.

5. B. D. Sommers, R. J. Blendon, E. J. Orav, and A. M. Epstein, "Changes in Utilization and Health Among Low-Income Adults After Medicaid Expansion or Expanded Private Insurance," *JAMA Internal Medicine* 176, no. 10 (2016): 1501–9.

6. Joseph P. Newhouse, *Free for All?: Lessons from the RAND Health Insurance Experiment* (Cambridge, MA: Harvard University Press, 1993).

7. Eli Ginzberg, "The Limits of Health Reform," *American Journal of Medicine* 69, no. 2 (1980): 174–76.

8. Newhouse, *Free for All*.

9. Ibid.

10. Amal N. Trivedi, Husein Moloo, and Vincent Mor, "Increased Ambulatory Care Copayments and Hospitalizations Among the Elderly," *New England Journal of Medicine* 362, no. 4 (2010): 320–28.

11. Zarek C. Brot-Goldberg, Amitabh Chandra, Benjamin R. Handel, and Jonathan T. Kolstad, "What Does a Deductible Do? The Impact of Cost-Sharing on Health Care Prices, Quantities, and Spending Dynamics," *Quarterly Journal of Economics* 132, no. 3 (2017): 1261–318.

12. Rajender Agarwal, Olena Mazurenko, and Nir Menachemi, "High-Deductible Health Plans Reduce Health Care Cost and Utilization, Including Use of Needed Preventive Services," *Health Affairs* 36, no. 10 (2017): 1762–68.

13. Oscar Wilde, *The Importance of Being Earnest: A Trivial Comedy for Serious People* (London: Methuen, 1908).

14. Newhouse, *Free for All*.

15. Trivedi, Moloo, and Mor, "Increased Ambulatory Care," 320–28.

16. Jay Helms, Joseph P. Newhouse, and Charles E. Phelps, "Copayments and Demand for Medical Care: The California Medicaid Experience," *Bell Journal of Economics* 9, no. 1 (1978): 192–208.

17. Ibid.

18. Tara S. Bernard, "Some Women Attain an Enviable Status: 401(k) Millionaire," *New York Times*, November 24, 2017, https://www.nytimes.com/2017/11/24/your-money/some-women-attain-an-enviable-status-401-k-millionaire.html.

19. David Y. T. Chen and Robert G. Uzzo, "Optimal Management of Localized Renal Cell Carcinoma: Surgery, Ablation, or Active Surveillance," *Journal of the National Comprehensive Cancer Network* 7, no. 6 (2009): 635–43.

20. W.-H. Chow, S. S. Devesa, J. L. Warren, and J. F. Fraumeni Jr., "Rising Incidence of Renal Cell Cancer in the United States," *JAMA* 281, no. 17 (1999): 1628–31.

21. A. Sidana, D. J. Hernandez, Z. Feng, A. W. Partin, B. J. Trock, S. Saha, and J. I. Epstein, "Treatment Decision-Making for Localized Prostate Cancer: What Younger Men Choose and Why," *Prostate* 72, no. 1 (2012): 58–64.

22. A. Bill-Axelson, L. Holmberg, H. Garmo, J. R. Rider, K. Taari, C. Busch, et al., "Radical Prostatectomy or Watchful Waiting in Early Prostate Cancer," *New England Journal of Medicine* 370, no. 10 (2014): 932–42; T. J. Wilt, K. M. Jones, M. J. Barry, G. L. Andriole, D. Culkin, T. Wheeler, W. J. Aronson, and M. K. Brawer, "Radical Prostatectomy Versus Observation for Localized Prostate Cancer," *New England Journal of Medicine* 367, no. 3 (2012): 203–13.

23. Michael J. Barry and Susan Edgman-Levitan, "Shared Decision Making—The Pinnacle of Patient-Centered Care," *New England Journal of Medicine* 366, no. 9 (2012): 780–81.

24. A. W. Partin, J. Yoo, H. B. Carter, J. D. Pearson, D. W. Chan, J. I. Epstein, and P. C. Walsh, "The Use of Prostate Specific Antigen, Clinical Stage and Gleason Score to Predict Pathological Stage in Men with Localized Prostate Cancer," *Journal of Urology* 150, no. 1 (1993): 110–14.

25. K. A. Scherr, A. Fagerlin, T. Hofer, L. D. Scherer, M. Holmes-Rovner, L. D. Williamson, et al., "Physician Recommendations Trump Patient Preferences in Prostate Cancer Treatment Decisions," *Medical Decision Making* 37, no. 1 (2017): 56–69.

26. Peter A. Ubel, Karen A. Scherr, and Angela Fagerlin, "Empowerment Failure: How Shortcomings in Physician Communication Unwittingly Undermine Patient Autonomy," *American Journal of Bioethics* 17, no. 11 (2017): 31–39.

27. K. A. Scherr, A. Fagerlin, L. D. Williamson, J. K. Davis, I. Fridman, N. Atyeo, and P. A. Ubel, "The Physician Recommendation Coding System (PhyReCS): A Reliable and Valid Method to Quantify the Strength of Physician Recommendations During Clinical Encounters," *Medical Decision Making* 37, no. 1 (2017): 46–55.

28. Anna D. Sinaiko, Ateev Mehrotra, and Neeraj Sood, "Cost-Sharing Obligations, High-Deductible Health Plan Growth, and Shopping for Health Care: Enrollees with Skin in the Game," *JAMA Internal Medicine* 176, no. 3 (2016): 395–97.

29. Peter A. Ubel, *Critical Decisions: How You and Your Doctor Can Make the Right Medical Choices Together* (New York: HarperOne, 2012).

4. What Patients and Doctors Talk About When They Talk About Money

1. Caleb Alexander, Lawrence P. Casalino, and David O. Meltzer, "Patient-Physician Communication About Out-of-Pocket Costs," *JAMA* 290, no. 7 (2003): 953–58.

2. B. Irwin, G. Kimmick, I. Altomare, P. I. Marcom, K. Houck, S. Y. Zafar, and J. Peppercorn, "Patient Experience and Attitudes Toward Addressing the Cost of Breast Cancer Care," *Oncologist* 19, no. 11 (2014): 1135–40.

3. Norbert Schwarz, *Cognition and Communication: Judgmental Biases, Research Methods, and the Logic of Conversation*, John M. MacEachran Memorial Lecture Series (Mahwah, NJ: L. Erlbaum Associates, 1996).

4. Norbert Schwarz, "Self-Reports—How the Questions Shape the Answers," *American Psychologist* 54, no. 2 (1999): 93–105.

5. W. G. Hunter, C. Z. Zhang, A. Hesson, J. K. Davis, C. Kirby, L. D. Williamson, J. A. Barnett, and P. A. Ubel, "What Strategies Do Physicians and Patients Discuss to Reduce Out-of-Pocket Costs? Analysis of Cost-Saving Strategies in 1,755 Outpatient Clinic Visits," *Medical Decision Making* 36, no. 7 (2016): 900–910.

6. G. D. Brown, W. G. Hunter, A. Hesson, J. K. Davis, C. Kirby, J. A. Barnett, D. Byelmac, and P. A. Ubel, "Discussing Out-of-Pocket Expenses During Clinical Appointments: An Observational Study of Patient-Psychiatrist Interactions," *Psychiatric Services* 68, no. 6 (2017): 610–17.

7. Hunter et al., "What Strategies Do Physicians and Patients Discuss," 900–910.

8. Daniel J. Simons and Christopher F. Chabris, "Gorillas in Our Midst: Sustained Inattentional Blindness for Dynamic Events," *Perception* 28, no. 9 (1999): 1059–74.

9. P. A. Ubel, C. J. Zhang, A. Hesson, J. K. Davis, C. Kirby, J. Barnett, and W. G. Hunter, "Study of Physician and Patient Communication Identifies Missed Opportunities to Help Reduce Patients' Out-of-Pocket Spending," *Health Affairs* 35, no. 4 (2016): 654–61.

10. Ibid.

11. Jessica R. Harris, "Communicating About Costs: A Qualitative Analysis to Understand the Out-of-Pocket Financial Burden Associated with Cancer Care" (Master's Thesis, Duke University, 2012), 1–36.

12. S. Yousuf Zafar, "Financial Toxicity of Cancer Care: It's Time to Intervene," *Journal of the National Cancer Institute* 108, no. 5 (2016): 1–4, cited ibid.

13. Danielle J. Brick, Karen A. Scherr, and Peter A. Ubel, "The Impact of Cost Conversations on the Patient-Physician Relationship," *Health Communication* 34, no. 1 (2019): 65–73.

14. G. Caleb Alexander, L. P. Casalino, C. W. Tseng, D. McFadden, and D. O. Meltzer, "Barriers to Patient-Physician Communication About Out-of-Pocket Costs," *Journal of General Internal Medicine* 19, no. 8 (2004): 856–60.

15. Peter A. Ubel, "Doctor, First Tell Me What It Costs," *New York Times*, November 3, 2013, https://www.nytimes.com/2013/11/04/opinion/doctor-first-tell-me-what-it-costs.html.

16. G. Caleb Alexander, Lawrence P. Casalino, and David O. Meltzer, "Physician Strategies to Reduce Patients' Out-of-Pocket Prescription Costs," *Archives of Internal Medicine* 165, no. 6 (2005): 633–36; Pauline W. Chen, "For New Doctors, 8 Minutes Per Patient," *New York Times* (Well blog), May 3, 2013, https://well.blogs.nytimes.com/2013/05/30/for-new-doctors-8-minutes-per-patient/.

17. K. A. Scherr, A. Fagerlin, J. T. Wei, L. D. Williamson, and P. A. Ubel, "Treatment Availability Influences Physicians' Portrayal of Robotic Surgery During Clinical Appointments," *Health Communication* 32, no. 1 (2017): 119–25.

5. The End of Life and the Limits of Healthcare Markets

1. Maeve Quigley, "Doting Parents Make Heartfelt Appeal to Help Save Brave Daughter Robyn from Rare Childhood Cancer," *Irish Mirror*, July 23, 2013, https://www.irishmirror.ie/lifestyle/health/parents-appeal-donations-save-brave-2081916.

2. James Arthur, "Big-Hearted Stars to Perform Special Gig to Raise Money for Life-Saving Treatment for 10-Year-Old Robyn," *Irish Mirror*, May 24, 2015, https://www.irishmirror.ie/news/irish-news/health-news/big-hearted-stars-perform-special-gig-5749680.

3. Nick Bramhill, "€300k Sought to Save 10-Year-Old Robyn Smyth," *Irish Examiner*, April 7, 2015, https://www.irishexaminer.com/ireland/300k-sought-to-save-10-year-old-robyn-smyth-322502.html.

4. Kenneth J. Arrow, "Uncertainty and the Welfare Economics of Medical Care," *American Economic Review* 53, no. 5 (1963): 941–73.

5. Valerie Michel Buck and Jed Winegar, "What Should I Expect to Pay for Funeral and Burial Expenses," National Care Planning Council, https://www.longtermcarelink.net/article-2016-2-16-What-Should-I-Expect-to-Pay-for-Funeral-and-Burial-Expenses.htm.

6. Steven Brill, *America's Bitter Pill: Money, Politics, Backroom Deals, and the Fight to Fix Our Broken Healthcare System* (New York: Random House, 2015).

7. Amos Tversky and Daniel Kahneman, "The Framing of Decisions and the Psychology of Choice," *Science* 211, no. 4481 (1981): 453–58.

8. Daniel Kahneman and Amos Tversky, "Prospect Theory: An Analysis of Decision Under Risk," *Econometrica* 47, no. 2 (1979): 263–91.

9. Cass R. Sunstein, "Incommensurability and Valuation in Law," *Michigan Law Review* 92, no. 4 (1994): 779–861.

10. Albert L. Siu, "Screening for Breast Cancer: U.S. Preventive Services Task Force Recommendation Statement," *Annals of Internal Medicine* 151, no. 10 (2009): 716–26.

11. Andrea V. Barrio and Kimberly J. Van Zee, "Controversies in the Treatment of Ductal Carcinoma in Situ," *Annual Review of Medicine* 68 (2017): 197–211.

12. J. G. Elmore, M. B. Barton, V. M. Moceri, S. Polk, P. J. Arena, and S. W. Fletcher, "Ten-Year Risk of False Positive Screening Mammograms and Clinical Breast Examinations," *New England Journal of Medicine* 338, no. 16 (1998): 1089–96.

13. Dan Munro, "Mark Cuban Ignites Digital Health Firestorm on Twitter," *Forbes*, April 5, 2015, https://www.forbes.com/sites/danmunro/2015/04/05/mark-cuban-ignites-digital-health-firestorm-on-twitter/#43facf8972b1.

14. J. W. O'Sullivan, A. Albasri, B. D. Nicholson, R. Perera, J. K. Aronson, N. Roberts, and C. Heneghan, "Overtesting and Undertesting in Primary Care: A Systematic Review and Meta-Analysis," *BMJ Open* 8, no. 2 (2018): 1–9.

15. Karen E. Jenni and George Loewenstein, "Explaining the 'Identifiable Victim Effect,' " *Journal of Risk and Uncertainty* 14, no. 3 (1997): 235–57.

16. D. P. Goldman, A. B. Jena, D. N. Lakdawalla, J. L. Malin, J. D. Malkin, and E. Sun, "The Value of Specialty Oncology Drugs," *Health Services Research* 45, no. 1 (2010): 115–32.

17. David Goldhill, *Catastrophic Care: Why Everything We Think We Know About Health Care Is Wrong* (New York: Vintage Books, Random House, 2013).

18. Julie A. Schoenman, *The Concentration of Health Care Spending* (Washington, DC: The NIHCM Foundation, 2012), 1–11, https://www.nihcm.org/pdf/Data -Brief3%20Final.pdf.

19. Mariacristina De Nardi, Eric French, John Bailey Jones, and Jeremy McCauley, "Medical Spending of the U.S. Elderly," *Fiscal Studies* 37, no. 3–4 (2016): 717–47.

20. P. A. Ubel, S. R. Berry, E. Nadler, C. M. Bell, M. A. Kozminski, J. A. Palmer, W. K. Evans, E. L. Strevel, and P. J. Neumann, "In a Survey, Marked Inconsistency in How Oncologists Judged Value of High-Cost Cancer Drugs in Relation to Gains in Survival," *Health Affairs* 31, no. 4 (2012): 709–17.

21. H. M. Kantarjian, T. Fojo, M. Mathisen, and L. A. Zwelling, "Cancer Drugs in the United States: Justum Pretium—the Just Price," *Journal of Clinical Oncology* 31, no. 28 (2013): 3600–3604.

22. David H. Howard, Peter B. Bach, Ernst R. Berndt, and Rena M. Conti, "Pricing the Market for Anticancer Drugs," *Journal of Economic Perspectives* 29, no. 1 (2015): 139–62.

23. Andrew Pollack, "Genentech Wins Approval for New Breast Cancer Drug," *New York Times*, June 9, 2012, https://www.nytimes.com/2012/06/09/business/genentech -wins-approval-for-new-breast-cancer-drug.html?mtrref=www.google.com.

24. E. B. French, J. McCauley, M. Aragon, P. Bakx, M. Chalkley, S. H. Chen, et al., "End-of-Life Medical Spending in Last Twelve Months of Life Is Lower Than Previously Reported," *Health Affairs* 36, no. 7 (2017): 1211–17.

25. Ibid.; Melissa D. Aldridge and Elizabeth H. Bradley, "Epidemiology and Patterns of Care at the End of Life: Rising Complexity, Shifts in Care Patterns and Sites of Death," *Health Affairs* 36, no. 7 (2017): 1175–83.

26. John K. Iglehart, "Future of Long-Term Care and the Expanding Role of Medicaid Managed Care," *New England Journal of Medicine* 374, no. 2 (2016): 182–87.

27. Gretchen Jacobson, Anthony Damico, Tricia Neuman, and Marsha Gold, "Medicare Advantage 2017 Spotlight: Enrollment Market Update," The Henry J. Kaiser Family Foundation, 2017, 1–23, http://files.kff.org/attachment/Issue-Brief-Medicare -Advantage-2017-Spotlight-Enrollment-Market-Update.

28. Rena M. Conti, Adam J. Fein, and Sumita S. Bhatta, "National Trends in Spending on and Use of Oral Oncologics, First Quarter 2006 Through Third Quarter 2011," *Health Affairs* 33, no. 10 (2014): 1721–27.

29. Robert Cunningham III and Robert M. Cunningham, *The Blues: A History of the Blue Cross and Blue Shield System* (DeKalb: North Illinois University Press, 1997).

30. Gilbert Welch and Juliana Mogielnicki, "Presumed Benefit: Lessons from the American Experience with Marrow Transplantation for Breast Cancer," *BMJ* 324 (2002): 1088–95.

31. Daniel J. Hopkins, "The Exaggerated Life of Death Panels? The Limited but Real Influence of Elite Rhetoric in the 2009–2010 Health Care Debate," *Political Behavior* 40, no. 3 (2017): 681–709.

32. Peter B. Bach, "Limits on Medicare's Ability to Control Rising Spending on Cancer Drugs," *New England Journal of Medicine* 360, no. 6 (2009): 626–33.

33. Walid F. Gellad and Aaron S. Kesselheim, "Accelerated Approval and Expensive Drugs—a Challenging Combination," *New England Journal of Medicine* 376, no. 21 (2017): 2001–4.

34. "NCCN Breast Cancer Panel Reaffirms Current Position and Recommendation Regarding the Use of Bevacizumab in Metastatic Breast Cancer," National Comprehensive Cancer Network, 2011, https://www.nccn.org/about/news/newsinfo.aspx?NewsID=289.

35. Peter A. Ubel and David A. Asch, "Creating Value in Health by Understanding and Overcoming Resistance to De-Innovation," *Health Affairs* 34, no. 2 (2015): 239–44.

36. Seyoung Lee and Thomas H. Feeley, "The Identifiable Victim Effect: A Meta-Analytic Review," *Social Influence* 11, no. 3 (2016): 199–215.

37. Bara Vaida, "For Super-Utilizers, Integrated Care Offers a New Path," *Health Affairs* 36, no. 3 (2017): 394–97.

38. Carl W. Gottschalk, "Report of the Committee on Chronic Kidney Disease" (Washington, DC: United States Bureau of the Budget, 1967).

39. Aaron Catlin and Cathy Cowan, "National Health Spending, 1960–2013," *Health Affairs* (blog), November 23, 2015, https://www.healthaffairs.org/do/10.1377/hblog20151123.051904/full/.

40. Kathi E. Hanna, ed., *Biomedical Politics* (Washington, DC: National Academies Press, 1991).

41. Ibid.

42. John McKie and Jeff Richardson, "The Rule of Rescue," *Social Science & Medicine* 56, no. 12 (2018): 2407–19.

6. Shining a Light on Healthcare Prices

1. E. A. Nalebuff, "The Rheumatoid Swan-Neck Deformity," *Hand Clinics* 5, no. 2 (1989): 203–14.

2. Harold C. Sox and Matthew H. Liang, "Diagnostic Decision: The Erythrocyte Sedimentation Rate: Guidelines for Rational Use," *Annals of Internal Medicine* 104, no. 4 (1986): 515–23.

3. M. B. Mac Bride, L. Neal, C. A. Dilaveri, N. P. Sandhu, T. J. Hieken, K. Ghosh, and D. L. Wahner-Roedler, "Factors Associated with Surgical Decision Making in Women with Early-Stage Breast Cancer: A Literature Review," *Journal of Women's Health* 22, no. 3 (2013): 236–42; Daniel Polsky, N. L. Keating, J. C. Weeks, and K. A. Schulman, "Patient Choice of Breast Cancer Treatment: Impact on Health State Preferences," *Medical Care* 40, no. 11 (2002): 1068–79.

4. Peter A. Ubel, *Critical Decisions: How You and Your Doctor Can Make the Right Medical Choices Together* (New York: HarperOne, 2012).

5. Peter A. Ubel, Amy P. Abernethy, and S. Yousuf Zafar, "Full Disclosure—Out-of-Pocket Costs as Side Effects," *New England Journal of Medicine* 369, no. 16 (2013): 1484–86.

6. Morgan Muir, Stephani Alessi, and Jaime S. King, "Clarifying Costs: Can Increased Price Transparency Reduce Healthcare Spending?" *William & Mary Policy Review* 2, no. 4 (2013): 319–66.

7. William Alden, "Castlight Health Soars in Stock Market Debut," *New York Times*, March 14, 2014, https://dealbook.nytimes.com/2014/03/14/castlight-health-soars-in-stock-market-debut/.

8. A. Kratka, C. A. Wong, R. Herrmann, K. Hong, A. Karediya, I. Yang, and P. A. Ubel, "Finding Health Care Prices Online: How Difficult Is It to Be an Informed Health-Care Consumer?," *JAMA Internal Medicine* 178, no. 3 (2018): 423–24.

9. "New Choice Health: Your Healthcare Marketplace," New Choice Health, https://www.newchoicehealth.com/.

10. "Pricing Healthcare: Busting Healthcare Pricing Wide Open," Pricing Healthcare, Inc., https://pricinghealthcare.com/.

11. Randy Cox, personal communication.

12. Jeffrey Rice, personal communication.

13. A. Mehrotra, P. J. Huckfeldt, A. M. Haviland, L. Gascue, and N. Sood, "Patients Who Choose Primary Care Physicians Based on Low Office Visit Price Can Realize Broader Savings," *Health Affairs* 35, no. 12 (2016): 2319–26.

14. Anna D. Sinaiko and Meredith B. Rosenthal, "Examining a Health Care Price Transparency Tool: Who Uses It, and How They Shop for Care," *Health Affairs* 35, no. 4 (2016): 662–70.

15. S. Desai, L. A. Hatfield, A. L. Hicks, A. D. Sinaiko, M. E. Chernew, D. Cowling, S. Gautam, S. J. Wu, and A. Mehrotra, "Offering a Price Transparency Tool Did Not Reduce Overall Spending Among California Public Employees and Retirees," *Health Affairs* 36, no. 8 (2017): 1401–7; A. Mehrotra, K. M. Dean, A. D. Sinaiko, and N. Sood, "Americans Support Price Shopping for Health Care, but Few Actually Seek Out Price Information," *Health Affairs* 36, no. 8 (2017): 1392–400.

16. "Compare Health Costs & Quality of Care in New Hampshire," New Hampshire Insurance Department, https://nhhealthcost.nh.gov/.

17. Health Care Cost Reduction and Transparency Act of 2013, H.B. 834.

18. Ed Sealover, "Colorado Hospitals Must Begin Posting Prices for Most Common Procedures on Jan. 1," *Denver Business Journal*, December 29, 2017, https://www.bizjournals.com/denver/news/2017/12/29/hospitals-must-begin-posting-prices-for-most.html.

19. Chris Kardish, "More States Create All-Payer Claims Databases," *Governing*, February 4, 2014, http://www.governing.com/topics/health-human-services/gov-states-serious-about-health-data.html; D. Newman, E. Barrette, A. Frost, and K. McGraves-Lloyd, "Losing the 'All' in All-Payer Claims Databases," *Health Affairs* (blog), July 18, 2016, https://www.healthaffairs.org/do/10.1377/hblog20160718.055873/full/.

20. Francois Brantes and Suzanne Delbanco, "2015 Report Card on State Price Transparency Laws," Catalyst for Payment Reform and Health Care Incentives Improvement Institute, Newtown, CT, 2015, 1–14, https://www.catalyze.org/wp-content/

uploads/woocommerce_uploads/2017/04/2015-Report-Card-on-State-Price
-Transparency-Laws.pdf.

21. Beth Kutscher, "Healthcare Underspends on Cybersecurity as Attacks Accelerate," *Modern Healthcare*, March 3, 2016, https://www.modernhealthcare.com/article/20160303/NEWS/160309922/healthcare-underspends-on-data-security-as-attacks-accelerate.

22. S. Wu, G. Sylwestrzak, C. Shah, and A. DeVries, "Price Transparency for MRIs Increased Use of Less Costly Providers and Triggered Provider Competition," *Health Affairs* 33, no. 8 (2014): 1391–98.

23. B. Elbel, R. Kersh, V. L. Brescoll, and L. B. Dixon, "Calorie Labeling and Food Choices: A First Look at the Effects on Low-Income People in New York City," *Health Affairs* 28, no. 6 (2009): w1110–21.

24. S. N. Bleich, J. A. Wolfson, M. P. Jarlenski, and J. P. Block, "Restaurants with Calories Displayed on Menus Had Lower Calorie Counts Compared to Restaurants Without Such Labels," *Health Affairs* 34, no. 11 (2015): 1877–84.

25. Francois Brantes and Suzanne Delbanco, "2016 Report Card on State Price Transparency Laws," Catalyst for Payment Reform and Health Care Incentives Improvement Institute, Newtown, CT, 2016, 1–18, https://www.catalyze.org/wp-content/uploads/woocommerce_uploads/2017/04/2016-Report-Card-on-State-Price-Transparency-Laws.pdf.

26. Erin Fuse Brown and Jaime King, "The Consequences of Gobeille v. Liberty Mutual for Health Care Cost Control," *Health Affairs* (blog), March 10, 2016, https://www.healthaffairs.org/do/10.1377/hblog20160310.053837/full/.

27. "Medicare.gov Hospital Compare," U.S. Centers for Medicare and Medicaid Services, https://www.medicare.gov/hospitalcompare/search.html.

28. Karl Y. Bilimoria and Cynthia Barnard, "The New CMS Hospital Quality Star Ratings: The Stars Are Not Aligned," *JAMA* 316, no. 17 (2016): 1761–62.

29. Ashish K. Jha, "The Stars of Hospital Care: Useful or a Distraction?," *JAMA* 315, no. 21 (2016): 2265–66.

30. Zosia Chustecka, "Senator Kennedy's Brain Cancer Followed a Typical Course," *Medscape Medical News*, August 28, 2009, https://www.medscape.com/viewarticle/708105.

31. "Duke University Hospital: Rankings & Ratings, #32 in Neurology & Neurosurgery," *U.S. News & World Report*, https://health.usnews.com/best-hospitals/area/nc/duke-university-medical-center-6360355/neurology-and-neurosurgery.

32. Bilimoria and Barnard, "Quality Star Ratings," 1761–62.

33. Justin B. Dimick, H. Gilbert Welch, and John D. Birkmeyer, "Surgical Mortality as an Indicator of Hospital Quality: The Problem with Small Sample Size," *JAMA* 292, no. 7 (2004): 847–51.

34. E. Batbaatar, J. Dorjdagva, A. Luvsannyam, M. M. Savino, and P. Amenta, "Determinants of Patient Satisfaction: A Systematic Review," *Perspectives in Public Health* 137, no. 2 (2017): 89–101.

35. Rachel M. Werner and David A. Asch, "The Unintended Consequences of Publicly Reporting Quality Information," *JAMA* 293, no. 10 (2005): 1239–44.

36. Rishi K. Wadhera and Deepak L. Bhatt, "Taking the 'Public' Out of Public Reporting of Percutaneous Coronary Intervention," *JAMA* 318, no. 15 (2017): 1439–40.

37. Ibid.; Bilimoria and Barnard, "Quality Star Ratings," 1761–62.

38. E. Peters, N. Dieckmann, A. Dixon, J. H. Hibbard, and C. K. Mertz, "Less Is More in Presenting Quality Information to Consumers," *Medical Care Research and Review* 64, no. 2 (2007): 169–90.

39. Vivian S. Lee, "Transparency and Trust—Online Patient Reviews of Physicians," *New England Journal of Medicine* 376, no. 3 (2017): 197–99.

40. B. L. Ranard, R. M. Werner, T. Antanavicius, H. A. Schwartz, R. J. Smith, Z. F. Meisel, D. A. Asch, L. H. Ungar, and R. M. Merchant, "Yelp Reviews of Hospital Care Can Supplement and Inform Traditional Surveys of the Patient Experience of Care," *Health Affairs* 35, no. 4 (2016): 697–705.

7. Pricing Healthcare to Reflect Value

1. Uwe E. Reinhardt, "The Disruptive Innovation of Price Transparency in Health Care," *JAMA* 310, no. 18 (2013): 1927–28.

2. Hans B. Christensen, Eric Floyd, and Mark Mafett, "The Effects of Price Transparency Regulation on Prices in the Healthcare Industry," *SSRN Electronic Journal*, 2014, https://www.bakerinstitute.org/media/files/event/01ce2e80/HPF-paper-AHEC-Floyd.pdf.

3. S. Wu, G. Sylwestrzak, C. Shah, and A. DeVries, "Price Transparency for MRIs Increased Use of Less Costly Providers and Triggered Provider Competition," *Health Affairs* 33, no. 8 (2014): 1391–98.

4. "Kineret (Anakinra)," U.S. Food and Drug Administration, 2001, 1–12, https://www.accessdata.fda.gov/drugsatfda_docs/label/2001/anakamg111401LB.pdf.

5. "Final Appraisal Determination: Anakinra for Rheumatoid Arthritis," National Institute for Clinical Excellence, 2003, 1–18, https://www.nice.org.uk/guidance/ta72/documents/final-appraisal-determination-anakinra-for-rheumatoid-arthritis2.

6. Michael E. Porter, "What Is Value in Health Care?," *New England Journal of Medicine* 363, no. 26 (2010): 2477–81.

7. Michael E. Porter and Thomas H. Lee, "From Volume to Value in Health Care: The Work Begins," *JAMA* 316, no. 10 (2016): 1047–48.

8. Phillip Miller and Kurt Mosley, "Physician Reimbursement: From Fee-for-Service to MACRA, MIPS and APMs," *Journal of Medical Practice Management* 31, no. 5 (2016): 266–69.

9. Donald M. Berwick, "Launching Accountable Care Organizations: The Proposed Rule for the Medicare Shared Savings Program," *New England Journal of Medicine* 364, no. 16 (2011): e32.

10. Karen E. Joynt and Ashish K. Jha, "Characteristics of Hospitals Receiving Penalties Under the Hospital Readmissions Reduction Program," *JAMA* 309, no. 4 (2013): 342–43.

11. Robert S. Kaplan and Michael E. Porter, "The Big Idea: How to Solve the Cost Crisis in Health Care," *Harvard Business Review*, September 2011, 46–52.

12. Daniel L. Riddle, William A. Jiranek, and Curtis W. Hayes, "Use of a Validated Algorithm to Judge the Appropriateness of Total Knee Arthroplasty in the United States: A Multicenter Longitudinal Cohort Study," *Arthritis & Rheumatology* 66, no. 8 (2014): 2134–43.

13. "Anakinra for Rheumatoid Arthritis," 1–18.

14. Paul Eastham, "Does Nice Have to Be Cruel to Be Kind?," *The Telegraph*, October 30, 2006, https://www.telegraph.co.uk/news/health/3344366/Does-Nice -have-to-be-cruel-to-be-kind.html.

15. Laura Donnelly and Gregory Walton, "25 Cancer Drugs to Be Denied on NHS," *The Telegraph*, January 12, 2015, https://www.telegraph.co.uk/news/politics/11340860/ 25-cancer-drugs-to-be-denied-on-NHS.html.

16. P. A. Ubel, R. A. Hirth, M. E. Cherney, and A. M. Fendrick, "What Is the Price of Life and Why Doesn't It Increase at the Rate of Inflation?," *Archives of Internal Medicine* 163, no. 14 (2003): 1637–41.

17. Leonard B. Saltz, "Perspectives on Cost and Value in Cancer Care," *JAMA Oncology* 2, no. 1 (2016): 19–21.

18. Jeremy Laurance, "NHS Watchdog Is Winning the Price War with Drug Companies," *The Independent*, December 21, 2009, https://www.independent.co.uk/ life-style/health-and-families/health-news/nhs-watchdog-is-winning-the-price-war -with-drug-companies-1846352.html.

19. Ezekiel J. Emanuel, "Skip Your Annual Physical," *New York Times*, January 8, 2015, https://www.nytimes.com/2015/01/09/opinion/skip-your-annual-physical. html.

20. Peter A. Ubel and David A. Asch, "Creating Value in Health by Understanding and Overcoming Resistance to De-Innovation," *Health Affairs* 34, no. 2 (2015): 239–44.

21. Peter J. Neumann, Allison B. Rosen, and Milton C. Weinstein, "Medicare and Cost-Effectiveness Analysis," *New England Journal of Medicine* 353, no. 14 (2005): 1516–22.

22. Susan B. Foote, "Why Medicare Cannot Promulgate a National Coverage Rule: A Case of Regula Mortis," *Journal of Health Politics, Policy and Law* 27, no. 5 (2002): 707–30.

23. Toni Clarke, "U.S. Lawmakers Blast Mylan CEO Over 'Sickening' EpiPen Price Hikes," *Reuters*, September 21, 2016, https://www.reuters.com/article/us-mylan-nl -epipen-congress-idUSKCN11R2OG.

24. Ben Popken, "Mylan CEO's Pay Rose over 600 Percent as Epipen Price Rose 400 Percent," *NBC News*, August 23, 2016, https://www.nbcnews.com/business/ consumer/mylan-execs-gave-themselves-raises-they-hiked-epipen-prices-n636591.

25. Sy Mukherjee, "Martin Shkreli Has a Lot to Say About Mylan's EpiPen," *Fortune*, August 26, 2016, http://fortune.com/2016/08/26/shkreli-testify-congress-drug -prices/.

26. Grace Donnelly, "Here's Martin Shkreli's Jail Sentence," *Fortune*, March 9, 2018, http://fortune.com/2018/03/09/martin-shkreli-jail-sentence/.

27. Nathan Bomey, "Martin Shkreli Pleads the Fifth, Then Tweets About 'Imbeciles' in Congress," *USA Today*, February 4, 2016, https://www.usatoday.com/story/money/2016/02/04/martin-shkreli-congressional-testimony-turing-pharmaceuticals-valeant-fda-drug-prices/79808004/.

28. J. Chhatwal, F. Kanwal, M. S. Roberts, and M. A. Dunn, "Cost-Effectiveness and Budget Impact of Hepatitis C Virus Treatment with Sofosbuvir and Ledipasvir in the United States," *Annals of Internal Medicine* 162, no. 6 (2015): 397–406.

29. Andrew Pollack, "Sales of Sovaldi, New Gilead Hepatitis C Drug, Soar to $10.3 Billion," *New York Times*, February 3, 2015, https://www.nytimes.com/2015/02/04/business/sales-of-sovaldi-new-gilead-hepatitis-c-drug-soar-to-10-3-billion.html.

30. A. L. Beckman, A. Bilinski, R. Boyko, G. M. Camp, A. T. Wall, J. K. Lim, E. A. Wang, R. D. Bruce, and G. S. Gonsalves, "New Hepatitis C Drugs Are Very Costly and Unavailable to Many State Prisoners," *Health Affairs* 35, no. 10 (2016): 1893–901.

31. Ubel et al., "Price of Life," 1637–41.

32. Jeremy S. Windsor and George W. Rodway, "Heights and Haematology: The Story of Haemoglobin at Altitude," *Postgraduate Medical Journal* 83, no. 977 (2007): 148–51.

33. Wolfgang Jelkmann, "The Disparate Roles of Cobalt in Erythropoiesis, and Doping Relevance," *Open Journal of Hematology* 3 (2012): 3–6.

34. Hyo B. Lee and M. Donald Blaufox, "Blood Volume in the Rat," *Journal of Nuclear Medicine* 26, no. 1 (1985): 72–76.

35. Merrill Goozner, *The $800 Million Pill: The Truth Behind the Cost of New Drugs* (Berkeley: University of California Press, 2005).

36. Ibid.

37. R. I. Griffiths, N. R. Powe, J. Greer, G. de Lissovoy, G. F. Anderson, P. K. Whelton, A. J. Watson, and P. W. Eggers, "A Review of the First Year of Medicare Coverage of Erythropoietin," *Health Care Financing Review* 15, no. 3 (1994): 83–102.

38. Joel W. Greer, Roger A. Milam, and Paul W. Eggers, "Trends in Use, Cost, and Outcomes of Human Recombinant Erythropoietin, 1989–98," *Health Care Financing Review* 20, no. 3 (1999): 55–62; Peter Whoriskey, "Anemia Drug Made Billions, but at What Cost?," *Washington Post*, July 19, 2012, https://www.washingtonpost.com/business/economy/anemia-drug-made-billions-but-at-what-cost/2012/07/19/gJQAX5yqwW_story.html?utm_term=.649d72ba6e70.

39. Aaron S. Kesselheim, Yongtian T. Tan, and Jerry Avorn, "The Roles of Academia, Rare Diseases, and Repurposing in the Development of the Most Transformative Drugs," *Health Affairs* 34, no. 2 (2015): 286–93.

40. David Dierking, "General Electric's 8 Most Profitable Lines of Business (GE)," *Investopedia*, February 20, 2016, https://www.investopedia.com/articles/markets/

022016/general-electrics-8-most-profitable-lines-business-ge.asp; Lacie Glover, "Why Does an MRI Cost So Darn Much?," *Time*, July 16, 2014, http://time.com/money/2995166/why-does-mri-cost-so-much/.

41. John Mallard, "Celebrated Scientist Donates Medal Collection," May 21, 2009, https://www.abdn.ac.uk/news/3095/.

42. J. Sijbers, P. Scheunders, N. Bonnet, D. Van Dyck, and E. Raman, "Quantification and Improvement of the Signal-to-Noise Ratio in a Magnetic Resonance Image Acquisition Procedure," *Magnetic Resonance Imaging* 14, no. 10 (1996): 1157–63.

43. Annette C. Bakker and Salvatore La Rosa, "Rethinking the Nonprofit Foundation: An Emerging Niche in the Rare Disease Ecosystem," *EMBO Molecular Medicine* 9, no. 9 (2017): 1179–82.

44. "Medicare Payments for Graduate Medical Education: What Every Medical Student, Resident, and Advisor Needs to Know," Association of American Medical Colleges, 2013, 1–11, https://members.aamc.org/eweb/upload/Medicare%20Payments%20ofor%20Graduate%20Medical%20Education%202013.pdf.

45. Catherine Rampell, "How Medicare Subsidizes Doctor Training," *New York Times*, December 13, 2013, https://economix.blogs.nytimes.com/2013/12/17/how-medicare-subsidizes-doctor-training/?mtrref=www.google.com; "Federal Student Loans," Association of American Medical Colleges, https://www.aamc.org/advocacy/meded/79232/federal_student_loans.html.

46. Laura J. V. Piddock, "The Crisis of No New Antibiotics—What Is the Way Forward?," *Lancet Infectious Diseases* 12, no. 3 (2012): 249–53.

47. Gregory Curfman, "PCSK9 Inhibitors: A Major Advance in Cholesterol-Lowering Drug Therapy," *Harvard Health* (blog), March 15, 2015, https://www.health.harvard.edu/blog/pcsk9-inhibitors-a-major-advance-in-cholesterol-lowering-drug-therapy-201503157801.

48. Robert P. F. Dullaart, "PCSK9 Inhibition to Reduce Cardiovascular Events," *New England Journal of Medicine* 376, no. 18 (2017): 1790–91.

49. "Evolocumab for Treating Primary Hypercholesterolaemia and Mixed Dyslipidaemia," National Institute for Clinical Excellence, 2016, 1–59, https://www.nice.org.uk/guidance/ta394/resources/evolocumab-for-treating-primary-hypercholesterolaemia-and-mixed-dyslipidaemia-pdf-82602910172869.

50. Henry Bodkin and Justin Stoneman, " 'Hugely Expensive' Cholesterol Drug Prescribed on NHS Does Not Prevent Fatal Heart Attacks or Strokes, Say Experts," *The Telegraph*, May 6, 2017, https://www.telegraph.co.uk/news/2017/05/06/nhs-wasting-tens-thousands-year-wonder-drug-stroke-heart-attacks/.

51. "Evolocumab for Treating Primary Hypercholesterolaemia," 1–59.

52. M. S. Sabatine, R. P. Giugliano, A. C. Keech, N. Honarpour, S. D. Wiviott, S. A. Murphy, et al., "Evolocumab and Clinical Outcomes in Patients with Cardiovascular Disease," *New England Journal of Medicine* 376, no. 18 (2017): 1713–22.

53. Liz Szabo, "Cholesterol Drug Prevents Heart Attacks—but Costs $14K a Year," *USA Today*, March 17, 2017, https://www.usatoday.com/story/news/2017/03/17/cholesterol-drugs-prevent-heart-attacks-but-they-dont-come-cheap/99286008/.

54. J. J. Carlson, S. D. Sullivan, L. P. Garrison, P. J. Neumann, and D. L. Veenstra, "Linking Payment to Health Outcomes: A Taxonomy and Examination of Performance-Based Reimbursement Schemes Between Healthcare Payers and Manufacturers," *Health Policy* 96, no. 3 (2010): 179–90.

55. Alan M. Garber and Mark B. McClellan, "Satisfaction Guaranteed—'Payment by Results' for Biologic Agents," *New England Journal of Medicine* 357, no. 16 (2007): 1575–77.

56. Peter B. Bach, "Indication-Specific Pricing for Cancer Drugs," *JAMA* 312, no. 16 (2014): 1629–30.

57. Peter B. Bach and Steven D. Pearson, "Payer and Policy Maker Steps to Support Value-Based Pricing for Drugs," *JAMA* 314, no. 23 (2015): 2503–4.

58. Eric Sagonowsky, "AbbVie's New Pan-Genotypic Hepatitis C Drug Mavyret Deeply Underprices the Competition," *FiercePharma*, August 3, 2017, https://www.fiercepharma.com/pharma/abbvie-s-new-pan-genotypic-hep-c-drug-mavyret-undercuts-competition.

59. Peter B. Bach, "Limits on Medicare's Ability to Control Rising Spending on Cancer Drugs," *New England Journal of Medicine* 360, no. 6 (2009): 626–33.

60. Thomas J. Hwang, Aaron S. Kesselheim, and Ameet Sarpatwari, "Value-Based Pricing and State Reform of Prescription Drug Costs," *JAMA* 318, no. 7 (2017): 609–10.

61. Robert Pear, "Massachusetts, a Health Pioneer, Turns Its Focus to Drug Prices. It's in for a Fight," *New York Times*, March 31, 2018, https://www.nytimes.com/2018/03/31/us/politics/massachusetts-drug-costs-medicaid-waiver.html.

62. Ankur Mani, Iyad Rahwan, and Alex Pentland, "Inducing Peer Pressure to Promote Cooperation," *Scientific Reports* 3, no. 1 (2013): 1735–44.

63. Peter J. Neumann and Joshua T. Cohen, "America's 'NICE'?," *Health Affairs* (blog), Drugs and Medical Innovation, July 17, 2018, https://www.healthaffairs.org/do/10.1377/hblog20180306.837580/full/.

64. "Evolocumab for Treatment of High Cholesterol: Effectiveness and Value, New Evidence Update," Institute for Clinical and Economic Review, 2017, 1–13, https://icer-review.org/wp-content/uploads/2017/06/ICER_PCSK9_NEU_091117.pdf; "PCSK9 Inhibitors for Treatment of High Cholesterol: Effectiveness, Value, and Value-Based Price Benchmarks, Final Report," Institute for Clinical and Economic Review, 2015, 1–113, https://icer-review.org/wp-content/uploads/2016/01/Final-Report-for-Posting-11-24-15-1.pdf.

65. "Overview of the ICER Value Assessment Framework and Update for 2017–2019," Institute for Clinical and Economic Review, 2017, 1–36, https://icer-review.org/wp-content/uploads/2018/03/ICER-value-assessment-framework-update-FINAL-062217.pdf.

8. Coverage for What Counts

1. B. G. Weinshenker, B. Bass, G. P. Rice, J. Noseworthy, W. Carriere, J. Baskerville, and G. C. Ebers, "The Natural History of Multiple Sclerosis: A Geographically Based Study: I. Clinical Course and Disability," *Brain* 112, no. 1 (1989): 133–46.

2. Dean M. Wingerchuk and Jonathan L. Carter, "Multiple Sclerosis: Current and Emerging Disease-Modifying Therapies and Treatment Strategies," *Mayo Clinic Proceedings* 89, no. 2 (2014): 225–40.

3. A. Kerbrat, S. Hamonic, E. Leray, I. Tron, G. Edan, and J. Yaouang for the West Neuroscience Network of Excellence, "Ten-Year Prognosis in Multiple Sclerosis: A Better Outcome in Relapsing-Remitting Patients but Not in Primary Progressive Patients," *European Journal of Neurology* 22, no. 3 (2015): 507–35.

4. Richard Harris, "Multiple Sclerosis Patients Stressed Out by Soaring Drug Costs," National Public Radio, May 25, 2015, https://www.npr.org/sections/health-shots/2015/05/25/408021704/multiple-sclerosis-patients-stressed-out-by-soaring-drug-costs.

5. "Cummings and Welch Launch Investigation of Drug Companies' Skyrocketing Prices for MS Drugs," August 17, 2017, https://democrats-oversight.house.gov/news/press-releases/cummings-and-welch-launch-investigation-of-drug-companies-skyrocketing-prices.

6. C. I. Starner, G. Caleb Alexander, K. Bowen, Y. Qiu, P. J. Wickersham, and P. P. Gleason, "Specialty Drug Coupons Lower Out-of-Pocket Costs and May Improve Adherence at the Risk of Increasing Premiums," *Health Affairs* 33, no. 10 (2014): 1761–69.

7. L. Goldberg, N. C. Edwards, C. Fincher, Q. V. Doan, A. Al-Sabbagh, and D. M. Meletiche, "Comparing the Cost-Effectiveness of Disease-Modifying Drugs for the First-Line Treatment of Relapsing-Remitting Multiple Sclerosis," *Journal of Managed Care & Specialty Pharmacy* 15, no. 7 (2009): 543–55.

8. "Financial Assistance Programs," National Multiple Sclerosis Society, https://www.nationalmssociety.org/Treating-MS/Medications/Financial-Assistance-Programs.

9. "How to Get Started on AMPYRA," Acorda Therapeutics, Inc., https://ampyra.com/prescription/coverage.

10. "HealthWell Foundation: When Health Insurance Is Not Enough," HealthWell Foundation, https://www.healthwellfoundation.org/.

11. Peter A. Ubel and Peter B. Bach, "Copay Assistance for Expensive Drugs: A Helping Hand That Raises Costs," *Annals of Internal Medicine* 165, no. 12 (2016): 878–79.

12. Leemore Dafny, Christopher Ody, and Matthew Schmitt, "When Discounts Raise Costs: The Effect of Copay Coupons on Generic Utilization," *American Economic Journal: Economic Policy* 9, no. 2 (2017): 91–123.

13. Carolyn Y. Johnson, "Pharma, Under Attack for Drug Prices, Started an Industry War," *Washington Post*, January 2, 2018, https://www.washingtonpost.com/business/economy/pharma-under-attack-for-drug-prices-started-an-industry-war/2017/12/29/800a3de8-e5bc-11e7-a65d-1acofd7f097e_story.html.

14. David H. Howard, "Drug Companies' Patient-Assistance Programs—Helping Patients or Profits?," *New England Journal of Medicine* 371, no. 2 (2014): 97–99.

15. Aaron Hakim and Joseph S. Ross, "High Prices for Drugs with Generic Alternatives: The Curious Case of Duexis," *JAMA Internal Medicine* 177, no. 3 (2017): 305–6.

16. Jessica R. Harris, "Communicating About Costs: A Qualitative Analysis to Understand the Out-of-Pocket Financial Burden Associated with Cancer Care" (Master's Thesis, Duke University, 2012), 1–36.

17. M. L. Maciejewski, D. Wansink, J. H. Lindquist, J. C. Parker, and J. F. Farley, "Value-Based Insurance Design Program in North Carolina Increased Medication Adherence but Was Not Cost Neutral," *Health Affairs* 33, no. 2 (2014): 300–308.

18. Michael E. Chernew, Allison B. Rosen, and A. Mark Fendrick, "Value-Based Insurance Design," *Health Affairs* 26, no. 2 (2007): 195–203.

19. A. Mark Fendrick and Michael E. Chernew, "Value-Based Insurance Design: A 'Clinically Sensitive' Approach to Preserve Quality of Care and Contain Costs," *American Journal of Managed Care* 12, no. 1 (2006): 18–20.

20. R. A. Hirth, E. Q. Cliff, T. B. Gibson, M. R. McKellar, and A. M. Fendrick, "Connecticut's Value-Based Insurance Plan Increased the Use of Targeted Services and Medication Adherence," *Health Affairs* 35, no. 4 (2016): 637–46.

21. N. K. Choudhry, J. Avorn, R. J. Glynn, E. M. Antman, S. Schneeweiss, M. Toscano, et al., "Full Coverage for Preventive Medications After Myocardial Infarction," *New England Journal of Medicine* 365, no. 22 (2011): 2088–97.

22. J. L. Lee, M. Maciejewski, S. Raju, W. H. Shrank, and N. K. Choudhry, "Value-Based Insurance Design: Quality Improvement but No Cost Savings," *Health Affairs* 32, no. 7 (2013): 1251–57.

23. Suzanne M. Goodwin and Gerard F. Anderson, "Effect of Cost-Sharing Reductions on Preventive Service Use Among Medicare Fee-for-Service Beneficiaries," *Medicare & Medicaid Research Review* 2, no. 1 (2012): e1–26.

24. C. E. Reeder and Arthur A. Nelson, "The Differential Impact of Copayment on Drug Use in a Medicaid Population," *Inquiry* 22, no. 4 (1985): 396–403.

25. Maciejewski et al., "Value-Based Insurance Design," 300–308.

26. Choudhry et al., "Full Coverage," 2088–97.

27. "Medicare Advantage Value-Based Insurance Design Model," Centers for Medicare & Medicaid Services, https://innovation.cms.gov/initiatives/vbid/.

28. Strengthening Medicare Advantage Through Innovation and Transparency for Seniors of 2015, H.R. 2570, 114th Cong. (2015).

29. Peter A. Ubel, "Value Promotion in Health Care: The Importance of Symmetry," *JAMA* 315, no. 2 (2016): 133–34.

30. Joseph P. Newhouse, *Free for All?: Lessons from the RAND Health Insurance Experiment* (Cambridge, MA: Harvard University Press, 1993).

31. Miriam Laugesen, *Fixing Medical Prices: How Physicians Are Paid* (Cambridge, MA: Harvard University Press, 2016).

32. Steve Brown and Helen Strain, "Costing Healthcare in Germany: Report of a Meeting Between INEK, the HFMA and Monitor," Healthcare Financial Management Association, 2015, 1–10, https://www.hfma.org.uk/docs/default-source/default-document-library/costing-healthcare-in-germany.pdf?sfvrsn=0.

33. Panos Kanavos and Uwe Reinhardt, "Reference Pricing for Drugs: Is It Compatible with U.S. Health Care?," *Health Affairs* 22, no. 3 (2003): 16–30.

34. James C. Robinson and Kimberly MacPherson, "Payers Test Reference Pricing and Centers of Excellence to Steer Patients to Low-Price and High-Quality Providers," *Health Affairs* 31, no. 9 (2012): 2028–36.

35. James C. Robinson, Timothy Brown, and Christopher Whaley, "Reference-Based Benefit Design Changes Consumers' Choices and Employers' Payments for Ambulatory Surgery," *Health Affairs* 34, no. 3 (2015): 415–22.

36. Kelly Gooch, "6 Things to Know About Facility Fees," *Becker's Hospital Review*, March 22, 2016, https://www.beckershospitalreview.com/finance/6-things-to-know -about-facility-fees.html.

37. J. L. Y. Lee, M. A. Fischer, W. H. Shrank, J. M. Polinski, and N. K. Choudhry, "A Systematic Review of Reference Pricing: Implications for U.S. Prescription Drug Spending," *American Journal of Managed Care* 18, no. 11 (2012): e429–37.

38. James C. Robinson, Christopher M. Whaley, and Timothy T. Brown, "Association of Reference Pricing with Drug Selection and Spending," *New England Journal of Medicine* 377, no. 7 (2017): 658–65.

39. David Kestenbaum and Robert Smith, "Pay Patients, Save Money," *Planet Money*, podcast audio, Episode 655, National Public Radio, October 2, 2015, https://www .npr.org/sections/money/2015/10/02/445371930/episode-655-pay-patients-save -money.

40. John Murawski, "Blue Cross to Pay NC Patients up to $500 Rebate for Choosing Cheaper Doctor," *News & Observer*, July 24, 2018, https://www.newsobserver .com/news/business/article215358360.html.

41. Jonathan R. Slotkin, Olivia A. Ross, M. Ruth Coleman, and Jaewon Ryu, "Why GE, Boeing, Lowe's, and Walmart Are Directly Buying Health Care for Employees," *Harvard Business Review*, June 8, 2017, https://hbr.org/2017/06/why-ge-boeing -lowes-and-walmart-are-directly-buying-health-care-for-employees.

42. Hui Zhang, David W. Cowling, and Matthew Facer, "Comparing the Effects of Reference Pricing and Centers-of-Excellence Approaches to Value-Based Benefit Design," *Health Affairs* 36, no. 12 (2017): 2094–101.

43. David M. Cutler, Mark McClellan, and Joseph P. Newhouse, "How Does Managed Care Do It?," *RAND Journal of Economics* 31, no. 3 (2000): 526–48.

44. Noam N. Levey, "Passing the Buck—or Empowering States? Who Will Define Essential Health Benefits," *Health Affairs* 31, no. 4 (2012): 663–66.

45. "10 Essential Health Benefits Insurance Plans Must Cover Under the Affordable Care Act," *Families USA: The Voice for Health Care Consumers,* February 9, 2018, https://familiesusa.org/blog/10-essential-health-benefits-insurance-plans-must -cover.

46. "Mental Health & Substance Abuse Coverage," U.S. Department of Health & Human Services, https://www.healthcare.gov/coverage/mental-health-substance -abuse-coverage/.

47. David Segal, "In Pursuit of Liquid Gold," *New York Times*, December 27, 2017, https://www.nytimes.com/interactive/2017/12/27/business/urine-test-cost .html.

9. Empowering Life-and-Death Decisions

1. "Two Ways to Deal with ED 'Frequent Flyers,' " *Physician's Weekly*, October 13, 2015, https://www.physiciansweekly.com/two-ways-deal-emergency-department -frequent-flyers/.

2. J. Bryk, G. S. Fischer, A. Lyons, S. Shroff, T. Bui, D. Simak, and W. Kapoor, "Improvement in Quality Metrics by the UPMC Enhanced Care Program: A Novel Super-Utilizer Program," *Population Health Management* 21, no. 3 (2018): 217–21.

3. Jordan Weissmann, "5% of Americans Made Up 50% of U.S. Health Care Spending," *The Atlantic*, January 13, 2012, https://www.theatlantic.com/business/ archive/2012/01/5-of-americans-made-up-50-of-us-health-care-spending/251402/.

4. Kristian Foden-Vencil, "How Oregon Is Getting 'Frequent Flyers' Out of Hospital ERs," *Kaiser Health News*, July 10, 2013, https://khn.org/news/emergency -room-frequent-flyers/.

5. Atul Gawande, "The Hot Spotters: Can We Lower Medical Costs by Giving the Neediest Patients Better Care?," *New Yorker*, January 24, 2011, https://www.newyorker .com/magazine/2011/01/24/the-hot-spotters.

6. Bara Vaida, "For Super-Utilizers, Integrated Care Offers a New Path," *Health Affairs* 36, no. 3 (2017): 394–97.

7. Nicholas A. Christakis and Elizabeth B. Lamont, "Extent and Determinants of Error in Doctors' Prognoses in Terminally Ill Patients: Prospective Cohort Study," *BMJ* 320, no. 7233 (2000): 469–73; D. Selby, A. Chakraborty, T. Lilien, E. Stacey, L. Zhang, and J. Myers, "Clinician Accuracy When Estimating Survival Duration: The Role of the Patient's Performance Status and Time-Based Prognostic Categories," *Journal of Pain and Symptom Management* 42, no. 4 (2011): 578–88.

8. R. Sean Morrison and Diane E. Meier, "America's Care of Serious Illness: 2015 State-By-State Report Card on Access to Palliative Care in Our Nation's Hospitals," Center to Advance Palliative Care National Palliative Care Research Center, 2015, 1–28, https://reportcard.capc.org/wp-content/uploads/2015/08/CAPC-Report-Card -2015.pdf.

9. J. M. Langton, B. Blanch, A. K. Drew, M. Haas, J. M. Ingham, and S. A. Pearson, "Retrospective Studies of End-of-Life Resource Utilization and Costs in Cancer Care Using Health Administrative Data: A Systematic Review," *Palliative Medicine* 28, no. 10 (2014): 1167–96.

10. Nicholas A. Christakis, *Death Foretold: Prophecy and Prognosis in Medical Care* (Chicago: University of Chicago Press, 1999).

11. Ziad Obermeyer and Ezekiel J. Emanuel, "Predicting the Future—Big Data, Machine Learning, and Clinical Medicine," *New England Journal of Medicine* 375, no. 13 (2016): 1216–19.

12. Mitchell Daitz, personal communication.

13. A. S. Kelley, P. Deb, Q. Du, M. D. Aldridge Carlson, and R. S. Morrison, "Hospice Enrollment Saves Money for Medicare and Improves Care Quality Across a Number of Different Lengths-of-Stay," *Health Affairs* 32, no. 3 (2013): 552–61; V. Colaberdino, C. Marshall, P. DuBose, and M. Daitz, "Economic Impact of an Advanced

Illness Consultation Program Within a Medicare Advantage Plan Population," *Journal of Palliative Medicine* 19, no. 6 (2016): 622–25.

14. Colaberdino et al., "Economic Impact of an Advanced Illness Consultation Program"; C. W. Kerr, K. A. Donohue, J. C. Tangeman, A. M. Serehali, S. M. Knodel, P. C. Grant, D. L. Luczkiewicz, K. Mylotte, and M. J. Marien, "Cost Savings and Enhanced Hospice Enrollment with a Home-Based Palliative Care Program Implemented as a Hospice–Private Payer Partnership," *Journal of Palliative Medicine* 17, no. 12 (2014): 1328–35.

15. B. Zhang, A. A. Wright, H. A. Huskamp, M. E. Nilsson, M. L. Maciejewski, C. C. Earle, S. D. Block, P. K. Maciejewski, and H. G. Prigerson, "Health Care Costs in the Last Week of Life: Associations with End-of-Life Conversations," *Archives of Internal Medicine* 169, no. 5 (2009): 480–88.

16. Arianne Brinkman-Stoppelenburg, Judith A. C. Rietjens, and Agnes van der Heide, "The Effects of Advance Care Planning on End-of-Life Care: A Systematic Review," *Palliative Medicine* 28, no. 8 (2014): 1000–1025.

17. R. L. Fine, Z. Yang, C. Spivey, B. Boardman, and M. Courtney, "Early Experience with Digital Advance Care Planning and Directives: A Novel Consumer-Driven Program," *Proceedings (Baylor University Medical Center)* 29, no. 3 (2016): 263–67.

18. Diane R. Rittenhouse, Stephen M. Shortell, and Elliott S. Fisher, "Primary Care and Accountable Care—Two Essential Elements of Delivery-System Reform," *New England Journal of Medicine* 361, no. 24 (2009): 2301–3.

19. "2011 Alzheimer's Disease Facts and Figures," *Alzheimer's & Dementia* 7, no. 2 (2011): 208–44.

20. "NHS Personal Health Budgets Spent on Holidays and Horse Riding," *BBC News*, September 1, 2015, https://www.bbc.com/news/health-34110964.

21. Luke O'Shea and Andrew B. Bindman, "Personal Health Budgets for Patients with Complex Needs," *New England Journal of Medicine* 375, no. 19 (2016): 1815–17.

22. "NHS Personal Health," https://www.bbc.com/news/health-34110964.

23. Gayle Shier, Michael Ginsburg, Julianne Howell, Patricia Volland, and Robyn Golden, "Strong Social Support Services, Such as Transportation and Help for Caregivers, Can Lead to Lower Health Care Use and Costs," *Health Affairs* 32, no. 3 (2013): 544–51.

24. "NHS Personal Health."

25. S. A. Berkowitz, H. K. Seligman, J. Rigdon, J. B. Meigs, and S. Basu, "Supplemental Nutrition Assistance Program (SNAP) Participation and Health Care Expenditures Among Low-Income Adults," *JAMA Internal Medicine* 177, no. 11 (2017): 1642–49.

26. James Krieger and Donna L. Higgins, "Housing and Health: Time Again for Public Health Action," *American Journal of Public Health* 92, no. 5 (2002): 758–68.

27. Harris Meyer, "A New Care Paradigm Slashes Hospital Use and Nursing Home Stays for the Elderly and the Physically and Mentally Disabled," *Health Affairs* 30, no. 3 (2011): 412–15; "Vermont Blueprint for Health 2010 Annual Report" (Williston: Department of Vermont Health Access, 2011), 1–62, https://blueprintforhealth

.vermont.gov/sites/blueprint/files/BlueprintPDF/AnnualReports/final_annual_
report_01_26_11.pdf.

28. H. Ding, L. Fang, W. Xin, Y. Tong, Q. Zhou, and P. Huang, "Cost-Effectiveness Analysis of Fulvestrant Versus Anastrozole as First-Line Treatment for Hormone Receptor-Positive Advanced Breast Cancer," *European Journal of Cancer Care* 26, no. 6 (2017): 1–6.

29. H. Mamiya, R. K. Tahara, S. M. Tolaney, N. K. Choudhry, and M. Najafzadeh, "Cost-Effectiveness of Palbociclib in Hormone Receptor-Positive Advanced Breast Cancer," *Annals of Oncology* 28, no. 8 (2017): 1825–31.

10. Simplifying Insurance Choices

1. George Loewenstein, Troyen Brennan, and Kevin G. Volpp, "Asymmetric Paternalism to Improve Health Behaviors," *JAMA* 298, no. 20 (2007): 2415–17.

2. Richard H. Thaler and Cass R. Sunstein, *Nudge: Improving Decisions About Health, Wealth, and Happiness* (New York: Penguin, 2009); Richard H. Thaler and Cass R. Sunstein, "Libertarian Paternalism," *American Economic Review* 93, no. 2 (2003): 175–79.

3. Peter A. Ubel, David A. Comerford, and Eric Johnson, "Healthcare.gov 3.0— Behavioral Economics and Insurance Exchanges," *New England Journal of Medicine* 372, no. 8 (2015): 695–98.

4. "Your Total Costs for Health Care: Premium, Deductible & Out-of-Pocket Costs," U.S. Department of Health & Human Services, https://www.healthcare.gov/choose-a-plan/your-total-costs/.

5. Charlene Wong, personal communication.

6. J. M. Kruser, M. J. Nabozny, N. M. Steffens, K. J. Brasel, T. C. Campbell, M. E. Gaines, and M. L. Schwarze, " 'Best Case/Worst Case': Qualitative Evaluation of a Novel Communication Tool for Difficult in-the-Moment Surgical Decisions," *Journal of the American Geriatrics Society* 63, no. 9 (2015): 1805–11.

7. Elisabeth Rosenthal, "After Surgery, Surprise $117,000 Medical Bill from Doctor He Didn't Know," *New York Times*, September 20, 2014, https://www.nytimes.com/2014/09/21/us/drive-by-doctoring-surprise-medical-bills.html.

8. Suzanne M. Kirchhoff, "Health Insurance Exchanges: Health Insurance 'Navigators' and In-Person Assistance," Congressional Research Service, 2014, 1–33, https://fas.org/sgp/crs/misc/R43243.pdf.

9. Neil MacKinnon and Ritu Kumar, "Prior Authorization Programs: A Critical Review of the Literature," *Journal of Managed Care & Specialty Pharmacy* 7, no. 4 (2001): 297–303.

10. Thomas Buchmueller and John DiNardo, "Did Community Rating Induce an Adverse Selection Death Spiral? Evidence from New York, Pennsylvania, and Connecticut," *American Economic Review* 92, no. 1 (2002): 280–94.

11. Michael Cooper, "Conservatives Sowed Idea of Health Care Mandate, Only to Spurn It Later," *New York Times*, February 14, 2012, https://www.nytimes

.com/2012/02/15/health/policy/health-care-mandate-was-first-backed-by-conservatives .html.

12. Katherine Baicker, William J. Congdon, and Sendhil Mullainathan, "Health Insurance Coverage and Take-Up: Lessons from Behavioral Economics," *Milbank Quarterly* 90, no. 1 (2012): 107–34.

13. J. C. Robinson, T. T. Brown, C. Whaley, and E. Finlayson, "Association of Reference Payment for Colonoscopy with Consumer Choices, Insurer Spending, and Procedural Complications," *JAMA Internal Medicine* 175, no. 11 (2015): 1783–89.

14. Amol K. Narang and Lauren Nicholas, "Out-of-Pocket Spending and Financial Burden Among Medicare Beneficiaries with Cancer," *JAMA Oncology* 3, no. 6 (2017): 757–65.

Epilogue

1. Peter A. Ubel, *Critical Decisions: How You and Your Doctor Can Make the Right Medical Choices Together* (New York: HarperOne, 2012).

2. Peter A. Ubel, " 'What Should I Do, Doc?': Some Psychologic Benefits of Physician Recommendations," *Archives of Internal Medicine* 162, no. 9 (2002): 977–80; Peter A. Ubel, Karen A. Scherr, and Angela Fagerlin, "Empowerment Failure: How Shortcomings in Physician Communication Unwittingly Undermine Patient Autonomy," *American Journal of Bioethics* 17, no. 11 (2017): 31–39.

ACKNOWLEDGMENTS

I would like to briefly acknowledge some of the many people who helped me bring this book across the finish line, beginning with the many patients who lent me their stories, whom I cannot thank by name as I have used pseudonyms to protect their identities. Some of the patients and clinicians I report on in this book were audio recorded by Verilogue Inc., whose CEO, Jamison Barnett, and all-around data-guru Dmytro Byelmac have been incredibly generous in providing my research team with access to some of their data.

Generous thanks to Yousuf Zafar and Brant Inman for letting me quote them at some length about specific patients they cared for at Duke University (excellent guys; fantastic physicians!). And an enormous thank you to Ravi Kanesvaran, who allowed me to review transcripts of oncology appointments in Singapore, providing me with insight into how physicians in that country address their patients' cost concerns.

I have received help from an absolutely stellar group of research assistants and students: Mary Carol Barks, Vinay Choksi, Robin Fail, Rachel Goldstein, Noelani Ho, Hanna Huffstetler, Allison Kratka, Helen Liu, Farrah Madanay, Lorena Millo, Laura Mortimer, Taruni Santanam, Natalie Trebes, Annabel Wang, and Iris Yang. Iris, Lorena, and Mary Carol were forced to review and re-review more draft chapters than any human should have to confront. Gracias!

My research team is off the charts. Special thanks to the team that analyzed all those cost conversations between clinicians and patients: Karen Scherr, Kelly Davis (da man!), Christine Kirby, Cecilia Zhang, and Wynn Hunter (da main man!). In other parts of the book, I revisit topics I have researched and written about with people like David Asch, Kevin Riggs, Amy Abernathy, Yousuf Zafar, Peter Bach, and Angie Fagerlin. They all advanced my thinking.

My agent, Jim Levine, was generous to help me out with a book I described, right off the start, as "academic": "Jim, it is academic; I won't contribute much to your income with this one." My editor, Seth Ditchik, helped me adjust the tone and depth of the book. I really appreciate his wisdom and experience. (We finally got to work together. Hope it was worth the wait!)

And finally, thanks to Paula for once again putting up with me while I snuck off to the third floor on weekend mornings to write. You are the sanest "crazy cat lady" I've ever met.

INDEX